Alex

D1680981

Implicature

H. P. Grice virtually discovered the phenomenon of implicature (to denote implications that are not strictly part of what is said) and provided the leading paradigm for research in pragmatics. Gricean theory claims that conversational implicatures can be explained and predicted using general psychosocial principles. This theory has established itself as one of the orthodoxes in the philosophy of language.

Wayne Davis argues controversially that Gricean theory does not work. He shows that any principle-based theory understates both the intentionality of what a speaker implicates and the conventionality of what a sentence implicates. In developing his argument the author explains that the psychosocial principles actually define the social function of implicature conventions, which contribute to the satisfaction of those principles.

By offering a searching and systematic critique of one of the established doctrines in the philosophy of language, this challenging book will be of particular importance to philosophers of language and linguists, especially those working in pragmatics and sociolinguistics.

CAMBRIDGE STUDIES IN PHILOSOPHY

General editor ERNEST SOSA (Brown University)

Advisory editors
JONATHAN DANCY (University of Reading)
JOHN HALDANE (University of St. Andrews)
GILBERT HARMAN (Princeton University)
FRANK JACKSON (Australian National University)
WILLIAM G. LYCAN (University of North Carolina at Chapel Hill)
SYDNEY SHOEMAKER (Cornell University)
JUDITH J. THOMSON (Massachusetts Institute of Technology)

RECENT TITLES

Implicature

Intention, convention, and principle in the failure of Gricean theory

Wayne A. Davis

CAMBRIDGE
UNIVERSITY PRESS

PUBLISHED BY THE PRESS SYNDICATE OF THE UNIVERSITY OF CAMBRIDGE
The Pitt Building, Trumpington Street, Cambridge CB2 1RP, United Kingdom

CAMBRIDGE UNIVERSITY PRESS
The Edinburgh Building, Cambridge CB2 2RU, UK   http://www.cup.cam.ac.uk
40 West 20th Street, New York, NY 10011-4211, USA   http://www.cup.org

First published 1998

Printed in the United States of America

Typeset in Bembo, in QuarkXPress [GH]

*A catalog record for this book is available from
the British Library.*

Library of Congress Cataloging-in-Publication Data
Davis, Wayne A., 1951–
Implicature : intention, convention, and principle in the failure
of Gricean theory / Wayne A. Davis.
p. cm. – (Cambridge studies in philosophy)
Includes bibliographical references and index.
ISBN 0–521–62319–7 (hb)
1. Grice, H. P. (H. Paul) Contributions in philosophy of language.
2. Implication (Logic) 3. Speech acts (Linguistics) 4. Language
and languages – Philosophy. I. Title. II. Series.
P85.G735D38   1998
306.44 – dc21   98-3021

ISBN 0–521–62319–7 hardback

To my wife, Kathy, on the occasion of our 20th anniversary

Contents

Introduction

H. P. Grice is justly famous for his work on implicature. He identified a theoretically important phenomenon and provided a theory that is still dominant. Grice's virtual discovery of implicature was a major achievement, a breakthrough in linguistics and philosophy of language. Nevertheless, his *theory* of implicature, I argue here, is a near-complete failure.

After explaining the concept of implicature and illustrating its theoretical importance, I review Grice's theory. It is distinguished by the claim that conversational implicatures arise from certain principles of cooperative behavior as they apply to conversation. I isolate and analyze four principal elements in Gricean theory: the *Theoretical Definition* of conversational implicature in terms of the conversational principles; the *Calculability Assumption,* which holds that conversational implicatures can always be worked out or inferred from the conversational principles; the *Generative Assumption,* which claims that conversational implicatures exist because of facts involving the conversational principles; and *Grice's Razor,* which holds that it is more economical to postulate conversational implicatures rather than senses because conversational implicatures can be derived from independently motivated principles. I use the

I would like to thank Anna Wierzbicka, Dan Sperber, an anonymous reviewer, and especially William Lycan for many helpful comments. I would also like to thank my colleagues in Linguistics at Georgetown: Ralph Fasold, Catherine Ball, Deborah Schiffrin, and Paul Portner, for the work they have done on pragmatics and implicature, from which I have profited. Finally, I am grateful to Ernest Sosa and Terence Moore for their support of this project, to Anne Lesser for copyediting, and to Françoise Bartlett for expert management of the production.

term *Gricean Theory* broadly to denote not just Grice's own theory, but any principle-based theory with these four or similar elements.

I develop four main lines of argument against Gricean theory. First, the theory generates erroneous predictions as readily as it generates correct ones. Indeed, it is the exception rather than the rule to find the implicatures predicted by Gricean derivations. Second, the conversational principles have insufficient power to enable rigorous derivation of specific implicatures. This holds for Grice's own Cooperative Principle and associated maxims as well as the supplementary or competing principles of his followers. Gricean derivations are seriously flawed. The problem is due not to any remediable imprecision of Gricean theorists, but to the inherent indeterminacy and conventionality of implicature. Third, conversational implicatures exist even when Grice's cooperative presumption and mutual knowledge conditions fail. These facts show that Gricean explanations of conversational implicatures are completely unsuccessful: they do not even begin to tell us *why* implicatures occur. The root problem is that any principle-based theory like Grice's understates both the intentionality of speaker implicature and the conventionality of sentence implicature.

I conclude by suggesting that the role of conversational principles in implicature is much more indirect than Grice imagined. Conversational principles partly define the social function of implicature conventions, which contribute to the satisfaction of those principles. I examine the similarities and differences between implicature conventions and the more familiar lexical and grammatical conventions, and offer alternative speculations about the reason for the universality of implicature conventions. The basis for a theoretical definition of conversational implicature should be found in a thorough revision of Grice's definition of speaker meaning in terms of intention, a project I have attempted elsewhere and do not pursue here.

Many of the criticisms I present have been known for some time. But the import and seriousness of the defects individually and collectively have not been widely appreciated, and the problems have had little impact on the general acceptance of Gricean theory. The best known critics of the Gricean theory have either expressed confidence that solutions would be found within the Gricean framework (Harnish 1976) or presented alternative theories with similar defects (Sperber and Wilson 1986a). Morgan (1978) and Searle (1975) observed the conventionality of sentence implicature, and Horn (1989) and Hirschberg (1991) noted the intentionality of speaker implicature, but all nonetheless affirmed calculability and other parts of Gricean theory. Only one author (Wierzbicka 1987) has argued that the conception is fundamentally flawed. But her evidence was limited to one type of implicature, one of the least discussed.

I suspect that extant criticisms have had little impact in part because they were presented piecemeal. Thus it always seemed that we were faced with a choice between a large, well-supported theory and a small piece of recalcitrant data, making it rational to expect that the problem was superficial and would in due course be explained away. I therefore plan to marshal the counterevidence en masse, and show that the theory has little success anywhere because it is fundamentally defective.

Some will resist this negative conclusion because they regard the Gricean theory as a fruitful if somewhat flawed paradigm, without which research on implicature will have no direction or interest. I argue that the Gricean theory has been barren, and that recognizing the role of intentions in speaker implicature and conventions in sentence implicature provides a better direction for research than a misplaced attention to general psychosocial principles. With the blinders off, we can see that the most familiar facts about implicature have not even begun to be explained. The goals of science have not been achieved. The illusion of understanding provided by the Gricean theory has only served to stifle inquiry. We can also see important new areas for empirical research. I raise many fascinating questions about implicature, requiring systematic historical and sociolinguistic research for their solution, which did not and could not arise when the Gricean theory held sway.

3

1

Concept and theory

Grice (1957) drew an important distinction between what a *speaker* means or implies and what a *sentence* or other expression means or implies. The sentence "The airplane is a mile long" means the airplane is 5,280 feet long and implies the plane is over 3,279 feet long. Nevertheless, it would be most unlikely for a speaker uttering the sentence to mean or imply such things unless he were pulling someone's leg. More likely, the speaker would be exaggerating, meaning simply that the airplane is enormous compared with typical planes. A speaker using the sentence in a coded message might mean something completely unrelated to its English meaning.

As a first approximation, word meaning may be characterized as *conventional* speaker meaning. Whereas we could conceivably use "bachelor" to mean just about anything, we conventionally mean "unmarried male," which is what the word means. Speaker meaning is determined by the intentions of the individual speaker. The exact intentions required are a matter of controversy. On my view, S means that the airplane is enormous only if S used the sentence to express the belief that the plane is enormous, which entails that S did something in order to provide an indication of that belief.[1] In one typical case, S would have the further intention of produc-

---

[1] I developed an account along these lines in Davis (1992a, 1992b), and will do so at even greater length in *Meaning, Expression, and Thought*. I will also give there a more adequate definition of sentence meaning in terms of speaker meaning. Grice's (1957, 1969) analysis of speaker intention has been very influential, but the specific intentions he singled out lead to a wide variety of serious objections.

ing the belief in the audience. Speaker *implication* is *indirect* speaker meaning: meaning one thing *by* meaning another. A boy who implies he cannot go to the movies by saying, "I have to study" has expressed the belief that he cannot go by expressing the belief that he has to study. Both word and speaker meaning differ from the *natural* sense in which smoke means fire. Natural meaning depends on causal connections, statistical correlations, laws of nature, and other relations among events, but not typically on intention or convention.

1.1 THE CONCEPT OF IMPLICATURE

Grice (1957) was the first to systematically study cases in which speaker meaning differs from sentence meaning. He introduced the verb *implicate* and the cognate noun *implicature* as technical terms denoting "the act of meaning or implying something by saying something else." Consider the following dialogue:

(1) ANN: Where can I get gasoline?
    BOB: There's a station around the corner.

We may suppose Bob to have implied that Ann can get gasoline at the station. Nevertheless, Bob did not actually *say* that Ann can get gasoline there. So Bob has *implicated* it. What Bob said, and therefore did not implicate, is just that there is a gasoline station around the corner. By *saying,* Grice meant not the mere locutionary act of uttering certain words. Instead, Grice focused on the illocutionary act of saying *that* something is the case.[2] If Bob had said, "There is a gasoline station around the corner," he would have said the same thing in the illocutionary sense, but not in the locutionary sense. It is not clear whether Grice restricted saying to *stating,* or allowed it to apply to *asking* and *ordering* as well. If Ann had said, "Where can I get petrol?" there is a sense in which she would have said the same thing, even though she would not have uttered the same words or made a statement. Even when "say" is restricted to stating, it can be used more or less narrowly, as Grice himself empha-

---

[2] Compare Grice (1975: 24–25; 1969: 87) and Bach (1994b).

sized. If Mary says, "The book is 12 inches long," we will count her as saying it is one-third of a yard long in some cases, but not others. The exact boundaries of implicature will not be an issue, so there is no need for us to focus on a specific interpretation of Grice's definition.

If Σ means that p, or if S says that p by uttering Σ, then p is a *truth condition* of Σ, either in general, or as used on that occasion. Truth conditions are "logical" or "a priori" implications. Assuming particular interpretations, p is a truth condition of sentence Σ iff it is absolutely impossible for Σ to be true without p being true. "There is a station" is a truth condition of "There's a station around the corner." For the latter cannot be true unless the former is true. But "Ann can get gasoline at the station" is not a truth condition of "There's a station around the corner." The station might be out of gasoline or closed. It follows that an implicature need not be a truth condition of the sentence uttered. It may be, though.[3] Suppose a taxpayer answers the auditor's question "Is it true that you or your spouse is 65 or older or blind?" by saying, "I am 67." The taxpayer said he is 67, which entails what he implicated, namely, that either he or his spouse is 65 or over or blind. The truth of what he implicated is thus a logically necessary condition of the truth of what he said. So being an implicature neither entails nor precludes being a truth condition.

Speakers who know that an implicature is false have *misled* their audience. But they have not thereby *lied* unless the implicature happens to be a truth condition. If Bob knows there is no gasoline at the station, then he has misled Ann in dialogue (1). But Bob has not lied because he did not actually say there was gasoline there. He would be lying only if he believed there was no station around the corner.

A *sentence* implicates, roughly, what speakers using the sentence with its regular meaning would commonly use it to implicate. Despite what Bob implicated in (1), the sentence Bob used does not itself implicate "Ann can get gasoline at the station." For in

---

[3] Contrast Grice (1975: 39).

most contexts, there would be no impropriety in using "There's a station around the corner" without that implicature. In contrast, (2)(a) itself implicates (2)(b):

(2) (a) Bill is sick, so he should rest.
    (b) Bill's being sick implies that he should rest.

For a speaker could not properly use (2)(a) without implicating (2)(b). And (3)(a) implicates (3)(b).

(3) (a) Some died.
    (b) Not all died.

For speakers would not normally use (3)(a) without that implicature.

Just as a speaker can implicate something the sentence he uttered does not implicate, so the sentence uttered can implicate something the speaker did not implicate. For example, someone uttering (3)(a) may have been engaging in understatement, knowing full well that everyone was massacred. S implicates a proposition which the sentence he uttered implicates only if S intended to provide an indication that he believes that proposition. Similarly, what S said may suggest or imply things that S did not suggest or imply. For example, if Bill said, "There is some oil on the shaft of my right front strut," then what he said implies that he needs new struts. But Bill need not have implied this at all. Indeed, believing the oil was supposed to be there, he may have been implying that his struts do not need replacing. Finally, S's saying what he said may mean or imply something that neither S nor what he said means or implies. When applied to an *act* of saying or uttering, "mean" and its relatives normally have their *natural* sense. What an act implies in this sense is what it is a natural sign of – what the act provides evidence for. Thus Bill's saying "There is some oil on the shaft of my right front strut" ordinarily implies all of the following: Bill speaks English, Bill is not brain dead, Bill is not paralyzed, Bill's senses are functioning, and so on. Bill himself would not ordinarily be implying any of these things, and what he said does not imply them either. In the literature on implicature, what a speaker's *utterance* implies (or means) is commonly equated with what the *speaker* implies rather than what the sentence uttered, or the uttering of it, implies. In my opinion this usage normally results from a technical stipulation rather than a mistake. To avoid confusion, I simply avoid applying "means," "implies," or "implicates" to "utterance."

The fact that "means" and its relatives have different meanings when applied to different things involved in a speech situation requires constant vigilance to avoid equivocation. Consider a fascinating ethnological report:

> On one occasion, a teenage boy mentioned to Keenan and Ochs that "Bosy's mother is a little sick," as a way of indirectly asking for some medicine. A European would normally assume that Bosy's mother is not the boy's mother, even if there was every reason to believe that Bosy is his sister. The European would assume that the boy would refer to his own mother as "my mother." But "Bosy's mother" was in fact the boy's mother, too. To refer to her as "my mother" would have called too much attention to him by Malagasy standards; it was much more appropriate to deflect that attention by identifying his mother through a third party, his sister. (Fasold 1990: 55)

Let us take it as given that if a European utters the sentence in question, that act implies that Bosy's mother is not his mother, whereas if a Malagasy speaker utters the sentence, this is not implied. The stipulated fact concerns natural implication. We are concerned with speaker implication. We cannot determine from the evidence provided what the teenage boy implied. It is possible, for example, that the boy knew how Europeans would read his utterance, and chose his words with his audience in mind, as a means of getting them to believe that Bosy's mother was not his mother. We have to know the speaker's intentions to know what the speaker has implicated.

Implicatures generated by the conventional meaning of the words uttered, as in (2), are classified as *conventional*. The implicature in (2) is due to the conventional meaning of the word *so*. Nonconventional implicatures that depend on the conversational context as in (1) and (3) are termed *conversational*. Spoken without some of their conventional implicatures or logical implications, sentences are used improperly. Spoken without a conversational implicature, they are at most misleading. Conversational implicatures differ further in being *cancelable*. The standard implicature of (3)(a) can be explicitly canceled by adding "indeed, all did." "Some died, indeed all did" is perfectly consistent, and does not imply "Not all died" in any way. In contrast, because "All died" logically implies "Some died," the sentence "All died, indeed none did" is self-contradictory. "Bill is sick, so he should rest, but Bill's being sick in no way implies that he should rest" is incoherent in a different way. Conversational implicatures can also be implicitly canceled by the context. Thus (3)(a) would not have its customary implication if uttered in full view of a garden in which every single plant was obviously dead. Conversely, conversational implicatures are *reinforceable*. Conjoining a sentence with one of its conversational implicatures is not redundant and logically implies what the original sentence implicates; witness "Some died, but not all did." In contrast, "All died, and some did" is redundant.

1.2 THEORETICAL IMPORTANCE

The main theoretical importance of implicature lies in the fact that to understand speakers fully we must know what they implicate. It does not suffice to know the truth conditions, or in some cases even the meaning, of all the sentences uttered, or what is said. We cannot fully understand Bob in dialogue (1) unless we recognize his implication that Ann can get gasoline at the station. Hence formal semantics, considered exclusively as the study of the meaning of words, cannot offer a complete account of all types of meaning. It is pointless to debate whether it is more important to understand speaker meaning or sentence meaning. Both are proper and important objects of study, as is their exact relationship.

Implicature must be considered even in truth conditional semantics. For example, readily available evidence suggests that the word "and" is ambiguous in English, having a strong sense connoting temporal or causal order in addition to the weak sense connoting joint truth alone. Compare "Joseph died and went to heaven" with "Joseph went to heaven and died." Yet before ambiguity can be accepted, the competing hypothesis that the sequential connotation is merely an implicature must be rejected. Many facts support implicature over ambiguity. For example, "Bill got sick and saw a doctor, but not necessarily in that order," does not have a contradictory reading.

Similarly, the thesis that certain implications are presuppositions can be accepted only if they are not mere implicatures. A sentence Σ is said to (semantically) *presuppose* p provided the truth of p is necessary for Σ to be either true or false. Following P. F. Strawson, and opposing Bertrand Russell, many have argued that a sentence like (4)(a) presupposes (4)(b).

(4) (a) Your crimes are inexcusable.
     (b) You have committed crimes.
     (c) Your crimes are not inexcusable.

The presupposition hypothesis is plausible because (4)(c) seems to imply (4)(b) just as strongly as (4)(a) does. Also supporting Strawson is the strong intuition that "Are your crimes excusable or not?" is a loaded question, which cannot be answered if you are innocent. Accepting presuppositions complicates logical theory, however. For example, if some declarative sentences are neither true nor false, then standard formulations of the Law of Excluded Middle must be modified. Furthermore, the identification of necessary truth as truth in all possible worlds becomes problematic. For it seems that cats are necessarily cats. Yet on the Strawsonian view, the proposition that cats are cats is not true in worlds in which there are no cats. One strategy for avoiding these complications hypothesizes that the negation's implication is *merely* an implicature. On this view, (4)(c) implicates (4)(b) without logically implying it. The fact that a sentence may be true when an implicature is false allows the Russellian to account for felt implications while insisting that (4)(c) is true and (4)(a) false when (4)(b) is false.

Implicature has also been invoked in accounts of lexical gaps. For example, Horn has observed an economical asymmetry in the lexicon of natural languages.[4] Logical concepts tend not to be lexical-

---

[4] Horn (1972: Ch. 4; 1989: §4.5), Levinson (1983: 164), Hirschberg (1991: 47). O'Grady, Dobrovolsky, and Aronoff (1993: 2) describe a related rule: "A new verb is rarely coined if a word with the intended meaning already exists."

ized if they are conveyed by implicature. As an illustration, English contains "No," which, appearing in "__S are P," results in a sentence meaning "*All* S are *not*-P." But English does not contain a word like "nall," which in the same context would produce a sentence meaning "*Not all* S are P." Horn correlates this with the fact that "Some S are P" conveys "Not all S are P" by implicature; no English sentence conveys "All S are not-P" by implicature. Similarly, English contains "neither" meaning "not either," but no term "noth" meaning "not both." Horn correlates this with the fact that "p or q" implicates "-(p&q)"; no sentence form conveys "-(pvq)" by implicature. Similarly, McCawley (1978: 245–246) observed that "pale" combines less freely with "red" and "black" than with "green" or "yellow," and attributed this fact to the existence of "pink" and "gray" and the nonexistence of any words meaning "pale green" or "pale yellow." As a result, a speaker who uses "pale red" rather than "pink" is usually implicating that the object described is not a typical pink.

More can be said about the importance of implicature. But we have done enough to establish that the theoretical importance of implicature is *independent* of the Gricean theory of implicature. We do not have to accept *any* theory of implicature in order to recognize the theoretical importance of the concept.

1.3 GRICEAN THEORY

Besides identifying the phenomenon of implicature and demonstrating its importance, Grice formulated a theory in terms of which he classified different sorts of conversational implicature and tried to explain how they arise and are understood. Grice (1975: 26–30) postulated a general "principle of cooperation" and four "maxims" specifying how to be cooperative. It is common knowledge, he asserted, that people generally follow these rules for efficient communication.

Cooperative Principle. Contribute what is required by the accepted purpose of the conversation.

11

Maxim of Quality. Make your contribution true; so do not convey what you believe false or unjustified.
Maxim of Quantity. Be as informative as required.
Maxim of Relation. Be relevant.
Maxim of Manner. Be perspicuous; so avoid obscurity and ambiguity, and strive for brevity and order.

Generalizations of these rules govern rational, cooperative behavior in general. If I am helping a man change the oil, I will hand him a can of oil rather than a tire iron (relevance), or a teaspoon of oil (quantity), or phony oil (quality), and I will not take all day doing it (manner). The maxims do not, therefore, have the characteristic arbitrariness of linguistic conventions.[5] Much of the literature is devoted to clarifying and strengthening the maxims, relating them, and extending the list. But Grice's formulations are still dominant. To my knowledge, none of the extant variants enable the Gricean to avoid the objections I will raise.

To sketch how the principles are thought to explain the way implicatures arise and are understood, consider (1). Bob would have infringed the Maxim of Relation, it is claimed, unless he believed Ann could get gasoline at the station. Because Bob was trying to cooperate, his utterance indicated that belief. Thus Bob could imply that Ann can get gasoline there and expect Ann to recognize that implication. Speakers using "Some died" would violate the Maxim of Quantity if they knew that all died. So by not making the stronger statement, they can imply that not all died, and expect hearers to recognize the implication. Unlike conventional implicatures, conversational implicatures are canceled, Griceans believe, when the maxims are in abeyance. Under cross examination of an uncooperative witness, "Some died" would not implicate "Not all died."

Some implicatures depend on *flouting* the maxims, Grice proposed. This occurs when what a cooperative speaker says so obviously fails to obey the maxims that the hearer must assume the speaker means something different. Irony and metaphor are thought to depend on flouting the Maxim of Quality. Hearing

---

[5] Compare Levinson (1983: 103); contrast Lycan (1984: 75) and Hirschberg (1991: 16).

"Fine day, isn't it?" in the middle of a blizzard, we recognize that the speaker cannot really believe it a fine day, and means the opposite. Hearing "The music danced lightly on his ears," we recognize that the speaker believes no such thing, and is waxing metaphorical. The speaker who says, "The singer produced a series of sounds closely corresponding to the score of *Oklahoma*," thereby meaning that the singing was terrible, is flouting the Maxim of Manner.

As we have seen, speaker implicature can be defined in terms of saying and meaning or implying: *S implicates that p iff S means or implies that p by saying something other than p.* Conversational speaker implicatures can be defined as implicatures that depend on the conversational context in the way illustrated by examples like (1) and (3). Generalizing from his analysis of selected examples, Grice went beyond these "analytic" definitions and offered a *theoretical* characterization of conversational implicature in terms of the Cooperative Principle.

Theoretical Definition I: S conversationally implicates p iff

(i) S implicates p;

(ii) S is presumed to be observing the Cooperative Principle (*cooperative presumption*);

(iii) The supposition that S believes p is required to make S's utterance consistent with the Cooperative Principle (*determinacy*); and

(iv) S believes (or knows), and expects H to believe that S believes, that H is able to determine that (iii) is true (*mutual knowledge*).[6]

---

[6] This is a lightly regimented paraphrase of Grice (1975: 30–31). Grice's definition is repeated with little change by Harnish (1976: 333), R. Lakoff (1977: 99), Brown and Levinson (1978: 63), Bach and Harnish (1979: xvii, 6), Atlas (1979: 272), Posner (1980), Grice (1978: 41; 1981: 185), Wilson and Sperber (1981: 160), Levinson (1983: 113), Green (1989: 93–97), Fasold (1990: 131–132), Hirschberg (1991: 16–24), Berg (1991), Blakemore (1992: 126, 137), and M. Green (1995: 98). The Sperber and Wilson definition is also similar, except their "Principle of Relevance" replaces the Cooperative Principle: "On this approach, the implicatures of an utterance are those contextual assumptions and implications which the hearer has to recover in order to satisfy himself that the speaker has observed the principle of relevance" (Wilson and Sperber 1986: 59); see later, section 3.12. For antecedents to Grice, see Hungerland (1960).

Thus Bob's implication that Ann can get gasoline around the corner was conversational on Grice's view because Bob was clearly trying to be cooperative, and would not have been unless he believed that Ann could get gasoline around the corner.

Definition I does not capture everything Grice viewed as essential to conversational implicature. He also held that conversational implicatures must be identifiable using conversational principles, which I call the *Calculability Assumption*.

Calculability Assumption: Conversational implicatures must be capable of being worked out.[7]

To *"work out"* an implicature is to infer it in a specific way from the Cooperative Principle together with particular facts such as the meaning of the sentence uttered and the context of utterance. The Calculability Assumption is thus an epistemological principle, and Grice's theory is in part a theory of interpretation or understanding:

The presence of a conversational implicature must be capable of being worked out; for even if it can in fact be intuitively grasped, unless the intuition is replaceable by an argument, the implicature (if present at all) will not count as a conversational implicature; it will be a conventional

---

[7] Calculability is also affirmed by Böer and Lycan (1973: 498–505), Searle (1975: 267), Morgan (1978: 246, 250, 252), Walker (1975: 176), Cole (1975: 260–261), Wright (1975: 380), Harnish (1976: 333–334, 336, 339), R. Lakoff (1977: 99), Sadock (1978: 368; 1981: 258, 261–262), Brown and Levinson (1978: 63, 288), Bickerton (1979: 236), Gazdar (1979: 41–42), Bach and Harnish (1979: 169, 171), Atlas (1979: 273, 276; 1989: 139–140), Grice (1981: 187), Atlas and Levinson (1981: 37–39), Nunberg (1981: 201, 207–208), Sag (1981: 275–276), Sperber and Wilson (1981: 165–167), Horn (1984: 13; 1989: 383; 1992: 260–262), Levinson (1983: 100, 113–114, 117), Leech (1983: 11, 17, 24–25, 30–31, 44, 153, 172), Lycan (1984: 75–78, 84), Martinich (1984: 509–511), Blakemore (1987a: 21, 34–39, 65), Carston (1988: 35), G. M. Green (1989: 88, 94, 115), Thomason (1990: 330, 334), Fasold (1990: 132), Hirschberg (1991: 3–4, 21–24, 38), Ward and Hirschberg (1991: 519 ff.), Bach (1994b: 12), Schiffrin (1994: 194–195, 367), M. Green (1995: esp. §3), and Matsumoto (1995: §1.1). Compare and contrast Stalnaker (1974: 475–476), Walker (1975: 157, 170), Miller and Johnson-Laird (1976: 636), Smith and Wilson (1979: Ch. 8), Wilson and Sperber (1979: 301; 1981: 157; 1986, 46, 49, 54, 59, 73), Sterelny (1982: 189), Searle (1982: 520, 532, 536), and Blakemore (1992: 126, 137).

implicature. To work out that a particular conversational implicature is present, the hearer will rely on the following data: (1) the conventional meaning of the words used, together with the identity of any references that may be involved; (2) the Cooperative Principle and its maxims; (3) the context, linguistic or otherwise, of the utterance; (4) other items of background knowledge; and (5) the fact (or supposed fact) that all relevant items falling under the previous headings are available to both participants and both participants know or assume this to be the case. A general pattern for the working out of a conversational implicature might be given as follows: "He has said that q; there is no reason to suppose that he is not observing the maxims, or at least the Cooperative Principle; he could not be doing this unless he thought that p; he knows (and knows that I know that he knows) that I can see that the supposition that he thinks that p is required; he has done nothing to stop me thinking that p; he intends me to think, or is at least willing to allow me to think, that p; and so he has implicated that p." (Grice 1975: 31)

To work out an implicature, then, is to engage in reasoning with the following key elements.

The Working-Out Schema for Speaker Implicature:

P1 S uttered a sentence with a particular meaning, in a given context, etc.

P2 S is observing the Cooperative Principle.

P3 Given P1, S could not be observing the Cooperative Principle unless he believed p.

. . .

C ∴ S implicated p.

P2, of course, is the content of the cooperative presumption required by definition I. Because P3 is the determinacy condition, the Calculability Assumption is true only if that part of definition I is.

Definition I and the Calculability Assumption are independent postulates. Despite the relationship between determinacy and calculability, definition I does not entail that conversational implicatures themselves are inherently calculable. What definition I states is that S's conversationally *implicating* that p depends on the determinacy of S's *believing* that p. Furthermore, provided S's beliefs are true, clauses (ii) and (iv) imply that H is capable of inferring that S believes p. For clause (ii) implies that H takes S to be observing the Cooperative Principle, and clause (iv) implies that H is able to determine that S must believe p if S is observing the Cooperative Principle. But to work out S's implicature as well as his belief, and thus arrive at the last line of Grice's "general pattern for the working out of a conversational implicature," H must know a rule connecting belief to implicature. It is no help for H to know definition I (which few if any hearers know anyway). For that definition does not enable anyone to infer clause (i) from clauses (ii) through (iv). Grice's Working-out Schema indicates that he does believe such an inference is warranted.

When Grice himself formulates his theoretical definition, determinacy, mutual knowledge, and the cooperative presumption appear simply as factors making conversational implicatures conversational, differentiating them from conventional implicatures. It is clear from other passages, however, that Grice assigned a stronger function to these factors. It is not just the *conversationality of the implicature* that is supposed to depend on determinacy and the two other conditions. The very *existence of the implicature* is supposed to depend on determinacy.

These analogies are relevant to what I regard as a fundamental question about the Cooperative Principle and its attendant maxims, namely, what the basis is for the assumption which we seem to make, and on which (I hope) it will appear that a great range of implicatures depends, that talkers will in general (ceteris paribus and in the absence of indications to the contrary) proceed in the manner that these principles prescribe. (Grice 1975: 28)

When someone, by using the form of expression *an X,* implicates that the X does not belong to or is not otherwise closely connected with some identifiable person, the implicature is present because the speaker has failed to be specific in a way in which he might have been expected to be specific, with the consequence that it is likely to be assumed that he is not in a position to be specific. (Grice 1975: 38)

Implicatures are thought of as arising in the following way; an implicatum (factual or imperatival) is the content of that psychological state or attitude which needs to be attributed to a speaker in order to secure one or another of the following results. (Grice 1989: 370)

Grice's characteristic view, which has been widely assimilated,[8] is that conversational implicatures are those that *depend on* the cooperative presumption and the other conditions, and so are present or absent *because of* them. The Gricean factors *make possible, give rise to,* and *generate* the implicatures. Grice is trying to define conversational implicatures in terms of underlying causes. If this is correct, then Bob's implication that Ann can get gasoline at the station depends on, and is present because of, the fact that Bob's possession of the belief that she can is inferable from the presumption that he is trying to be cooperative.

Grice thus holds what I call the *Generative Assumption,* according to which satisfaction of the first clause of definition I is due to satisfaction of the remaining three clauses when the implicature is conversational.

Generative Assumption: Conversational implicatures exist because of the fact that the cooperative presumption, determinacy, and mutual knowledge conditions hold.

Whereas the Calculability Assumption is epistemological, the Generative Assumption is ontological, concerned with the constitution of implicatures rather than their recognition, with explanation rather than prediction. The reasons why something occurs need not enable us to recognize it, and the evidence we use to detect a phenomenon need not explain why it exists. Given the Generative Assumption, definition I could be simplified by omitting clause (i),

---

[8] By Stalnaker (1974: 476), Kempson (1975: 144), Walker (1975: 170, 175), Searle (1975: 266), Harnish (1976: 330, 332), Sadock (1978: 366), McCawley (1978: 245), Bach and Harnish (1979: 167, 169, 171), Gazdar (1979: 51), Wilson and Sperber (1979: 301), Levinson (1983: 99–100), Leech (1983: 9, 91–92), Lycan (1984: 75–76), Martinich (1984: 510), G. M. Green (1989: 89, 93), Atlas (1989: 148), Thomason (1990: 330, 350, 352, 355–357), Fasold (1990: 129–130), Hirschberg (1991: 1–2, 16), Bach (1994b: 12), Schiffrin (1994: 193), and Matsumoto (1995).

as Levinson (1983: 113) does. Although logically independent, the condition would be theoretically superfluous. Moreover, the definiens could be strengthened without affecting the strength of the definition by adding *because:* at the end of condition (i).

In one respect, the Generative Assumption helps interpret definition I. Consider clause (iii), which says the supposition that S believes p is required to make S's utterance consistent with the Cooperative Principle. The satisfaction of clause (iii) seems automatic in light of clause (i) and the Maxim of Quality, which is subsumed under the Cooperative Principle. Clause (i) says that S implicates p. The Maxim of Quality says, "Do not convey what you believe false." If S is implicating p and obeying the Maxim of Quality, then S must believe p. But Grice did not intend anything so trivial. The fact that S has implicated p was not intended to be a determinant of what is required to make S's utterance compatible with the Cooperative Principle. On the contrary, the relevant determinants must be such that the fact that S has to believe p can give rise to the fact that S has implicated p. The sorts of factors Grice had in mind were the linguistic meaning of the sentence uttered, the perceptually salient features of the physical context, and so on.

The final tenet of the Gricean theory is a methodological principle I call *Grice's Razor* because it is a specific application of Ockham's rule. Grice's Razor is usually formulated briefly as saying that *Senses are not to be multiplied beyond necessity.* Griceans typically invoke Ockham in their arguments that certain interpretations should be classified as implicatures rather than meanings. For example, Grice's Razor is used to support the conclusion that the sequential interpretation of "and" is an implicature rather than a second sense. It is also used against claims that natural language connectives like "or" and "if-then" have different meanings from their logical counterparts *"v"* and *"⊃."*

The usual formulation of Grice's Razor is zippy and unexceptionable. Unfortunately, it is useless for Gricean purposes. It is certainly true that senses should not be postulated beyond necessity. But it is just as true that implicatures should not to be multiplied beyond necessity. The simple formulation of Grice's Razor does not favor implicatures over senses: both are "extra entities."

More fully expressed, Grice's view is this. It is more economical to postulate implicatures rather than senses because implicatures can be accounted for in terms of general psychosocial principles of conversation, whereas senses require specific linguistic conventions. The postulation of senses rather than implicatures thus results in a more complex overall theory. In addition to the general rules of rational, cooperative behavior represented by the Cooperative Principle, senses imply specific conventions governing the use of particular words.

A further argument is that the ambiguist will often have to postulate several independent but suspiciously similar ambiguities. Just as "some" implies "not all" in some contexts, so do "many," "most," and "nearly all"; furthermore, "possible" usually implies "not necessary," and "warm" often implies "not hot." The Gricean accounts for all these facts in terms of one principle, the Maxim of Quantity. The ambiguist, it seems, must treat them as unconnected.

It is clear from this line of thought that only conversational implicatures are favored over senses. Indeed, the same reasoning favors postulation of conversational implicatures over conventional implicatures or semantic presuppositions. We therefore formulate Grice's Razor as follows:

Grice's Razor: Other things equal, it is preferable to postulate conversational implicatures rather than senses, conventional implicatures, or semantic presuppositions because conversational implicatures can be derived from independently motivated psychosocial principles.[9]

The *ceteris paribus* clause acknowledges that the evidence in favor of ambiguity might be sufficiently strong to warrant its postula-

---

[9] Grice's Razor is affirmed by Ziff (1960: 44), Grice (1978: 47), Cohen (1971: 56), Stalnaker (1974: 475), Walker (1975: 158 ff.), Kempson (1975: 142), Searle (1975: 269), McCawley (1978: 257–258), Sadock (1981: 258), Atlas and Levinson (1981: 56), Sperber and Wilson (1981: 317), Wilson and Sperber (1981: 155), Levinson (1983: 97–100, 132), Leech (1983: 48, 88), Bach (1987: 69, 77–79), Blakemore (1987a: 21), Schiffer (1987b: §IV), Horn (1989: 213–214, 365, 383). Compare and contrast Carston (1988) and Thomason (1990: 329). Van Kuppevelt (1996: 393) affirms the derivability clause without addressing ambiguity.

tion, as in the case of "bank." The force of the rule is only that unless the direct evidence for ambiguity is strong enough to outweigh the indirect evidence represented by the added theoretical complexity, implicature is preferred.

William Lycan suggested that Grice's Razor can be sharpened by a Davidsonian consideration. "It is not just that positing extra senses complicates the semantics," he remarked. "It is that every single extra sense would have to be *learned* separately."[10] Positing conversational implicatures, in contrast, places no such demands on the learning process. For implicatures can be worked out by general reasoning from common knowledge and situational perception. It is not clear to me that this argument really establishes a theoretical advantage for the postulation of conversational implicatures over senses. Although the ambiguist does impose extra demands on the learning process, the Gricean appears to place extra demands on the interpretation process. Instead of the familiar process of selecting the most likely sense from the list of previously learned senses on the basis of contextual clues, the Gricean asks the interpreter to engage in the sophisticated reasoning represented by the Working-out Schema. Grice's general pattern for the working out of a conversational implicatures certainly appears to be more difficult than the reasoning by which we infer that "bank" most likely means "commercial bank" in a sentence like "John deposited $50 in the bank."[11] Without a reason to think that it is better to complicate the interpretation process rather than the learning process, or a compelling argument that recognizing previously learned senses is no easier than working out implicatures, the Davidsonian consideration creates no presumption in favor of implicatures over senses.

1.4 GRICE'S RAZOR

The last clause in Grice's Razor states that *conversational implicatures can be derived from independently motivated principles.* The term *"derived from"* in this clause should be understood as implying that

---

[10] Personal communication.   [11] I pursue this question further in section 4.5

the conversational implicatures can be *inferred from and explained by* the conversational principles. The derivation clause of Grice's Razor is an independent postulate of Gricean theory. It does not follow from definition I. Defining conversational implicature in terms of certain principles, as definition I does, explains the concept of a conversational implicature in terms of those principles, but does not explain any conversational implicatures. To see the point starkly, note that if one defines miracles as acts of God that contravene the laws of nature, then one has explained the concept of a miracle in terms of laws of nature without explaining any miracles in terms of laws of nature.

Even the Generative Assumption falls short of saying that conversational implicatures are explained by the Cooperative Principle and associated maxims. The Generative Assumption says that conversational implicatures depend on three conditions, none of which is a principle of conversation. The cooperative *presumption* is not the Cooperative Principle itself, but the act of believing or assuming that S is obeying the Cooperative Principle. It is S's audience, of course, who presumes that S is obeying the Cooperative Principle. The fact that S's audience presumes something about S is not a general psychosocial principle. The vague wording of Grice's theory, coupled with the "act-object" ambiguity of "presumption" – it can mean either the principle presumed or the presuming of that principle – may have led to some confusion on this point.

In fact, the Generative Assumption and the derivability clause of Grice's Razor are concerned with the explanation of different things. The Generative Assumption is concerned with providing an account of *speaker* implicatures, whereas Grice's Razor is concerned with the explanation of *sentence* implicatures. Grice called the former "*particularized* implicatures," the latter "*generalized* implicatures." It is at least plausible that "Some died" implicates "Not all died" because people generally observe the Maxim of Quantity. Because people tend to be as informative as required, they generally use sentences of the form "Some _____" to implicate "Not all _____". And because speakers generally use *some* in that way, the sentence "Some died" implicates "Not all died." I criticize this reasoning later (sections 3.7–3.8), but it is at least plausible.

21

In the case of speaker implicatures, the order of explanation must be reversed. The fact that people *tend* to be cooperative does not begin to explain why a particular speaker is cooperative on a given occasion, or why he says or implicates what he does. The mere existence of a general behavioral tendency does not suffice to explain why it happens to be manifested when it is. Even the fact that S *was* cooperative on a given occasion does not explain what he said or implicated. For S obeys the Maxim of Quantity in the paradigm case *by* using "Some S is P" with a quantity implicature. Using "Some S is P" to implicate that not all S is P is one way of being as informative as required. Hence S obeyed the maxim *because* he used the quantity implicature, not vice versa. Suppose an army official reporting on the results of a raid to free hostages says, "Some hostages died." In such a situation, the official would be obligated to convey that all died if he knew that to be a fact. So if in this situation the official gave as much information as required, he did so by saying "Some hostages died" and thereby implicating "Not all did."[12] He gave as much information as required in virtue of saying and implicating what he did. It would make no sense to claim that he said or implicated anything in virtue of giving as much information as required.

Grice assumed that speakers *intentionally* conform to the Maxim of Quantity. When they do, it is the *intention* to obey the maxim that leads them to use sentences with quantity implicatures, and thereby to obey the maxim. In the same way, I comply with the tax code by paying my taxes. But it is my intention to comply with the tax code that leads me to pay taxes and thereby comply with the law. Whereas *obeying* a law cannot explain the act in virtue of which you obey it, the act of *trying* to obey the law can. So can the desire to obey the law, or the belief that you ought to obey. We focus on intention as the explanatory factor.

(5) **Order of Explanation, Speaker Implicature:**
    (a) *S intends to observe the Cooperative Principle.*
    (b) ▶ *S uses Σ to implicate that p.*
    (c) ▶ *S does observe the Cooperative Principle.*

[12] In Goldman's (1970) terminology, the official's speech act "generated" his compliance with the maxim.

The symbol "▶" in (5) may be read "consequently." The move from (5)(a) to (5)(b) involves a broadly causal explanation. The move from (5)(b) to (5)(c) specifies what makes it true that S is observing the Cooperative Principle. Given that S observes the Cooperative Principle by implicating certain things, rather than vice versa, it would immediately falsify the Generative Assumption if "the cooperative presumption" were changed to "the Cooperative Principle."

The explanatory factors identified in the Generative Assumption – determinacy, mutual knowledge, and the cooperative presumption – are not *causes* of implicatures or any sort of *antecedent conditions* that lead to them. Nor are they laws of nature under which implicatures are subsumed. The Gricean factors are only plausible as conditions that *constitute* the implicatures. Nothing in Grice's theory is suited to tell us *why* Bill implicated that Ann could get gasoline around the corner rather than telling her that she could, remaining silent, or being insolent. Nor can the Gricean factors explain *how* S implicates things: the factors are not ways of implicating. The Generative Assumption could only describe the conditions *in virtue of which* implicatures occur – the conditions *making it true* that Bill implicated that Ann could get gasoline around the corner rather than telling her. The theory may tell us how metaphorical and ironic meaning arises, but it says nothing about why people use figurative speech at all rather than speaking literally.[13] Nor does the theory tell us how speakers manage to use metaphors.

An analogy may make the distinction I am drawing clearer. The fact that Tom was driving 100 miles an hour may be what makes it true that he violated the law. But it does not explain why Tom violated the law. To know why Tom violated the law, we would have to know what led him to drive 100 miles per hour. Was it a desire to get there quickly? Or inadvertence? Similarly, Horowitz may be playing the *Waldstein* Sonata beautifully by virtue of the fact that he is playing a certain sequence of notes on the piano. But this does not explain why he is playing that sonata or how he does it so beautifully.

Does the fact that people generally obey the Cooperative

---

[13] Compare Sperber and Wilson (1981: 296) and Leech (1983: 80).

Principle perhaps explain why the Gricean conditions are satisfied on a given occasion, thereby explaining particular implicatures? Even that indirect link is unlikely. The Cooperative Principle cannot explain why a certain belief is required by the Cooperative Principle, or why S expects that H can see it is required by the Cooperative Principle. General obedience may explain in an indirect fashion why S is presumed to be following the principle. For H may presume that S is obeying the principle because H has observed that people in general tend to obey it. But that is hardly enough to say that the Cooperative Principle explains any particular implicature. For H may for the same reason presume that any number of people around her are obeying the Cooperative Principle. Yet S may be unique in implicating what he does. The Cooperative Principle would not tell us, therefore, why S implicated what he did or why the others did not.

Now let us return to the case of sentence implicature. Is it really the fact that *people tend to be cooperative* that explains why *speakers generally use Σ to implicate that p?* That would be like saying that the fact that people tend to obey the law explains why Americans generally drive on the right and Britons generally drive on the left. If there is any explanation here, it is extremely low powered. A much more satisfactory explanation of why Americans drive on the right and Britons on the left is provided by observing that they generally know the laws of their land and *intend* to obey them. Similarly, it is the fact that speakers intend to be cooperative that explains why they use sentences the way they do. So complementing (5) we have:

(6) **Order of Explanation, Sentence Implicature:**
   (a) *People intend to observe the Cooperative Principle*
   (b) ▶ *Speakers use sentence Σ to implicate that p.*
   (c) ▶ *Sentence Σ implicates that p.*

In going from (6)(a) to (6)(b), we would be explaining common usage of a sentence in terms of a common intention. In going from (6)(b) to (6)(c), we are specifying what makes it true that a sentence has a particular implicature.[14] We could extend (6) in a

---

[14] Only under specific conditions, however, will (6)(c) be derivable from (6)(b). See *Meaning, Expression, and Thought,* Chapters 8 through 10.

different direction by observing that the fact that speakers generally use sentence Σ to implicate that p contributes to the fact that they tend to be cooperative.

The plausibility of Grice's Razor, therefore, depends on distinguishing two different forms of the Gricean conversational principles, a distinction that is obscured by their usual imperatival formulation. One form specifies a general *behavioral* tendency, the other a general *motivational* tendency. Both must be distinguished from further *normative* and *cognitive* formulations.

Cooperative Principle: "Contribute what is required by the accepted purpose of the conversation."

> **Normative:** People *ought to* contribute what is conversationally required.
>
> **Behavioral:** People *do* contribute what is conversationally required.
>
> **Motivational:** People *intend to* contribute what is conversationally required.
>
> **Cognitive:** People *believe they ought to* contribute what is conversationally required.[15]

The maxims, of course, all have parallel formulations. The motivational principles are clearly deeper in the order of explanation than the behavioral; the cognitive formulations are deeper still. For people generally do what is required because they intend to, and they intend to because they believe they ought to. Furthermore, only the motivational and cognitive forms of the Cooperative Principle can serve to explain why sentences have conversational implicatures. Whereas Grice's Razor must therefore be interpreted as referring to the cognitive or motivational forms, the Theoretical Definition, calculability, and determinacy must be interpreted as

---

[15] Four more principles can be obtained by modifying "people" with *rational,* and still more can be obtained by iterating the operators: people *ought to want to, believe they ought to want to, believe that people believe they want to,* and so on. Finally, the principles must all be interpreted *nonuniversally,* as saying that people *generally* rather than *always* do/ought to/want to/ . . . tell the truth. Interpreted universally, all the principles would be false.

referring to the *normative* form of the Cooperative Principle. What we *observe,* and in the relevant sense *obey,* are normative rules.

We have been clarifying Grice's Razor by trying to understand and make plausible the claim that conversational implicatures can be derived from the Cooperative Principle. In additional to meaning that the implicatures can be explained by the principle, this must also imply that the implicatures can be inferred from the principle. If it did not, Grice's Razor would be blatantly false. For semantic conventions and conventional implicatures are also at least partly explained by the fact that people intend to be cooperative. Because people intend to contribute what is required in daily conversations, they use words with their conventional meanings. In conversation (1), surely, Bob spoke English rather than a language he did not think Ann would understand because he wanted to provide her with useful information. He used the words he did with their standard English meanings in order to communicate the information Ann needed. Similar decisions made daily by speakers of English around the world sustain the conventions by virtue of which words have the meaning they do in English.

The intention to communicate cooperatively thus leads to and partly explains why words have the meanings they do. But that intention does not explain why one convention sprang up rather than another, and thus does not completely explain why words have their standard meanings. Given that the intention to be cooperative could have led to and sustained two very different conventional uses, neither can be derived from the principle alone. Similarly, the fact that people intend to obey the law leads them to obey the law, and partly explains why they do. The intention leads Americans to drive on the right and Britons to drive on the left. One of my reasons for driving on the right is to obey the law. One of a Briton's reasons for driving on the left will be the same. But the intention to obey the law cannot explain why it is conventional or legal for Americans to drive on the right or Britons on the left. Thus the intention does not fully explain why Americans drive on the right or Britons on the left.

Grice's Razor appears to rely on the Calculability Assumption, which says that conversational implicatures can be "worked out," that is, inferred in a specific way from the Cooperative Principle. But "working out" in Grice and his followers has been understood as a process for inferring what a *speaker* implicates. Observe, for example, that a key consideration, according to Grice, is that "the speaker has done nothing to stop me thinking that p." Grice's Razor therefore implies that there is also a working-out schema for *sentence* implicature. Facts about a particular context or speaker will never play a role in deriving a sentence implicature. We have to substitute reference to contexts of the *type* Grice described.

The Working-Out Schema for Sentence Implicature:

P1 Sentence Σ is commonly used with a particular meaning in contexts of type G.

P2 Speakers in G-contexts are observing the Cooperative Principle.

P3 Users of Σ in G-contexts could not be observing the Cooperative Principle unless they believed p.

  . . .

  ∴ Speakers use Σ to implicate that p.

C ∴ Σ implicates that p.

Equivalently, P3 could be replaced with a premise stating that the Working-out Schema for speaker implicature can be used to infer that users of Σ in G-contexts implicate that p. We look more critically at this schema in Chapter 3.

1.5 SUFFICIENCY

The Generative Assumption states, among other things, that the satisfaction of conditions (ii) through (iv) of definition I implies condition (i), according to which S implicates p. By definition, to implicate that p is to mean or imply that p by saying something else. The fact that nothing in conditions (ii) through (iv) addresses what S has said is therefore a minor defect. One option is to qualify the Generative Assumption with the proviso that S has said something other than p, and to drop the claim that condition (i) of definition I is superfluous given the Generative Assumption.

Another option would be to add a fifth clause to definition I stating that S has said something other than p, and to strengthen the Generative Assumption to say that the satisfaction of the first condition is implied by and due to the satisfaction of the other four.

We focus on a more fundamental consequence of the Generative Assumption, which I call the *Sufficiency Implication.*

Sufficiency Implication: If the cooperative presumption, determinacy, and mutual knowledge conditions are satisfied, then S means or implies that p.

Grice is as famous for his definition of speaker meaning (Grice 1957, 1969) as he is for his theory of implicature. Because his definition of speaker meaning was published before the 1967 William James Lectures in which he presented his theory of implicature, one would have expected some effort on Grice's part to derive the Sufficiency Implication from his theory of speaker meaning. The closest he came to doing this was the passage quoted earlier in which Grice (1975: 31) presented his Working-out Schema. Grice makes no explicit reference there to his definition of speaker meaning. The last few lines of the quoted passage, however, seem to have Grice's (1957) definition in mind.

According to Grice (1957), *S means that p iff S intends to produce in H the belief that p by means of recognition of intention.* Speaker meaning, on Grice's view, is a species of speaker intention. Nothing in clauses (ii) through (iv), however, implies that S has *any* intentions. Clause (iv) attributes to S certain beliefs, but not intentions. In particular, nothing in (iv) implies that S intends H to believe p. This fact is no problem for definition I. For in that definition, S's implicating p is an independent condition. All clauses (ii) through (iv) do is differentiate conversational implicature from other forms of implicature. But as we saw in section 1.3, Grice made the further, and much more interesting claim, that in cases of conversational implicature, condition (i) is satisfied *because* the others are. That is the claim we are examining now.

In his Working-out Schema, Grice has H assume that *S has done nothing to stop H from thinking that p.* The truth of this assumption is neither assured nor excluded by clauses (ii) through (iv), and it is not sufficient even with them to yield the result that S intends H to believe that p. The fact that S has done nothing to stop H from thinking p might provide evidence that S intends H to believe p together with the fact that S is being cooperative. But nothing in clauses (ii) through (iv) requires that S is being cooperative. Clause (ii), of course, states that S is *presumed* to be observing the Cooperative Principle. But nothing guarantees that that presumption is correct. Suppose, for example, that S does not much care for H and wants her to suffer at least momentarily. H has just been informed that her family was involved in a bad auto accident. She fearfully asks S, "Are they alive?" S says, "Some are," cruelly implicating that not all of H's family survived the accident. No bridge from "S has done nothing to stop me from believing that not all of my family survived" to "S intends me to believe that not all survived" is provided by the fact that S is being cooperative. For he isn't. He is trying to hurt H by misleading her. Of course, because H mistakenly believes that S is being cooperative, she will arrive at the true conclusion that S intends her to believe that not all of her family survived. But H's reasoning is unsound, involving as it does a false premise.

Even if we add in the fact that S is being cooperative, clauses (ii) through (iv) do not imply that S intends H to believe p. What clause (iv) says is that S believes that H is *able* to determine that the supposition that *S believes p* is required to make S's utterance consistent with the Cooperative Principle. It does not say that S believes H *will* determine anything. And H may well conclude that S believes p without drawing the further conclusion that p. Consider this variant of case (1). Ann asks Bob where she can get gasoline, but she is racially bigoted and jumps to the conclusion that Bob is an ignoramus. She plans to ignore what Bob says, and asks only because she thinks that is the quickest way to dispatch him. Bob notes her somewhat condescending attitude, and he concludes that she does not consider him reliable. Nevertheless, he intends to be a good citizen, and answers, "There's a station around the corner," implicating as before that she can get gasoline there. Bob may believe that Ann will infer that he thinks there is a station around the corner. But he does not expect her to conclude there is a station around the corner. As a final variation on the case, it is easy to imagine Bob answering, "There's a station around the corner" without caring at all about what Ann believes, even if he is observing the Cooperative Principle.

I have been arguing here that the satisfaction of conditions (ii) through (iv) does not entail that Grice's (1957) definition of speaker meaning is satisfied. Elsewhere, I have reviewed a wide variety of evidence showing that Grice's definition is very wide of the mark.[16] Would use of a superior definition of speaker meaning sustain the Sufficiency Implication? I think not. Grice's (1969) definition is superior in a number of respects, but its definiens is not implied by the determinacy, mutual knowledge, and cooperative presumption conditions either. The same goes for my own definition. *Every* plausible definition of speaker meaning will require S to have certain intentions. But nothing in clauses (ii) through (iv) requires any particular intentions.

Other cases show that the Sufficiency Implication fails even if belief is strengthened to intention in clause (iv), making it a "mutual intention" rather than "mutual knowledge" condition. Let (iv) now read: *S intends, and intends H to recognize that S intends, that H be able to determine that (iii) is true.*[17] It is still not implied that S has implicated p. Suppose S and H are having a brainstorming session aimed at determining who committed the crime. To this end, S and H are critically reviewing evidence establishing that the butler did it. At one point in the conversation, H asks S to describe the butler. S says, "He is 6 feet tall, thin, and 55 years old." The supposition that S believes he is describing the butler is required to make S's utterance consistent with the Cooperative Principle, we may presume. And S may well intend H to determine that he believes he is describing the butler. It is presumably not true, though, and certainly need not be, that by saying "He is 6 feet tall . . ." S meant or implied *that he (S) is describing the butler.*

This example is an instance of a familiar sort of problem. Suppose S and H later reach a point in the conversation at which they

---

[16] See Davis (1992a, 1992b). [17] Compare Walker (1975: 157).

agree that what they really need is evidence substantiating S's belief that the butler knew Mrs. Smith. S thereupon produces a photograph of the butler with Mrs. Smith. The supposition that S believes the butler knew Mrs. Smith, and the supposition that the photograph is evidence the butler knew her, are presumably required by the accepted purpose of the conversation. But by producing the photograph, S did not mean or imply that the butler knew Mrs. Smith or that the photograph was evidence to that effect. It might be insisted that S's "contribution" here is not a speech act, and thus not the sort of action covered by clauses (ii) through (iv). This observation would be more than a technicality if we were just concerned with what S implicated. For by definition, implicatures are generated by speech acts. But we are now concerned with whether certain conditions are sufficient for meaning or implying something. And it is both possible and common to mean something by completely nonlinguistic actions.

Indeed, if the Generative Assumption were correct, and the cooperative presumption, determinacy, and mutual knowledge conditions really *generated* implicatures, then one should expect analogous conditions involving generalizations of the Cooperative Principle to generate speaker meaning outside the narrowly linguistic realm. They do not. Consider the case cited by Grice (1975: 28), in which S cooperatively hands H four screws because that is what H needs at that stage of repairing a car. The supposition that S believes there are four screws in his hand is presumably required to make his action consistent with the generalized principle of cooperation, as H presumably recognizes. But by handing H four screws, S did not mean that he has four screws. Indeed, S was not attempting to communicate and did not mean anything by that act. (S did mean to help, of course, but that is a different sense of *mean*.)

Grice (1957) handled "showing" by his condition that the speaker must intend to produce belief at least in part *by means of recognition of intention*. According to Grice, if S means that p, then S must intend not only that H will recognize his intention to produce the belief that p; S must also intend H to infer that p from the very fact that S intends to make him believe that p. In the photograph case, Grice thought, S intends the photo to do all the convincing. This treatment is inadequate, however. First, S may well have intended H to infer that the butler knew Mrs. Smith not from the photograph alone, but also from the fact that S intends the photo to produce that belief; photographs, after all, are neither self-authenticating nor self-interpreting. S still would not have meant anything by showing the photograph. Second, there are other cases in which S does mean something by showing a photograph, even though he expects the photo to do most or even all of the convincing. For example, S may be momentarily unable to speak, and in order to convey the idea that the butler knew Mrs. Smith, he produces the photograph. Third, there are plenty of cases in which S means something despite the fact that he does not expect H's recognition of his intentions to play any role in the formation of H's beliefs, as when S yells out, "I'm over here!" in a crowd to let H know where he is (Recanati 1986: 225), or more radically when S sends out anonymous, unsigned letters (Davis 1992a: 240). My main point here, though, is that clauses (ii) through (iv) contain nothing designed to distinguish between proving or showing that p and meaning or implying that p, and thus are far from sufficient for meaning or implying that p.

Chapters 3 and 4 are concerned with failures of the parallel "Necessity Implication," the assumption that S means or implies p *only if* the cooperative presumption, determinacy, and mutual knowledge conditions are satisfied. Chapter 2 is concerned with cases in which either the Sufficiency Implication or the Necessity Implication fails.

2

Differentiation

A number of writers have observed that for nearly every implicature correctly predicted by Gricean theory, others are falsely predicted.[1] That is, the rules of inference used to "work out" observed implicatures can usually be used just as well to work out nonexistent implicatures. I call these *failures of differentiation*. By a simple application of Mill's Methods, failures of differentiation mean that the observed implicatures do not exist *because of* the Gricean factors or maxims and that Gricean theory does not provide a satisfactory account of implicatures. To make the point, I examine three of the most familiar applications of Gricean theory and one less familiar. Other examples are plentiful. I also observe the converse failure of differentiation, in which implicatures exist that cannot be derived from conversational principles.

2.1 QUANTITY IMPLICATURES

The most thoroughly studied implicatures are *quantity implicatures,* those in which a weaker statement is used to implicate the denial of a stronger statement.[2] A large number of implicatures follow this pattern. Let ⊐ mean *implicates,* and − mean *it is not the case that.*

[1] Kroch (1972), Kempson (1975: 152–156), Harnish (1976: 332, 334, 352), Horn (1989: 15, 18–19, 332–335), Sadock (1978: 369), Levinson (1983: 122), Burton-Roberts (1984: 200–201), Sperber and Wilson (1986a: 37, 93; 1987: 699), Brown and Levinson (1987: 11), and Thomason (1990: 353–356).

[2] See especially Horn (1972, 1984, 1989), Gordon and Lakoff (1975: 92), Gazdar (1979), Atlas and Levinson (1981: §9), Leech (1983: §4.2), Levinson (1983: 106, 132–146; 1987b: 63), Fasold (1990: 138–139), Hirschberg (1991), Rooth (1992), Matsumoto (1995), and Van Kuppevelt (1996).

(1)   Some [Many, At least 90% . . .] died ⊐ –(All died).
      It is possibly true ⊐ –(It is necessarily true).
      The food is warm ⊐ –(The food is hot).
      Steve believes the plant is alive ⊐ –(Steve knows the plant is alive).

Griceans attempt to explain these implicatures in terms of the Maxim of Quantity, according to which one is to be just as informative as required. The idea is that if the speaker were in a position to make the stronger statement, he should have. Because he did not, he must believe that the stronger statement is not true.

To show that these regular scalar inferences are indeed implicatures we need now to produce a Gricean argument deriving the inference. . . . A short version of the argument might go as follows:

> The speaker has said $A(e_2)$; if S was in a position to state that a stronger item on the scale holds – i.e. to assert $A(e_1)$ – then he would be in breach of the first maxim of Quantity if he asserted $A(e_2)$. Since I the addressee assume that S is cooperating, and therefore will not violate the maxim of Quantity without warning, I take it that S wishes to convey that he is *not* in a position to state that the stronger item e_1 on the scale holds, and indeed knows that it does not hold.

More generally, and somewhat more explicitly:

> (i)   S has said p
> (ii) There is an expression q, more informative than p (and thus q entails p), which might be desirable as a contribution to the current purposes of the exchange (and here there is perhaps an implicit reference to the maxim of Relevance)
> (iii) q is of roughly equal brevity to p; so S did not say p rather than q simply in order to be brief (i.e. to conform to the maxim of Manner)
> (iv) Since if S knew that q holds but nevertheless uttered p he would be in breach of the injunction to make his contribution as informative as is required, S must mean me, the addressee, to infer that S knows that q is not the case (K–q), or at least that he does not know that q is the case (–Kq).

The important feature of such arguments to note is that they derive an implicature by reference to what has *not* been said: the absence of a statement $A(e_1)$, in the presence of a weaker one, legitimates the inference that it is not the case that $A(e_1)$, via the maxim of Quantity. (Levinson 1983: 134–135)

Given the perceived success of Gricean theory in explaining the implicatures of the sentences in (1), Grice's Razor has been used to argue that certain alleged senses are really implicatures. Thus it is argued that the exclusive interpretation of "p or q" can and therefore should be considered a quantity implicature rather than a second sense.[3]

The existence of quantity implicatures is undeniable. What is false is the claim that quantity implicatures are *derived from* or *explained by* the Maxim of Quantity. Note that I have defined quantity implicatures as those in which a weaker statement is used to implicate the denial of a stronger statement. By this definition, there are lots of quantity implicatures. Quantity implicatures are sometimes defined, however, as those *due to the Maxim of Quantity*. I argue that that class is empty. The ex post facto "derivations" Levinson and others give cannot be explanatory, because they can be given just as well when there are no implicatures to explain. Suppose, for example, that S is asked, "Did anyone die?" He might answer, "Some did," or he might simply say, "Yes." If he answered, "Yes," he would be affirming that some died, just as if he had answered, "Some did." But he would not have implicated anything further.

(2) "Did anyone die?"
   Some did ⊐ −(All died).
   Yes ⊉ −(All died).

If we can use Levinson's Gricean argument to derive the implicature of "Some did," then we should also be able to use it to show that a "Yes" answer has the same implicature. It does not.[4]

Cases in which weaker statements are *not* used to implicate the denial of stronger statements are at least as common as cases in which they are.

(3) Some died ⊉ −(Only some [a few, a minority] died).
   Some died ⊉ −(Some were killed [murdered, assassinated, executed, . . .])

---

[3] See later, section 5.5.
[4] M. Green (1995: 96–98) noted the difference described in (2), and used it in an argument that the Maxim of Quantity is preferable to a principle of "Volubility" (see §3.8). He failed to observe that the difference also shows the Maxim of Quantity cannot be used to derive the implicature of "Some S is P."

Some died ⊅ –(35.72% died).

Over 50% died ⊅ –(Over 51% died).

Some people died ⊅ –(Some women [mothers, grandmothers, . . .] died).

The repairs will take some time ⊅ –(The repairs will take a long time).

Hummel wrote some fine music ⊅ –(Hummel wrote only fine music).

Some odd numbers are prime ⊅ –(Many [most] are).

John may win ⊅ –(John will win).

John sees a book on the table ⊅ –(John sees all [many, most] books on the table).

2 is an even number ⊅ –(2 is necessarily an even number).

2 is an even number ⊅ –(S knows that 2 is an even number).

2 is a number ⊅ –(2 is an even [odd, prime, composite, . . .] number).

The food is not hot ⊅ –(The food is nearly hot).

John is not happy ⊅ –(John is unhappy [miserable, depressed, . . .]).

John is in California ⊅ –(John is in southern California).

It is snowing ⊅ –(It is snowing and cold [wintry, cloudy, . . .]).

It is snowing or raining ⊅ –(It is snowing).

It is hot and/or humid ⊅ –(It is both hot and humid).

John kicked the dog ⊅ –(John kicked the dog intentionally [unintentionally, softly, . . .]).

John lost a book ⊅ –(John lost his book [Mary's book, the red book . . .]).

John didn't shop and buy wine ⊅ –(John neither shopped nor bought wine).

I'll pay you $5 if you mow the lawn ⊅ –(I'll pay you $5 if and only if you mow the lawn).

In some cases, contrary implications are present or strongly suggested. For example, "John lost a book" implicates "John lost his own book," and "John kicked the dog" at least suggests "John did kick the dog intentionally." The fact that "John is not happy" implicates "John is unhappy" illustrates a general figure of speech known as *litotes*. When you realize that (3) can be extended endlessly, it becomes evident that as common as they are, *quantity implicatures are the exception rather than the rule*. Hence quantity implicatures cannot possibly be due to any general psychosocial principles.

The point can be reinforced by examining a contrast noted by Grice (1975: 38). Consider (4):

(4) (a) John entered a house ⊐ −(John entered his house).
    (b) John entered a house ⊅ −(John entered S's house).
    (c) John lost a book ⊐ John lost his book.
    (d) John drove a car ⊅ John drove his car.
    (e) John drove a car ⊅ −(John drove his car).

(4)(a) is a quantity implicature because the weaker statement implicates the denial of a stronger statement. But we would be guilty of post hoc reasoning if we concluded that (4)(a) holds *because of* the Maxim of Quantity. For the denials of other equally relevant statements are not implicated (see (4)(b)), and sentences that do not seem to differ in any way relevant to the Maxim of Quantity have contrary implicatures (see (4)(c)), or none at all (see (4)(d) and (4)(e)).[5] Cross-culturally, Keenan provided evidence that in Malagasy society, (4)(a) would not hold. "When someone in a Malagasy village says *I see a person,* those listening do not infer that the speaker is not closely associated with the referent. Such a format is simply a conventionalized mode of personal reference" (Keenan 1975: 261–262). It appears to be just a coincidence that "John did not enter his house" can be "derived" from "John entered a house" in the manner Levinson set out.[6]

Horn (1972: Chs. 1 & 2; 1984: 15) similarly noted the contrast between (5)(a) and (5)(b).

(5) (a) John could have solved the problem ⊐ −(John did solve it).
    (b) John was able to solve the problem ⊐ John did solve it.[7]

Horn says that the Maxim of Quantity is "in force" in (5)(a) whereas the Maxim of Relation is "in force" in (5)(b). But given

---

[5] This problem was noted by Harnish (1976: 334), who saw no way to explain it; and by Atlas and Levinson (1981: 49), Horn (1984: 15, 19), and Mey (1993: 78–80), who offer an unconvincing solution. Leech (1983: 91) offered the standard Gricean explanation in a case like (4)(a) without noting the problem represented by the contrary cases.
[6] It might be noted in defense of the Gricean explanation that (4)(b) does hold in contexts in which S's house is under discussion. But (4)(c) through (4)(e) hold even if someone else's book or car is under discussion.
[7] We present evidence in Chapter 6 suggesting that (5)(b) involves ambiguity rather than implicature. But Grice's Razor militates against exploiting this possibility to defend the Gricean against the differentiation problem noted in the text.

the similarity in meaning between "could have solved" and "was able to solve," how could one maxim be in force but not the other? How in general could a body of general psychosocial principles generate diametrically opposed implicatures from nearly identical utterances? The difference cannot be attributed to contextual differences, because no context has been specified and the difference would exist even if both sentences were uttered in the same context. It would again be post hoc reasoning to conclude that (5)(a) was due to the Maxim of Quantity and (5)(b) to the Maxim of Relevance.

In some cases, Levinson's working-out schema can be used to "derive" contradictory implicatures for one and the same sentence. For example, Harnish (1976) observes that "Bill and Tom moved the piano" implicates that Bill and Tom moved it *together*. This could be "derived" by noting that if S could have asserted the stronger "Bill and Tom moved it separately," he would have. Because he did not, he must believe they moved it together. But then the same reasoning could be used to "show" that "Bill and Tom moved the piano" implicates that they moved it *separately*.[8] For there is just as much reason to think that if S could have asserted the stronger "They moved it together," he would have.

A further problem for the Gricean is that stressing the word "able" in (5)(b) blocks the implicature that John solved the problem, and at least suggests he did not solve it. Stressing "was" emphasizes the implicature. Stress will actually induce an implicature in some of the examples in (3). Thus, unlike the unstressed form, "Hummel wrote *some* fine music" does implicate "Hummel did not write only fine music." "*Hummel* wrote some fine music" implicates that some other composers did not.[9] Nothing in the Cooperative Principle or the maxims suggests that stress should have such a role in generating implicatures.

Consider next the classic "letter of recommendation." Suppose that Dr. Jones is being considered for the most distinguished chair

---

[8] Compare Kroch (1972), Kempson (1975: 152–156), and Atlas and Levinson (1981: 47).

[9] Compare Hirschberg (1991, Ch. VI) and Rooth (1992, 82–83).

in history of philosophy. Then by writing "Dr. Jones knows how to spell Descartes's name," and nothing else, the evaluator can implicate that Dr. Jones is a poor philosopher. This "damning by faint praise" is typically explained as a quantity implicature: if the evaluator could have said more, he would have. Because he didn't, and yet is trying to be cooperative, he must regard more informative statements as false. But now consider the related phenomenon of "praising by faint damns" (Sainsbury 1984: 423). An evaluator could implicate that Dr. Jones is a remarkably knowledgeable philosopher by writing, "Dr. Jones does not know anything about Pseudo-Albertus"[10] and nothing else. We might reason that more strongly negative statements are false, but we do not infer that all more informative statements are false. For clearly, the latter will include many positive statements, such as "Jones does not know anything about Pseudo-Albertus but does know everything there is to know about every major philosopher." In the case of damning by faint praise, similarly, it is not that every more informative statement is regarded as false. For some of those will be negative, such as "The most important thing Dr. Jones knows is how to spell Descartes's name."

Finally, many implicatures appear to operate in the same way quantity implicatures do, but do not involve the implied denial of a *stronger* statement.

(6) A: Did anyone get an A?
     B: Some got Bs.

(7) A: Did you get Hillary Clinton's photograph?
     B: I got Bill Clinton's.[11]

In (6), B implicated that no one got an A. But "Someone got an A" is neither stronger nor weaker than "Someone got a B." The two statements are similar in content but logically independent. There is no sense in which one is "more informative" than the other. Even the fact that an A is higher than a B in the grading

---

[10] An obscure sixth-century Andorran philosopher.
[11] This is a variant of Hirschberg's (1991: 50, 134) example. See also M. Green (1995: 92) and Van Kuppevelt (1996: 423).

scale is irrelevant to the implicature, as can be seen by switching from A and B to D and C, or by examining (7). So the implicature here is not a quantity implicature and cannot be explained by the Maxim of Quantity. In (7) similarly, B implicated that she did not get President Clinton's photograph, but not by asserting a statement weaker than the one she denied by implication. I refer to the class of implicatures represented by (6) and (7) as *close-but implicatures*. In them, the speaker explicitly provides information that is close to what is required by the conversation, but not quite; by doing so, the speaker implies the requisite further information. All quantity implicatures are close-but implicatures, but not all close-but implicatures are quantity implicatures.

The close-but implicatures that are not quantity implicatures present two differentiation problems for Gricean theory. The first concerns particularized implicatures, that is, speaker implicatures. How can quantity implicatures be *explained* by the Maxim of Quantity when that principle does not even apply to implicatures that seem to work in the same way? The second concerns generalized implicatures – sentence implicatures. If "Some students got A's" implicates "Not all students got A's" in virtue of Gricean principles, then why doesn't "Some students got Bs" implicate "No students got an A" as B used it in (6)? We return to close-but implicatures in Chapter 3.

Grice's Razor asserts that conversational implicatures can be explained by independently motivated principles. We observed in section 1.4 that this could hold only for generalized conversational implicatures, that is, sentence implicatures. We have argued in this section that generalized quantity implicatures cannot be explained by the Maxim of Quantity or any other general psychosocial principles. For such implicatures are the exceptions rather than the rule, and Gricean derivations of implicatures work just as well when they do not exist. Indeed, for every observed implicature that can be derived, unobserved implicatures can also be derived.

The Generative Assumption, in contrast, concerns how particularized conversational implicatures, or speaker implicatures, are generated by what the speaker says. What the evidence we have reviewed shows is that quantity implicatures are not generated in accordance with that assumption. The fact that quantity implicatures are the exception rather than the rule shows that either sufficiency or determinacy fails. That is, unless determinacy fails, and observed quantity implicatures are not derivable from the Maxim of Quantity as Griceans have assumed, we have to conclude that determinacy (together with common knowledge and the cooperative presumption) is not sufficient for implicature. The fact that quantity implicatures are members of the broader class of close-but implicatures, whose other members cannot be worked out in the Gricean fashion from the Maxim of Quantity, shows that Gricean derivations of quantity implicatures are not genuinely explanatory.

It is worth recalling that nothing in the Gricean Theory is designed to explain why a speaker says "Some died" and implicates "Not all died" rather than saying "Not all died" and implicating "Some died" (section 1.4). The theory does attempt to explain how by saying "Some died" speakers can implicate "Not all died." But that attempt, I am arguing, is unsuccessful.

2.2 TAUTOLOGY IMPLICATURES

Grice and his followers believe that the implicatures carried by tautologies can be explained in terms of the Maxim of Quantity even though they are quite different from quantity implicatures. Grice asserted that utterances of patent tautologies involve flouting the Maxim of Quantity because what is said is totally uninformative. He did not, however, explain how the implicature is to be worked out, or what is implicated. Levinson gives a bit more detail:

The uttering of simple and obvious tautologies should, in principle, have absolutely no communicative import. However, utterances of (38)–(40) and the like can in fact convey a great deal.

> (38) War is war
> (39) Either John will come or he won't
> (40) If he does it, he does it

Note that these, by virtue of their logical forms . . . are necessarily true; ergo they share the same truth conditions, and the differences we feel to lie between them, as well as their communicative import, must be almost entirely due to their pragmatic implications. An account of how they come to have communicative significance, and different communicative significances, can be given in terms of the flouting of the maxim of Quantity. Since this requires that the speakers be informative, the asserting of tautologies blatantly violates it. Therefore, if the assumption that the speaker is actually co-operating is to be preserved, some informative inference must be made. Thus in the case of (38) it might be "terrible things always happen in war, that's its nature and it's no good lamenting that particular disaster"; in the case of (39) it might be "calm down, there's no point in worrying about whether he's going to come because there's nothing we can do about it" and in the case of (40) it might be "it's no concern of ours." Clearly these share a dismissive or topic-closing quality, but the details of what is implicated will depend upon the particular context of utterance. (Incidentally, exactly how the appropriate implicatures in these cases are to be predicted remains quite unclear, although the maxim of Relevance would presumably play a crucial role.) (Levinson 1983: 110–111)

Note first that Levinson *claims* in the middle of the passage that an account of these implicatures can be given in terms of the Maxim of Quantity. But at the end he concedes that he does not know how to provide such an account.[12] Levinson's claim is therefore a mere assertion. Neither Grice nor Levinson attempted to *show* that the Maxim of Quantity had anything to do with generating the implicature.

[12] Compare Harnish (1976: 332) and Ward and Hirschberg (1991: 509). Ward and Hirschberg (1991: 511) later attempt to show how the implicatures can be calculated. But their working-out schema wrongly assigns the same implicature to all tautological utterances, one that none of them conveys. According to their schema, H is supposed to infer that in uttering 'a is a', "S has said as much as she or he truthfully can that is relevant about 'a'." H is supposed to infer further that because S has chosen not to assert any nontautological proposition about **a,** "S implicates that these alternatives are not relevant for the purposes of the exchange." But someone who utters "War is war" or "Boys will be boys" does *not* implicate that there is nothing more informative that he could truthfully say about the subject. On the contrary, he would implicate that terrible things happen in war, or that boys always do naughty things, depending on which tautology he uttered. No speaker tempted to use "War is war" with its customary implicature would believe that he could not say anything truthful, informative, and relevant about war.

Observe next that whatever the account of tautology implicature is, it must be different from that given for quantity implicature. For tautologies like "War is war" are not used to deny some stronger statement, the way "Some died" is used to implicate "Not all died." The question is, why not? Why should the Maxim of Quantity have a different sort of effect on "Some died" than it has on "War is war"? Why should the Maxim of Relation play a role in producing an implicature in the latter when it plays no role in producing an implicature in the former? The lack of an evident answer to these questions argues against the idea that sentences have the implicatures they do *because of* the maxims.

Let us nevertheless assume for the sake of argument that there is an as yet undiscovered method of calculating the implicature briefly recorded in (8).

(8)   War is war ⊐ It is the nature of war that terrible things happen.

Grice's view was that with the exception of manner implicatures, conversational implicatures are generated by what is said, which in turn is determined by the linguistic meaning of the sentence uttered. Hence substitution of synonyms should not affect implicatures, a property Grice (1975: 39) termed "nondetachability." Now "War is war" does not differ too much in meaning from "A war's a war." Yet the latter would ordinarily carry a very different implicature.

(9)   A war's a war ⊐ One war is as bad (or as good) as another.

Imagine a speaker getting impatient with a hairsplitting debate over whether intervention in Bosnia would result in another Korea as opposed to another Vietnam, and tossing out "A war's a war" dismissively. Contrast that with a speaker, impatient with those concerned that an attack will produce civilian casualties, who ends discussion with "War is war." What is there in the Maxim of either Quantity or Relation, or in the minuscule difference in meaning of these sentences, that could account for the fact that despite (8), "A war's a war" does not ordinarily implicate that terrible things always happen in wars, and that despite (9), "War is war" does not ordinarily implicate that one war is as bad as another?[13] Why doesn't the equally tautologous "War was war" have any implicatures? Why does "A war's a war" lack the characteristic implication of "A deal's a deal"? And why should "Wars will be wars" be perceived as a joke, a play on "Boys will be boys"? Wierzbicka (1985: 145; 1987: 110; 1991: Ch. 10) describes the Gricean view that tautological implicatures are somehow calculable from general, language-independent principles as an ethnocentric illusion. She gives many fascinating examples. One is that "in French one can hardly say *La guerre est la guerre* 'War is war'; to express a similar idea, one would say *C'est la guerre* 'That's war,' just as one says *C'est la vie* 'That's life'" (1987: 96). In Polish, "the *co X to X* construction ('What is X is X') implies that there is something uniquely good about X, and that the speaker feels he must admit it" (Wierzbicka 1987: 97). Whereas the Spanish *Que sera, sera* expresses a fatalistic attitude toward future events, *Co będzie to będzie* is used in Polish to express one's determination to act, regardless of possible negative consequences, as before a battle (Wierzbicka 1987: 102). Brown and Levinson provided evidence of further cross-cultural differences:

In Tamil, tautologies serve similar functions, for example a refusal of a request:

(43) kuTukkamaaTTeennaa, kuTukkamaaTTeen.
   If I won't give it, I won't. (c.i. I mean it!)

or a complaint:

(44) rooTunnaa rooTu!
   If it's a road, it's a road! (c.i. Boy, what a terrible road!)

---

[13] I say "ordinarily" here, because "War is war" can also be used to implicate that one war is as bad as another. If S said "War is war" to dismiss H's claim that another war with Iraq would be justified because Saddam Hussein is a madman, we would have to interpret S as implicating that one war is as bad as another, not that it is the nature of war that terrible things happen. The fact that the interpretation we give to tautologies depends in this way on the context may have contributed erroneously to the belief that tautology implicatures are due in some way to the Maxim of Relation. What we have here is not a relevance implicature like example (1) of Chapter 1, but rather contextual disambiguation. Compare Sadock (1978), Carston (1988), and Blakemore (1992: Ch. 5).

And a tautological statement like:

(45) amerikka amerikkataan.
America is exactly America.

may be used to implicate disapproval (as when Jacqueline Kennedy married Onassis), or approval (as when Apollo landed on the moon). Tamil also has a conventionalized tautology which conveys the attitude 'to hell with X' . . . :

(46) avaar-aam avaaru.
He they say is he. (c.i. 'Big deal him')

(Brown and Levinson 1978: 225)

Ward and Hirschberg (1991: 509–510) do note many cross-linguistic correlations among tautology implicatures. Wierzbicka's point, however, is that the correlation is not as perfect as it should be if Gricean theory were correct.

Incidentally, how could the fact that "War is war" involves flouting the Maxim of Quantity have anything to do with *why* certain implicatures exist when "That's war" has the same implicatures even though it is not tautologous and does not involve flouting the maxim?

Finally, note that tautology implicatures are far and away the exception rather than the rule. Just think of "No tables are nontables," "If it rains then it will rain or snow," "It won't both rain and not rain," "The red car is red," "The red car is either red and fast or red but not fast," and so on. Get out your logic book if you need more examples. The fact that most tautologies lack implicatures undermines the claim that observed tautology implicatures can be derived from general psychosocial principles. More specifically, the exceptional nature of tautology implicatures casts further doubt on the claim that the uninformativeness of tautologies, and thus their flouting of the Maxim of Quantity, has anything to do with their bearing certain implicatures. Think about the sorts of contexts in which one would use implicature-free tautologies. When looking at a number of different cars, Mary might ask John why he likes the red car best. John might well reply, "Because the red car is red." Similarly, "x can't be both less than zero and not less than zero" would most naturally be used to show that a given system of equations has no solution. "War is a state of armed conflict between groups" would normally be interpreted as a definition. It carries no implicature despite being very close if not identical in meaning to "War is war."

Again, the moral is clear. Generalized tautology implicatures like (8) and (9) are not explained by the Gricean maxims. *Convention* seems to be the only answer as to why specific tautologies have the implicatures they do.[14] The conventions, moreover, are language specific. Grice's Razor thus fails doubly for tautological implicatures. As for particularized implicatures, the evidence reviewed shows that either the observed tautological implicatures are not calculable from the Cooperative Principle, or else calculability plus the other Gricean factors are not sufficient for implicature.

2.3 CONJUNCTION IMPLICATURES

As we noted in section 1.2, it is well known that (10)(b) differs significantly from (10)(a).

(10) (a) John took off his trousers and went to bed.
      (b) John went to bed and took off his trousers.

In both these cases, the conjunction has an asymmetric temporal implication. Griceans argue that this implication is a conversational implicature generated by the nontemporal, symmetrical "and," not a part of one of the meanings of "and." One argument for this conclusion is quite convincing: the implication is cancelable. "John took off his trousers and went to bed, but not necessarily in that order" is not heard as contradictory. This argument is not completely conclusive, however, because it could be that the but-clause forces us to give the "and" its nontemporal meaning. That is, the but-clause may not be canceling an implicature but rather disambiguating the "and."[15] An analogy is provided by "John picnicked on a bank, but not on a riverbank." This sentence is not heard as a

---

[14] Compare Harnish (1976: 332), Fraser (1988), and especially Wierzbicka (1987; 1991: Ch. 10).

[15] Compare Crimmins (1992: 24).

contradiction either, even though "bank" is ambiguous and does have a meaning ("riverbank") on which the sentence does express a contradiction.

A further piece of evidence for implicature rather than ambiguity is that sentences like (11) have the same sequential interpretation even though they lack the word "and."[16]

(11)   John took off his trousers; he went to bed.

All (11) asserts is the joint truth of what the two concatenated sentences claim. The fact that (11) has the same sequential interpretation as (10)(a) implies that the implication is not due to any special meaning of "and" other than its purely truth-functional meaning, which asserts the joint truth of what the conjoined sentences claim. Moreover, the fact that (11) has a sequential interpretation that "Triangles have three sides; squares have four" lacks cannot be due to the ambiguity of any of the words in the sentences, because they have no words in common.

Another argument for holding that the implications are conversational implicatures rather than senses is an application of Grice's Razor. This second argument claims that it is preferable to hold that the temporal implications of conjunctions are conversational implicatures rather than senses, because conversational implicatures can be accounted for by general, psychosocial principles. I will not try to refute the claim that the temporal implication of sentences like (10) is a conversational implicature. I assume that it is on the basis of the sort of linguistic evidence presented earlier. What I seek to show is that the assumed implication cannot be explained in the Gricean manner. Conjunction implicatures cannot be attributed to Gricean maxims. And the implications of speakers who use conjunctions either cannot be worked out, or cannot be inferred from their calculability together with the other Gricean factors.

In the case of conjunctions, Grice suggested that their sequential interpretation results from the Maxim of Manner:

[16] Gazdar (1979: 70–71), Posner (1980: 187), Bar-Lev and Palacas (1980: 139), Blakemore (1987a: 113–114; 1992: 79).

It was suggested by Strawson, in *An Introduction to Logical Theory,* that there is a divergence between the ordinary use or meaning of the word *and* and the conjunction sign of propositional or predicate calculus, because *He took off his trousers and went to bed* does not seem to have the same meaning as *He went to bed and took off his trousers.* The suggestion here is, of course, that, in order properly to represent the ordinary use of the word *and,* one would have to allow a special sense (or subsense) for the word *and* which contained some reference to the idea that what was mentioned before the word *and* was temporally prior to what was mentioned after it, and that on that supposition, one could deal with this case. I want to suggest, in reply, that it is not necessary, if one operates on some general principle of keeping down, as far as possible, the number of special senses of words that one has to invoke, to give countenance to the alleged divergence of meaning. It is just that there is a general supposition which would be subsidiary to the general maxim of Manner ("Be perspicuous.") that one presents one's material in an orderly manner and, if what one is engaged upon is a narrative (if one is talking about events), then the most orderly manner for a narration of events is an order that corresponds to the order in which they took place. So, the meaning of the expression *He took off his trousers and he got into bed* and the corresponding expression with a logician's constant "&" (i.e., "He took off his trousers & he got into bed") would be exactly the same. And, indeed, if anybody actually used in ordinary speech the "&" as a piece of vocabulary, instead of as a formal device, and used it to connect together sentences of this type, they would collect just the same implicata as the ordinary English sentences have without any extra explanation of the meaning of the word *and.* (Grice 1981: 186)[17]

As an initial hunch as to where an explanation might lie, Grice's suggestion was brilliant. The fact that it has been repeated approvingly for years is inexplicable. For counterevidence is readily available, and the litany of problems is very long.

First, Grice's "test" involving the use of "&" as a piece of vocabulary is flawed by the fact that "&" customarily *is* used in ordinary written English as an abbreviation for "and." When instead I use a

[17] See also Kempson (1975: 198), Harnish (1976: 338), Walker (1975: 136–144), Gazdar (1979: 45, 69–71), Posner (1980: §§7–9), Wilson and Sperber (1981: 174), Levinson (1983: 108; 1987), Fasold (1990: 135–136), Blakemore (1992: 78–83), Mey (1993: 24), and Schiffrin (1994: 195).

symbol whose connection with "and" is much weaker, I find that Grice's test fails. For example, I hear no sequential interpretation in (12) at all.

(12)   (John took off his trousers) • (John went to bed).

The fact that (12) does not appear here in a piece of ordinary speech seems completely irrelevant; (10) does not appear in ordinary speech here either, yet the sequential interpretation is quite perceptible. And I could easily enough write a letter to my wife using •, v, − , (,), and so on. The absence of implicature would contribute to the stiltedness and formality of the writing. Sticking to ordinary English, it is most remarkable that the addition of "both" eliminates the sequential implicature while emphasizing that joint truth is being claimed.

(13)   John both took off his trousers and went to bed.
        It is true both that John took off his trousers and that John went to bed.

The sentences in (13) do not have a sequential interpretation even though they assert exactly what Grice assumes (10)(a) unambiguously asserts.[18]

Second, the Maxim of Manner could at best provide a very partial explanation of the sequential interpretation of conjunctions. The fact that people tend to be orderly might possibly explain why speakers arrange conjuncts in *some order*. But it does not predict that conjuncts are arranged in *temporal* order specifically. Indeed, whereas (10) implicates a temporal ordering between the conjuncts, other conjunctions implicate different orderings.[19]

(14)   (a)   John dropped the glass and it broke.
        (b)   John flipped the switch and turned on the light.
        (c)   John was in the kitchen and he was baking bread.

(14)(a) implicates that John's dropping the glass *caused* it to break,

---

[18] Compare and contrast Schmerling (1975: 222, 226).
[19] Compare Geis and Zwicky (1971), Böer and Lycan (1973: 502–505), Schmerling (1975: 214–215, 226–227), Posner (1980: 186), and Blakemore (1992: 80).

in addition to implicating that the former preceded the latter. (14)(b) implicates that John turned on the light *by* flipping the switch, and therefore implicates that John's flipping of the switch neither caused nor preceded his turning on of the light. (14)(c) implicates that John was baking bread *while* he was in the kitchen. The Maxim of Manner provides no explanation for why the sentences in (10) implicate a temporal ordering whereas those in (14) implicate different orderings.

Furthermore, it would be just as orderly to arrange sentences in reverse temporal or causal order, the way they appear in "p after q" or "p because q." The Maxim of Manner therefore provides no explanation for why (10) fails to imply that John went to bed before he put on his trousers. In fact, conjunctions can be found which *do* imply reverse orderings, as in (15).

(15)   John set a record and cleared 15 feet.

(15) implies that John set a record by clearing 15 feet, not – as we would expect from (14)(b) – that he cleared 15 feet by setting a record. And whereas some unconjoined sequences convey "forward" causation, others imply reverse causal order.

(16)   (a)   John dropped the glass; it broke.
       (b)   John slipped; the road was icy.[20]

(16)(a) implies that the first event mentioned caused the second. But (16)(b) implies that the second event mentioned caused the first. Note that conjoining the sentences in (16)(a) and (16)(b) preserves the implication of the former but not that of the latter.

(17)   (a)   John dropped the glass and it broke.
       (b)   John slipped and the road was icy.

This is completely inexplicable in Gricean theory.

Walker (1975: 137, fn.4) maintains that it is "most natural" to describe events in the order in which they occur, and that the reverse order is "unnatural." Whether this is true or not, the implicatures of

[20] Gazdar (1979: 44, fn. 9), Bar-Lev and Palacas (1980), Blakemore (1992: 90). Examples (17)(b) and (15), incidentally, refute Bar-Lev and Palaca's thesis that *S′ and S″* means that S″ is "not prior (chronologically or causally)" to S′.

(15) and (16)(b), and the lack of a sequential implicature in (17)(b), show that the naturalness of the order of description has nothing to do with the presence or absence of sequential implicatures.

Similarly, Grice (1981: 186) asserted that "the most orderly manner for a narration of events is an order that corresponds to the order in which they took place." This may well be true, but it is no help in explaining the sequential interpretation of conjunctions. For (10) carries its temporal implication whether it is part of a narrative or not. If Grice's claim is defended against this charge by maintaining that (10) by itself is a one-sentence narrative, then his claim founders on sentences like (15) and (16)(b). They could just as well be counted as one-sentence narratives. But their implicatures reverse the normal causal or temporal sequence. Furthermore, the sentences carry the same implication when they are embedded in complex sentences where they cannot do any narrating.

(18)   (a)   If John went to bed and took off his trousers, he did things the hard way.[21]

     (b)   John did not go to bed and take off his trousers.

     (c)   I hope that John took off his trousers and went to bed.

Sentences in the imperative or interrogative moods have similar meanings even though they are not used to give part of a narrative.

(19)   (a)   Take off your trousers and go to bed!

     (b)   Did you take off your trousers and go to bed?

John fails to obey the command given by (19)(a) if he goes to bed first and then takes off his trousers. And (19)(b) could not be answered affirmatively under the same conditions.

---

[21] Compare Cohen (1971: §ii), Walker (1975: 136–144), Gazdar (1979: 69–70), Posner (1980: §9), Bar-Lev and Palacas (1980: 142–143), and Blakemore (1987a: 114–118; 1992: 80–81). The debate among these authors centers around a different issue, however. They are concerned with whether examples like (18) prove that the sequential meaning of conjunctions is part of their sense rather than an implicature. I am merely using the examples to show that facts about narrative are no help in explaining the sequential interpretation of conjunctions, because that interpretation is present even when the conjunctions are not used to narrate events. In light of a mistake made by both Walker and Gazdar, note that I am not claiming that any of the compound sentences in (18) themselves implicate that John went to bed before he put on his trousers.

The fact that the injunction to be orderly does not provide specific guidance and appears to be completely uninvolved in the generation of conjunction implicatures may explain why it is hard to *flout* the submaxim. Whereas one can utter an obvious understatement to convey a much more informative statement, or an obvious falsehood to convey a truth, I do not think anyone can produce an unordered series of statements in order to convey their proper order. "She had a baby and got pregnant" is a tad playful, but that appears to be the best we can do. It is playful, I believe, only because it is obviously misleading despite being literally true. Hence the presence of the standard implicature explains the effect, meaning this is not a case in which a special implicature is due to the flouting of the submaxim.

There are three further problems with the Gricean theory of conjunction implicatures. First, if the submaxim "Be orderly" predicts the sequential interpretation of conjunctions, it should also predict an "ordinal" interpretation for disjunctions. When listing alternative courses of action, for example, it would surely be natural and orderly to list the alternatives in order of preference, with the first option being preferred to the second, which is preferred to the third, and so on. But (20) does not imply in any way that I prefer racquetball to tennis or tennis to squash.

(20)   I will play racquetball, tennis, or squash.

It would also be natural to list alternative possibilities in order of probability, with the most probable outcome first. Yet (20) does not imply that I am more likely to play racquetball than tennis.

Second, the Maxim of Quantity can be applied to conjunctions using the same sort of reasoning that Griceans use to explain observed quantity implicatures.

S said that John took off his trousers and went to bed. If S had known that John took off his trousers *before* going to bed, he should have said so. Because he did not, he must be implicating that John did not take off his trousers before going to bed.

However, this use of the Maxim of Quantity would yield the result that the various implicature-bearing conjunctions displayed in this section implicate the *denial* of what they are observed to implicate. Thus if Gricean theory correctly predicted that "Some died" implicates "Not all died," it should also incorrectly predict that "John took off his trousers and went to bed" implicates "John did not take off his trousers before going to bed."[22] It seems obvious that the theory actually predicts neither implicature. If the Maxims of Quantity and Manner were genuinely predictive, it would be post hoc reasoning at its worst to attribute the sequential interpretation of conjunctions to the Maxim of Manner when the Maxim of Quantity predicts the opposite implicature just as well.

Third, countless conjunctions have no sequential interpretation at all.

(21) (a) Jack married Jill, and Ted married Alice.

      (b) Steve and Terry helped move the piano.

      (c) John bought apples, oranges, and pears.

      (d) Cats are animals, vertebrates, and mammals.

      (e) It will be rainy and cold today.

      (f) John visited London, and didn't see Big Ben.

      (g) John saw Bill, and met either Charles or Andrew.

      (h) John took the exam, and I'll be amazed if he passed.

      (i) "John got into bed" is true and "John took off his trousers" is true.

      (j) Some violinists are pianists, and some pianists are violinists.

      (k) 6 is an even number, and 7 is odd.

It is probably an overstatement to say that conjunctions with a sequential implication are the exception rather than the rule. But it is surely incorrect to say that they are the rule. Hence general psychosocial principles cannot provide an adequate explanation of a sequential interpretation where it does happen to exist. In par-

---

[22] The same failure of differentiation occurs in an even more parallel case, namely the Gricean theory that the exclusive interpretation of "or" should be reckoned an implicature rather than a sense because the Maxim of Quantity suffices to predict that "p or q" implicates "not both p and q." The completely unambiguous "p or q or both" does not implicate "not both p and q" as it should if the Gricean explanation of the exclusive interpretation were correct. See later, section 5.5.

ticular, it would be post hoc reasoning to attribute the sequential implication of (10) and (11) to the Maxim of Manner when the maxim applies just as well to examples like those in (21) lacking such an implication.

Despite attributing the implicature of (10)(a) to the Maxim of Manner, Levinson invokes a *Principle of Informativeness* to account for the implicatures of sentences like (14), (15), and (16):

Principle of Informativeness: Read as much into an utterance as is consistent with what you know about the world.[23]

This principle is not a "general psychosocial principle," nor a principle of rational cooperation, but a specifically linguistic rule – an interpretation guide. Nevertheless, it is still too general to account for the observed implicatures. Suppose that "consistent with" is taken to mean "*possible* given." Then Levinson's principle wrongly predicts that many of the examples in (21) have a causal implication. An example is (21)(a): it is quite possible that Ted married Alice because Jack married Jill. Levinson's principle wrongly predicts that many of the examples have temporal implicatures: with regard to (21)(b), it is quite possible that Terry helped move the piano after Steve did. Levinson's principle wrongly predicts that some of the examples have logical implications: "and" should imply "and so" in (21)(j) because the second conjunct follows from the first. The principle also wrongly predicts that (21)(a) implicates that Franklin married Eleanor, and that (21)(b) implicates that Tom helped too, because those implications are quite consistent with what those sentences explicitly say together with the known facts.

Some of these incorrect predictions can be avoided by taking "consistent with" to mean something stronger, like "*probable* given." But on that interpretation, Levinson's principle would

[23] Levinson (1983: 146–147); see also Böer and Lycan (1973: 495, 502–505), Atlas and Levinson (1981: 40–50), Lycan (1984: 77–78), Horn (1984: 18), Sperber and Wilson (1986a), Carston (1988: 36–37), Levinson (1987b: 62–79), Blakemore (1987a: 117, 119), and Bach (1987, 77).

wrongly predict: that (10)(b) and (21)(i) both implicate that John took off his trousers before going to bed; that (10)(a) also implicates that John took off his shoes; that (17)(b) implicates that John slipped because the road was icy; and that "and" should imply "and so" in (21)(j). When one starts with the data, it is hard to see *any* generalization emerging that fits it all.

Levinson notes that his Principle of Informativeness contrasts markedly with the Maxim of Quantity:

The problem here is that by the maxim of Quantity the inference from [*He turned on the switch and the motor started*] to [*He turned on the motor and consequently the motor started*] should be specifically banned. For if I had meant the informationally richer [*He turned on the motor and consequently the motor started*] I should have said so; having not said so, I implicate that as far as I know [*He turned on the motor and consequently the motor started*] does not obtain. But that of course is the wrong prediction. There therefore seems to be an independent principle or maxim, which we may call the **principle of informativeness,** that in just some circumstances allows us to read into an utterance *more* information than it actually contains – in contrast to Quantity, which only allows the additional inference that (as far as the speaker knows) no stronger statement could be made. The problem that now besets the analyst is to provide a principled account of how in just some cases this additional principle . . . takes precedence over the maxim of Quantity, while in other circumstances (e.g. most of the examples in this Chapter) the reverse precedence holds (see here Atlas and Levinson 1981). (Levinson 1983: 146–147)[24]

The notion of one principle "taking precedence" over another makes sense when we are dealing with *normative* principles. When faced with a clash between the imperative to save lives and the imperative not to lie, we have to weigh the two moral principles and follow the more important of the two. But whereas Gricean principles are usually stated as imperatives – "contribute this" or "be that," we are concerned with explanations of observed linguistic phenomena, specifically, the presence or absence of certain implicatures. To explain observed implicatures, we must appeal to *descriptive* principles, specifically *motivational* or *cognitive* principles.

[24] See also Levinson (1987b: 62–79).

We must therefore distinguish four forms of the Gricean maxim, as we did in Chapter 1.

Maxim of Quantity: "Be as informative as required."

Normative: People *ought to* be as informative as required.
Behavioral: People *are* as informative as required.
Motivational: People *intend to* be as informative as required.
Cognitive: People *believe they ought to* be as informative as required.

The normative principle that people *ought to be* as informative as possible cannot possibly predict that "Some died" implicates "Not all died" unless it is combined with a descriptive rule such as that people intend to do what they ought to do. Even then, what would explain the observed implicature is not the normative principle that people ought to be as informative as required, but the descriptive principle that people believe the normative principle and intend to follow it.

The only way in which a "weighting" of the normative principles of quantity and informativeness could indirectly yield a prediction that "John took off his trousers and went to bed" has a sequential implicature rather than a quantity implicature would be if the Principle of Informativeness (or Maxim of Manner) generally has greater normative weight than the Maxim of Quantity in the circumstances in which that sentence would be uttered. But it would be astounding if such a generalization were true. The cases we are examining are not at all like the sorts of cases discussed by Leech (1983: 80–84, 145–149). Leech observes that sentences typically lack their customary quantity implicatures in circumstances in which the speaker wishes to be modest, to avoid insulting the speaker, and so on. For example, if a skilled tennis player was asked whether he could beat members of the team and answered, "Many," we would ordinarily infer he was implicating he could not beat all of them. But if the athlete were excessively modest, we would not acknowledge such an implicature. Leech plausibly observes that a "Politeness Principle" takes precedence over the Maxim of Quantity in such situations, at least in the speaker's mind. Coupled with the premise that the speaker tries to do what he ought to do, Leech can provide a plausible explanation for why the quantity implicatures are absent. But nothing whatsoever in the meaning of "John took off his trousers and went to bed" suggests it would be more important for speakers uttering it to provide as much information as possible explicitly rather than providing it implicitly and allowing the hearer to read the extra information into the utterance.

Given the precedence problem, Levinson concedes that substantial problems face the Gricean theory of implicature:

> Nevertheless enough progress has been made to show that the various attacks that have been made on the theory of implicature, usually on the grounds that the concepts involved are too vacuous to be formalizable or testable (see, e.g., Cohen 1971; Kroch 1972) are quite ill-founded. (Levinson 1983: 147)

Even if we grant Levinson that individual Gricean maxims yield testable predictions – a point I am also arguing against – it does not follow that the whole theory yields testable predictions. For the theory contains several principles, which may individually yield predictions that collectively conflict. Because the theory contains nothing to tell us which principles to apply in such cases, the theory yields no predictions, and thus as a whole is untestable. Postulation of the Principle of Informativeness to save the theory from erroneous predictions of the Maxim of Quantity will remain completely ad hoc and ineffective until Levinson can explain why the Principle of Informativeness applies in some cases, the Maxim of Quantity in others.[25]

Atlas and Levinson (1981: section 11) do attempt to *specify* the Maxim of Quantity and the Informativeness Principle in such a way that the two principles apply in different cases (see also Levinson 1987b: 69). However, the proposed specifications are completely ad hoc, and the resulting rules are neither general psychosocial principles nor items of common knowledge. For example, the Maxim of Quantity becomes something like this: "If

---

[25] Compare Bird (1979: 143) and Fasold (1990: 154–155).

you are going to assert any proposition on a given scale, assert the strongest proposition on the scale that you believe to be true." Scales must be sequences of propositions that differ only in concepts that are "lexicalized" in the speaker's natural language and are all "about" the same thing in some peculiar sense. The particular specification of the Quantity Maxim found in Atlas and Levinson is falsified by many of the cases noted in (3) earlier. Nevertheless, the general notion of a scale may be useful in providing a general *description* of the implicatures in a large class of cases. But such descriptions are unlikely to *explain why* the cases have the implicatures they do (see section 3.8). Furthermore, quantity implicatures are found even when the terms are not all lexicalized.[26] For example, "Some S are P" implicates "It is not the case that *nearly all* S are P." And "The work was *good or very good* " implicates "The work was not excellent."

Furthermore, Atlas and Levinson still find conflicts even after their specification. At this point, they offer the following:

> For the class of indefinite descriptions just discussed, the upshot seems to be that where there is an implicature at all (not all indefinite descriptions yield them) Quantity takes precedence over Informativeness unless the result contradicts our background Conventions of Noncontroversiality. If that occurs, the Informativeness implicatum is adopted. This is the first genuine case of clash between Quantity and Informativeness that we have discussed. It is resolved by a general preference for the Quantity implicatum. After all, where the Quantity implicature may be employed appropriately, it is reasonable to do so on the grounds that speakers are being cooperative. (Atlas and Levinson 1981: 50)

First, it is not apparent why it would be uncooperative for speakers to exploit the Principle of Informativeness when they expect their audience to observe it. Second, the Maxim of Quantity produces no results contradicting their Convention of Noncontroversiality in the case of "John took off his trousers and went to bed," and yet there is a conjunction implicature rather than a quantity implicature. Atlas and Levinson's proposed resolution of the conflict they cite is thus an example of a pervasive tendency in the

---

[26] Compare Matsumoto (1995: 45).

Gricean literature to dismiss serious problems with the most superficial solutions.

2.4 IDIOMS

Sadock observed that conversational implicatures can become conventionalized:[27]

That is, what starts life as a metaphor can grow into an idiom. Euphemisms fairly rapidly come to MEAN what they were originally intended to circumlocute and so cease to be euphemisms, and indirect speech acts can in time metamorphose into direct forms. But except for the limiting case in which the original meaning is entirely lost, conversational principles can always be called upon to explain the force of an originally indirect form, since those principles were indeed important in the history of the reanalyzed forms. (Sadock 1978: 369)

To use Sadock's example, (22)(a) was originally a euphemism, but is now an idiom.

(22) (a) NP went to the bathroom.
       (b) NP urinated or defecated.

That is, at one time (22)(a) implicated but did not mean (22)(b). Now (22)(a) means rather than implicates (22)(b). Evidence is provided by the fact that "NP went to the bathroom *on the carpet*" is now completely grammatical. If implicatures must be capable of being worked out, then it was once possible to derive the implicature that NP defecated or urinated from the literal meaning of (22)(a) and the conversational principles. But if it was possible then, it must still be possible now. Hence Gricean theory wrongly predicts that (22)(a) is not an idiom and does not mean (22)(b). Grice's Razor would shave too closely in this case. Put another way, the theory cannot differentiate between an implicature and an idiomatic meaning.

Gricean theory could be saved from this particular embarrassment by insisting that (22)(b) never was derivable from the con-

---

[27] See also R. Lakoff (1975), Walker (1975: 158), Morgan (1978), Nunberg (1981: 202), Levinson (1983: 165–166; 1987b: 99), and Fasold (1990: 155).

versational principles. But then we are stuck with the conclusion that the determinacy requirement failed back when (22)(a) was a live euphemism, which leads to the next chapter.

2.5 NON-GRICEAN SPEECH

We have focused in this chapter on *false positives:* cases in which Gricean theory would seem to predict implicatures that are not found. *False negatives* represent another failure of differentiation. A false negative arises when an implicature is found that Gricean theory says should not be found. False negatives show equally well that even if many observed implicatures can be worked out on the basis of Gricean conversational principles, those principles cannot explain why the implicatures occur. Because the same implicatures can be found when the principles do not apply.

The Cooperative Principle fails to apply when *nothing is "required by the accepted purpose of the conversation,"* either because there is no conversation, or because it has no accepted purpose, or because the accepted purpose is not specific enough to require a particular contribution. Let us refer to this case as *non-Gricean speech.* Suppose Jack and Jill are lying on a hill enjoying a beautiful spring day. After a long silence Jack says, "Some of the clouds look like big fluffy pillows," implying as usual that not all do. He said this for no particular reason and without expecting any response from Jill; afterward they return to silent embraces. Jack's utterance does not count as a conversation, and it has no purpose that Jill accepted in any way. Because Jack had "no particular reason" to say what he did, even his own purposes did not require him to say what he did. Consequently, the Cooperative Principle does not apply. The same goes for the Maxim of Quantity. Whatever his reason for speaking, it was not specific enough to require that he provide more information than he communicated explicitly. It would be completely out of place for Jill to reason, "If Jack knew that all the clouds looked like big fluffy pillows, it would have been incumbent on him to say so. Because he did not, he must have intended me to think that not all of them do." If Gricean Theory were accurate, there should be no implicature. But the idle nature of the utterance does not stop Jack from intending a typical quantity implicature, nor Jill from recognizing it. The fact that Jack's implicature cannot be derived from or explained by the Cooperative Principle in this case casts doubt on the claim that quantity implicatures are genuinely explained by Gricean principles when they do apply.

The problem is not special to quantity implicatures. Jack could just as well have idly used a tautology implicature (*Que sera, sera*), a conjunction implicature ("The sun came out and it got warm"), or a metaphor ("The clouds are big fluffy pillows"). Chapter 4 sets out more cases of non-Gricean speech: refusing to cooperate, talking to the dead, and so on. Implicatures can nonetheless be found in all of them. The focus in Chapter 4, however, is on the fact that the Cooperative Principle is not even presumed to apply. Chapter 3 shows that observed implicatures cannot be derived from the Cooperative Principle even when it does apply.

3

Determinacy and calculability

Gricean theory holds that conversational implicatures must be capable of being worked out, which I call the Calculability Assumption. A key premise in the Working-out Schema is that *the supposition that S believes p is required to make S's utterance consistent with the Cooperative Principle,* which is the determinacy condition. Thus the Calculability Assumption holds only if the determinacy condition does. Grice's Razor entails that conversational implicatures can be derived from Grice's conversational principles. We observed in Chapter 1 that this derivability clause depends on the calculability assumption for sentence implicatures. Determinacy is thus the foundation of Gricean theory. In this chapter, we see that the determinacy condition, and therefore the Calculability Assumption and Grice's Razor, are untenable.

3.1 BACKGROUND CONSTRAINTS

Taken at face value, the determinacy condition is impossible to satisfy. There are too few constraints for the Cooperative Principle to *require* any particular beliefs. Unless word meanings are fixed, for example, the Maxim of Quality will not pick out a definite belief S has to possess for his utterance to be truthful. The most we could say is that *if* the sentence S uttered means "It is raining," then S must believe it is raining; *if* the sentence S uttered means "It is snowing," then S must believe it is snowing, and so on. Grice was aware of this fact, and he specified a fuller set of determinants in the following passage, quoted earlier:

To work out that a particular conversational implicature is present, the hearer will rely on the following data: (1) the conventional meaning of the words used, together with the identity of any references that may be involved; (2) the Cooperative Principle and its maxims; (3) the context, linguistic or otherwise, of the utterance; (4) other items of background knowledge; and (5) the fact (or supposed fact) that all relevant items falling under the previous headings are available to both participants and both participants know or assume this to be the case. (Grice 1975: 31)

I treat factors like the meanings and references of the words S utters, and the context, as *background constraints,* relative to which the supposition that S believes p is supposed to be required to make S's utterance consistent with the Cooperative Principle. I assume that "the accepted purpose of the conversation," as referred to in the Cooperative Principle, is a background constraint, presumably by being part of the context.

The background constraints must make the key element of the Working-out Schema true: *S could not be observing the Cooperative Principle unless he believed p.* I argue that no background constraints suffice to provide this element. A variety of problems show not only that the Gricean definition of conversational implicatures is too strong, but also that Gricean conversational principles do not have sufficient power to predict or explain conversational implicatures. Whereas Chapter 2 mainly explored the problem of false positives, this chapter focuses on false negatives.

3.2 THE MEANING CONSTRAINT PROBLEM

The background constraints must include more than the *conventional* meanings (and referents) of the words S utters. We must in addition know what the words mean *on the occasion of S's utterance.* Consider dialogue (1) of Chapter 1, repeated here:

ANN: Where can I get gasoline?
BOB: There's a station around the corner.

To know whether conformity with the Maxim of Quality requires Bob to believe there is a *gasoline* station around the corner rather than a *police* station, and whether the Maxim of Relation requires him to believe Ann can get gasoline there rather than that Ann can ask a police officer where to get gasoline there, we would have to know whether "station" meant "police station" or "gasoline station" on that occasion. To determine that, we have to know what Bob meant *then* by the word. This "applied" word meaning, as Grice (1969) called it, is determined by both conventional word meaning and speaker meaning.[1]

If this line of thought is extended, however, it will become apparent that the conventional meanings of the words the speaker utters are not operative *constraints* on determinacy at all. It is possible that Bob misspoke, for example, saying "coroner" when he meant to say "corner." In that case, the maxims would still seem to require that Bob believe there is a station around the corner, where Ann can get gasoline. As long as Bob believes those things, he is in no way lying or misleading his audience. Bob is not required in any way to believe that Ann can get gasoline at the station around the coroner, wherever that might be, despite what the sentence he uttered means. The fact that the sentence Bob uttered refers to a coroner rather than a corner would actually be a distraction in trying to figure out what Bob implicated.

More radically, Bob might have been using "There's a station around the corner" in a secret code known only to Bob and Ann, in which the sentence meant that Bob has a can of gasoline in his trunk. In that case, consistency with the Maxim of Quality would require Bob to believe he has a can of gasoline in his trunk, and consistency with the Maxim of Relation would require him to believe Ann can use that gasoline. Bob would not need to believe anything about gasoline stations or police stations. Alternatively, Bob could have said, "Go to the corner, Ralph it,[2] and there's a filler-up" to convey the same beliefs, even though the sentence he uttered makes little sense in English. In general, the operative background constraint is what the *speaker* means by the sentence he utters.[3]

---

[1] For a definition, see my *Meaning, Expression, and Thought,* §7.6.

[2] As in "Hang a Ralph," that is, turn right.

[3] The relevant sort of speaker meaning is "cogitative" rather than "cognitive" – meaning "p" by the sentence Σ rather than meaning that p by uttering Σ. Compare Grice (1969: 148–150), Schiffer (1972: 2–3), and Davis (1992b).

What the sentence itself means in any particular language, or on that occasion, is relevant to what the speaker believes only insofar as it is an indicator of what the speaker means by it. The same can be said, of course, for word and speaker reference.

3.3 THE RHETORICAL FIGURE PROBLEM

The meaning constraint problem has a solution within the Gricean framework. Other problems do not. Consider the example of irony given earlier. If Sam says, "It is a fine day!" in the middle of a blizzard, is the assumption that Sam believes it *isn't* a fine day required to make his utterance consistent with the Cooperative Principle, specifically the Maxim of Quality? No. His utterance would also be consistent with the Cooperative Principle if he genuinely believed it is a fine day and was speaking literally. If we are determining whether a certain belief is required by something, we obviously have to determine whether contrary beliefs would do the job. And here they would. Grice (1978: 53) himself notes that determinacy fails in this case.

Another possibility is that Sam might be using a figure of speech other than irony. Sam might be engaged in what Leech (1983: 145) called "mock-irony," meaning, and believing, that it is a fine day. Or Sam might have been overstating things, believing the day is good but not fine. To change the example, suppose Pam and Ted are looking out at a ticker-tape parade, and Pam says, "It's a blizzard!" Pam might be using irony, and meaning it is not a blizzard; or Pam might be using metaphor, meaning it is like a blizzard; or Pam might be using a combination of metaphor and irony, meaning the amount of ticker tape is puny; or Pam might be speaking literally. Finally, suppose Jane, looking at a snowstorm, engages in hyperbole and says, "It is a blizzard." Then she implicated, and believes, it is a heavy snowstorm, but not a blizzard. However, Jane could have been speaking literally, meaning and believing falsely it is a blizzard. She could also be engaging in understatement, meaning and believing the snowstorm exceeds even a blizzard. We can generalize from these cases: *The determinacy requirement will always fail in the case of irony and other figures of speech, because S COULD have been speaking literally, believing what is said, or using a different figure of speech.* Even more generally, whenever S is flouting a maxim, S could have been observing it, or flouting it in a different way, and that possibility undermines the determinacy requirement.[4]

The possibility of figurative speech also undermines the determinacy requirement when S is actually speaking literally. Consider dialogue (1) of Chapter 1 again. When Bob said, "There's a station around the corner," he could have been speaking ironically, parodying the depression era bromides "Prosperity is just around the corner" and "There's a chicken in every pot." Bob could have thought it would be obvious to Ann he was doing this, and that he was trying to convey the idea that there is no gasoline anywhere near. Hence it is just false that consistency with the Cooperative Principle *requires* Bob to believe Ann can get gasoline at the station, which is what he actually implicated. Similarly, suppose S says, "Most people died," implicating that not all died. The Gricean idea is that S's utterance conforms to the Cooperative Principle only if S believes that not everyone died. Because if S could have made a more informative statement, he would have. But there is another possibility. S could have been engaging in hyperbole, in which case he would have implicated that many died, but not most people. *Because S COULD be speaking figuratively, the determinacy requirement will also fail in the case of literal speech.* More generally, the possibility that S is flouting a maxim undermines the determinacy requirement even when the speaker is obviously observing it. Even with the background factors Grice identified, there are not enough constraints for the Cooperative Principle to determine a unique belief.

One might object that I have been placing too much weight on the word *required* in Grice's formulation of the determinacy requirement. It might be suggested that Grice was not claiming, or need not have claimed, that no contrary belief is *possible* given the Cooperative Principle, but only that no contrary belief is *likely* given the Cooperative Principle. Indeed, many have argued that the working-out

---

[4] Compare Walker (1975: 171–172) and Harnish (1976: 333). Compare and contrast Hugly and Sayward (1979), Sperber and Wilson (1981: 296–309), Wilson and Sperber (1981: 160–161), and Levinson (1983: 158–159).

process is inductive rather than deductive reasoning.[5] Nothing would be lost, I believe, if the key element in the Working-out Schema were taken to be as follows: *S probably is not observing the Cooperative Principle unless he believes p.* This possibility suggests a variant of definition I. Leave the other clauses the same and rewrite clause (iii) as follows:

Theoretical Definition II: S conversationally implicates p iff . . . (iii) The supposition that S believes p is probable given that S is observing the Cooperative Principle. . . .

Although this substitution works well in the Gricean framework and eliminates many counterexamples, it does not get to the root of the problem. When Sam says, "It is a fine day!" ironically, there might be no background constraints that make irony more likely than literal speech. The available evidence need not enable the hearer to figure out whether Sam meant what he said. Hearers are far from omniscient about speakers. Indeed, we are often in situations in which we do not know how to take certain remarks. A speaker can mean something even though there is not enough evidence for the hearer to determine with certainty or probability what the speaker either means or believes. A nearly paradigm example was provided by Leech:

> Considering that I am a hostage, I should say that I have been treated fairly.

This highly ambivalent utterance is reported to have been said by an American hostage in Iran in 1980, when he was due for early release. It was said to reporters who asked how he had been treated. (Leech 1983: 23)

His American audience may suspect the hostage meant that, being a hostage, he was forced to say he was treated fairly. His captors

---

[5] For example, Stalnaker (1974: 475), Harnish (1976: 333), Bach and Harnish (1979: 92–93), Levinson (1983: 115–116), and Leech (1983: 30–44, 153). Compare and contrast Sperber and Wilson (1986a: Ch. 2), Wilson and Sperber (1986), and Blakemore (1987a: 36–39; 1992: 129–130), who agree that the reasoning is nondemonstrative.

may believe he meant he was treated fairly as a hostage. There may be no way to settle the question. Leech's example is slightly imperfect for my purposes because the ambiguity may well have been deliberate. The normal case is exemplified amply in any set of undergraduate term papers.

Furthermore, the probability that S believes p given that S is observing the Cooperative Principle is influenced by a host of factors that are not determinants of implicature. Suppose Jack listened to the Mendelssohn Violin Concerto this morning, and said, "That is my favorite piece of music." Imagine further that Jack had listened to that concerto and made the same remark a thousand times in the past when he was being cooperative, and on every single occasion he was using irony, expressing his belief that the music is not his favorite. Moreover, he insists now that he really meant the opposite of what he said this morning. Then we have imagined a situation in which it is extremely unlikely that Jack believed the Mendelssohn is his favorite concerto given that he was obeying the Cooperative Principle. It does not follow, however, that Jack was not implicating that the Mendelssohn is his favorite concerto on that occasion. Despite all the previous cases in which he used irony, he could have been speaking literally this morning. He might finally have come to appreciate the music; or he might just have been lying. The testimonial and analogical evidence makes it unlikely that he believed certain propositions, but it does not prevent him from having believed or implicated them.

Alternatively, the rhetorical figure problem could be alleviated somewhat by replacing S believes p with S implicates p in the determinacy clause of definition I. The resulting definition fits the common claim that it is S's implicature that brings S into conformity with the cooperative principle when what S said does not.[6] If a similar change were made in P3 of the Working-out Schema, enabling the ellipsis to be deleted, the Calculability Assumption would be a theorem rather than an independent postulate.

[6] Compare Grice (1975: 31), Walker (1975: 157), Harnish (1976: 336), Sadock (1978: 368), Levinson (1983: 113, 117, 122), Leech (1983: 24–25), Martinich (1984: 509), Wilson and Sperber (1986), and Searle (1982: 520). Walker and Martinich use this version of the determinacy clause in their official definitions.

Theoretical Definition III: S conversationally implicates p iff . . . (iii) The supposition that S implicates p is required to make S's utterance consistent with the Cooperative Principle. . . .

Suppose that, instead of asking whether the supposition that Sam believes it is a lousy day is required to make Sam's utterance consistent with the Cooperative Principle, we ask whether the supposition that Sam is implicating it is a lousy day is required. When we ask the second question, unlike the first, we can take it as a fixed background condition that Sam *does* believe it is a lousy day. Then the Maxim of Quality would seem to dictate that Sam must mean and therefore implicate it is a lousy day.

Despite this advantage, serious problems plague the third version of the determinacy requirement, too. First, the Generative Assumption would be completely implausible if its antecedent referred to the conditions of definition III. How could any fact about the supposition that S implicates something *make it true* that S implicates it? Because it contains the term "implicates," the satisfaction of clause (iii) of definition III could not generate any implicatures definitionally. And no other form of generation seems plausible. I would guess that this is why Grice chose definition I rather than III. Second, the treatment of irony using definition III creates problems concerning literal speech. Suppose Tommy blatantly lies, saying, "I did not eat the cookies" despite the chocolate and crumbs smeared all over his face. If he was responding to his mother, who said, "You're a bad boy!" Tommy may have been implicating he is a good boy. If we take it as a fixed background condition that Tommy *does* believe he ate the cookies, we will be led to the erroneous conclusion that he is speaking ironically, meaning and therefore implicating he did eat them, and not implicating he is a good boy. The Cooperative Principle and associated maxims provide no reason to think that Sam must be implicating the opposite of what he said, whereas Tommy need not be.[7] Third, the

---

[7] The Gricean might try defending definition III by observing that the cooperative presumption fails here and using that to explain why Tommy is not implicating that he ate the cookies. But then the Gricean would have to deny that Tommy implicated anything. Yet he may well have been implicating, as I suggested, that he is a good boy. Failures of the cooperative presumption are discussed in section 4.1.

suggested treatment of irony is completely ad hoc. When Sam says, "It is a fine day!" we know he believes many relevant facts other than that it is a lousy day. For example, he undoubtedly knows it is snowing at least a little. The Cooperative Principle gives us no more reason to believe Sam is implicating it is a lousy day than to believe Sam is implicating it is snowing.[8]

A final solution to the rhetorical figure problem is to treat the figure S is using as a background constraint. Let *Fig(u)* be the variable whose range of possible values includes S's speaking literally, S's speaking ironically, S's speaking metaphorically, and so on. Then we could treat the actual value of *Fig(u)* as a fixed part of the context, using it together with the meaning of S's utterance and the Cooperative Principle to work out what S believes. But then the Cooperative Principle would play little or no role in the prediction or explanation of the implicature. The fact that Sam said, "It is a fine day!" together with the fact that Sam is being ironic entails that Sam is implicating it is not a fine day. If the background constraints all by themselves enable us to derive the conclusion that S believes p, without using the Cooperative Principle, the derivation will not show that the supposition that S believes p is required to make S's utterance consistent with the Cooperative Principle.

3.4 "INDETERMINATE" IMPLICATURES

Grice concluded his first article on conversational implicature with the following observation:

Since, to calculate a conversational implicature is to calculate what has to be supposed in order to preserve the supposition that the Cooperative Principle is being observed, and since there may be various possible specific explanations, the list of which may be open, the conversational implicatum in such cases will be a disjunction of such specific explanations; and if the list of these is open, the implicatum will have just the kind of indeterminacy that many implicata do in fact seem to possess. (Grice 1975: 39–40)[9]

[8] Compare Harnish (1976: 333).
[9] See also Kempson (1975: 144, 159), Leech (1983: 23), Sperber and Wilson (1987: 705–706), and Fasold (1990: 132).

Martinich (1984: 512) has argued that metaphors have just this sort of vagueness and indeterminacy:

Suppose someone writes the sentence, "My love is a red rose," in the context of a poem, singing the praises of his lover. . . . Since the poet is signifying by implication, he must believe that the audience is able to work out the implication. For this reason, the features of the rose that are exploited will be those that the audience is as likely to know as the poet. . . . Not all salient properties are meant by the speaker; there are too many of them. Thus the set of salient properties r̄ ... be further reduced. There are two further principles that limit the properties the speaker intends to be operative in the metaphor. . . . The pattern of inference involved in calculating what the speaker conversationally implies typically involves the maxim of relation: Be relevant. In order to interpret what the poet means, it is necessary to understand his utterance as relevant to the context. The poet is comparing his lover to a rose and hence, given that his comparison is apt, only those salient properties will be considered that are relevant to the poet's attitude towards his love. The other principle that limits the salient properties is this: the properties intended are only those that contribute to a true conclusion. One plausible statement of the salient features of a rose, relevant to the context of utterance and leading to a true conclusion, is that a red rose is beautiful, or sweet-smelling, or highly-valued. . . . Putting the poet's sentence and the statement of salience together and drawing an obvious inference, we construct the following argument:

> My love is a red rose.
> A red rose is beautiful, or sweet-smelling, or highly valued. . . .
> Therefore, my love is beautiful, or sweet-smelling or highly
>   valued. . . .

(Martinich 1984: 511)

Thus by "My love is a red rose," the poet implicates his love is beautiful, *or* sweet-smelling, *or* highly valued. . . .

This account has several serious problems. First, nothing in the Gricean maxims or Cooperative Principle tells us the poet's utterance is to be interpreted metaphorically rather than ironically. We have already made that point. Second, as Sadock (1978: 368) observed, a metaphor lacking aptness might be a poor metaphor, but it is not no metaphor at all. Third, the poet surely does not mean anything as weak as a disjunction. He is not merely implying she is beautiful *or* sweet-smelling *or* highly valued *or*. . . . If someone else said, "I agree with you: your love smells good, but she's ugly and worthless," the poet would surely take umbrage. And he would probably not be prepared to maintain his metaphor should her personality and looks turn ugly while her scent remains sweet. Moreover, the Maxim of Quantity says that one should provide as much information as required. Many purposes are better served by a conjunction rather than a disjunction. In that case, conformity to that maxim would require the poet to implicate that his love is beautiful *and* sweet-smelling *and* highly valued *and*. . . . But a conjunctive interpretation is surely too strong. The poet might not have been thinking of the fact that his love was sweet-smelling, and he might have no disposition to withdraw his metaphor should it turn out that she had no discernible odor, or the scent of gardenias rather than roses. Furthermore, many salient and relevant properties of roses would never be part of what the poet means. For example, roses are hairless, toothless, brainless, breastless, and legless. Finally, a more plausible interpretation is that the poet implicates his love is *like a red rose in certain respects relevant to her being his love.* This interpretation is supported by the Maxim of Manner ("Be brief"), but may be counterindicated by the Maxim of Quantity ("Be as informative as required"). Nothing in the Gricean principles predicts that this "implicit simile" interpretation has the optimal strength to brevity ratio.[10]

The most fatal problem with the idea of an indeterminate implicature is that it contradicts the determinacy requirement! If, as Grice and Martinich suggest, there are several possible alternative ways in which the speaker could be observing the Cooperative Principle, then the conclusion that must ordinarily be drawn is that the determinacy requirement fails. There is no belief the speaker is *required* to possess. The only way the determinacy requirement could hold is if one of the alternatives is a disjunction that includes all the other alternatives, as Grice suggests. But disjunctive implicatures are rare in the sorts of cases Martinich points to. Furthermore, if the list of alternative ways is literally *open,* as Grice and Martinich also suggest, then there could not even be a disjunctive implicature

10 Compare Harnish (1976: 333).

satisfying the determinacy requirement. To say the list of disjuncts is open is just to say we cannot work out all of them. But if we cannot work out all the disjuncts, we cannot work out the disjunction.

Sperber and Wilson resolve the indeterminacy problem by counting all the alternative ways in which the speaker could be observing their conversational principle as "weak implicatures."

An utterance that can be given an interpretation consistent with the principle of relevance on the basis of different – though of course related – sets of premises and conclusions has a wide range of weak implicatures. (Sperber and Wilson 1987: 706)[11]

For us, as for the romantics, metaphor has a genuine cognitive content which, particularly with the more creative metaphors, is not para-phrasable without loss. This content we have proposed to analyse in terms of an indefinite array of weak implicatures whose recovery is trig-gered by the speaker, but whose content the hearer actively helps to determine. (Sperber and Wilson 1986b: 549)

Satisfaction of the determinacy requirement is taken to be defini-tive of "strong implicatures." The first problem with this resolu-tion is that it contradicts the authors' repeated claim:

In our theory, we show that an utterance cannot have more than one interpretation consistent with the principle of relevance. (Sperber and Wilson 1987: 739)

and:

On this approach, the implicatures of an utterance are those contextual assumptions and implications which the hearer has to recover in order to satisfy himself that the speaker has observed the principle of relevance. (Wilson and Sperber 1986: 383)

which affirm calculability. The main problem with their "weak implicature" notion, however, is that it eliminates the distinction between what the speaker actually implicated and what he might have implicated but did not. That is, Sperber and Wilson wrongly count *all* of the things the speaker could have been implicating as things he did implicate. Someone who writes, "My love is a red

---

[11] See also Wilson and Sperber (1981: 163–164), Sperber and Wilson (1986a: 193–200), and Blakemore (1987a: 70–71; 1992: 129–130).

rose" could – compatibly with the Cooperative Principle, the Principle of Relevance, or any other conversational principle – have meant that his love smells like a rose, has rosy color hair, and is very delicate. He may not actually have intended to convey any of these particular thoughts, however. He may have meant only that his love is as beautiful as a red rose, another thing he could have implicated.

Clearly, the weaker the implicatures, the less confidence the hearer can have that the particular premises or conclusions he supplies will reflect the speaker's thoughts, and this is where the indeterminacy lies. However, people may entertain different thoughts and come to have different beliefs on the basis of the same cognitive environment. The aim of communication in general is to increase the mutuality of cognitive environments rather than guarantee an impossible duplication of thoughts. (Sperber and Wilson 1986a: 200)

The last two claims may be conceded, but do nothing to ameliorate the problem identified in the first. To implicate something is to mean or imply it in a certain way. That involves the intentions of the speaker and the expression of thoughts. If there is indeterminacy about the speaker's thoughts, we have not figured out what he has implicated. For calculability to hold, we need some way of distinguishing which, among all the things the speaker might have implicated, he actually implicated. And that requires determining which thoughts the speaker intended to convey.

3.5 RELEVANCE IMPLICATURES

Let us consider a variation on dialogue (1) of Chapter 1.

(1) CARL: I am sick.
    DIANE: A flying saucer is nearby.

Carl may be dumbfounded by Diane's response because he believes that it is false, and that even if it were true it would not be relevant to his being sick. Nevertheless, Diane may well have been implicating that Carl could get help from the doctors on the flying saucer. Alternatively, she may have been implicating that Carl may have gotten sick because of the flying saucer. She might even have been implicating that the flying saucer would take him to a hospital, or that either the doctors on the saucer would help him or the aliens would take him to the hospital. Diane might have been implicating many things, because there are any number of ways her remark could have been relevant to the accepted purpose of the conversation. But this means that Diane may be implicating p even though the supposition that she believes p is not *required* to make her utterance consistent with the Cooperative Principle.

Suppose Diane is implicating that Carl got sick because of the flying saucer. We can conclude from this assumption that Diane must believe that Carl got sick because of the flying saucer, for she would otherwise be violating the Maxim of Quality. But as noted in our exposition of Gricean theory (section 1.3) and again in section 3.3, the fact that S implicated p is not intended to be a determinant of what is required to make S's utterance consistent with the Cooperative Principle. For the theory is trying to identify the determinants of the fact that S is implicating p. Antecedent to the fact that Diane is implicating that Carl got sick because of the flying saucer, many other beliefs would have made her utterance consistent with the Cooperative Principle. She could have believed, and implicated, that Carl could get help from the doctors on the flying saucer or that the flying saucer would take him to the hospital. The determinacy principle fails because there are too few constraints for the Cooperative Principle to require, or even make probable, any particular beliefs. There are just too many ways of being relevant. Calculability fails because conversational principles do not enable us to determine which of all the things Diane might have been implicating she actually implicated.

3.6 CLOSE-BUT IMPLICATURES

In section 2.1, we introduced the class of "close-but" implicatures, which includes quantity implicatures as a special case. The speaker implicates the denial of one statement by asserting another statement that is close in content but not the same. The examples given before are repeated here:

(2) A: Did anyone get an A?
     B: Some got Bs.

(3) A: Did you get Hillary Clinton's photograph?
     B: I got Bill Clinton's.

The point made in section 2.1 was that these implicatures cast doubt on the claim that quantity implicatures are actually explained by the Maxim of Quantity. The question now is how such implicatures are to be calculated. It might be suggested that although the Maxim of Quantity does not apply here, another maxim does, one not isolated by Grice. It is quite plausible that the Cooperative Principle implies that cooperative speakers ought to *provide requested information,* which we might call the "Maxim of Request." But whereas this maxim does indeed apply to (2) and (3), it is still not specific enough to enable us to calculate the observed implicatures. For B would be "providing the requested information" whether he implied that the answer to the question is yes or no. So the Maxim of Request gives us no reason to predict that B used "Some got Bs" to implicate "No one got As" rather than "Some got As," or "I did not get Hillary Clinton's photograph" rather than "I did get hers."

Furthermore, we can find the same close-but implicatures when the Maxim of Request does not apply.

(4) A: Everyone in my class got an A.
     B: Some in mine got Bs.

(5) A: I'd love to have Hillary Clinton's photograph.
     B: I have Bill Clinton's.

We cannot even use the Cooperative Principle to derive what B implicated in these cases. The conversations do not *require* B to contribute the information she implicated – or asserted, for that matter. Hence determinacy fails: it is not true that B could not be observing the Cooperative Principle without believing that no one in her class got an A, or that she does not have President Clinton's photograph. B would have been plenty cooperative if she had implicated that some students in her class got As and that she does have the president's photograph. Of course, quality may make one case more cooperative than another, but that is an independent consideration. Indeed, in the actual case, B might have been falsely implicating that she does not have President Clinton's photograph, to keep A from pestering her for it.

76

3.7 QUANTITY IMPLICATURES:
THE POSSIBILITY OF IGNORANCE

Determinacy, and with it calculability, fail even in the case receiving the most detailed attention from Griceans, that in which a weaker statement is used to implicate the denial of a stronger statement. According to the determinacy requirement, a general who says "Some died" thereby implicates "Not all died" only if the supposition that the general believes not all died is required to make his utterance consistent with the Cooperative Principle. The Maxim of Quantity would seem to be the operative principle here because it requires the speaker to be as informative as is required. But the general *could* be observing the Maxim of Quantity without believing that not all died. For he would also be in conformity with the Maxim of Quantity if he knew that some died, but had no idea whether all died.

It might be suggested that in those cases in which the general does implicate that not all died, the context provides a background constraint relative to which the supposition that he believes not all died is required. Leech (1983: 86) remarked, "One context will suggest that *s* has withheld the information because of lack of knowledge, and another that *s* has withheld it because of a definite belief to the contrary." But over and above the very fact that the general has implicated that not everyone died, nothing in the context need rule out one possibility or the other. When the general says, "Some died" and thereby implicates that not all died, the context may not even provide enough evidence for the hearer to make an educated guess as to whether or not the general believes or is implicating that not all died.[12]

Levinson (1983: 134–135) also showed some recognition of the alternative possibility I am citing when he tried to show how

---

[12] Following Leech (1983: 86) and Horn (1989: 233–234), Matsumoto (1995: 24) asserts, "The weaker implicature ["S does not know whether all died"] is produced when the speaker's knowledge ... is assumed to be incomplete, the stronger implicature ["Not all died"] when it is not." But as we show in Chapter 4, what anyone *presumes about S* in no way *produces S's implicature*. The most we can say is that H's presumption about S *influences the implicatures H understands S to be making.*

quantity implicatures could be worked out. In the "more explicit" version of the derivation, Levinson said the following:

Since if S knew that q holds but nevertheless uttered p he would be in breach of the injunction to make his contribution as informative as is required, S must mean me, the addressee, to infer that S knows that q is not the case (K–q), *or at least that he does not know that q is the case (–Kq).* (Levinson 1983: 135; emphasis added)

Levinson has not succeeded in working out "S implicated –q" because he has not shown that S is *required* to believe –q. Levinson acknowledges here that S would also conform to the quantity maxim if he were ignorant as to q. In the sentence immediately following, however, Levinson implies that S is required to believe –q:

The important feature of such arguments to note is that they derive an implicature by reference to what has *not* been said: the absence of a statement $A(e_1)$ [= q], in the presence of a weaker one, legitimates the inference that it is not the case that $A(e_1)$, via the maxim of Quantity. Another feature to note is that the inference is implicitly or explicitly **epistemically modified;** that is to say that from the utterance of $A(e_2)$ [= p] one actually infers "speaker knows that not $A(e_1)$" . . . rather than just $–A(e_1)$. . . . Since I the addressee assume that S is cooperating, and therefore will not violate the maxim of Quantity without warning, I take it that S wishes to convey that he is *not* in a position to state that the stronger item e_1 on the scale holds, and indeed knows that it does not hold. (Levinson 1983: 134–135)

The Maxim of Quantity together with the assertion of the weaker statement $A(e_2)$ does *not* entitle us to infer *S knows that $–A(e_1)$.* For another possibility is *S does not know that $A(e_1)$.* Because the Maxim of Quantity provides no reason to infer the former rather than the latter, the determinacy requirement fails. Levinson is not alone in insisting on determinate belief in the contradictory despite pointing out that the Quantity Maxim only requires lack of belief in the implicated proposition.

If I tell you that some of my friends are Buddhists, *I license you to draw the inference that not all my friends are Buddhists.* (If I knew they all were, and this knowledge was relevant to your interests, it would have been incumbent on me to obey the Q Principle and say so; the assumption that I am obeying *Quantity allows you to infer that I did not know for a fact that the stronger pre-diction* – "All of my friends are Buddhists" – held.) (Horn 1984: 13)[13]

Only in a very special case will your inferring *I do not know whether all S are P* allow you to infer *Not all S are P.* Quantity implicatures are not restricted to that case. Levinson's final view is that negative knowledge is indicated in some cases, ignorance in others, and "Why this should be so remains one of the many mysteries in this area" (1983: 136).

We might take Levinson and Horn to be suggesting the following reformulation of the determinacy requirement:

Theoretical Definition IV: S conversationally implicates p iff . . . (iii) The supposition that S either believes p or does not believe –p is required to make his utterance consistent with the Cooperative Principle. . . .[14]

If we let p be "Not all died," then the determinacy requirement of definition IV may appear satisfied in the general's case. For Levinson and Horn would maintain that the general is required to know that not all died, or at least not know that all died. However, definition IV would be much too weak with this change in clause (iii). Let p be "I am not talking to little green men on Alpha Centauri," and suppose Peter is here on earth having a conversation with Mary about the weather. The positive supposition that Peter believes he is not talking to little green men on Alpha Centauri hardly seems to be necessary for Peter's utterance to be required by the accepted purpose of the conversation. But the negative supposition that Peter does not believe he is talking to little green men on Alpha Centauri would seem to be required. How could

---

[13] (I added the emphasis, and used quotation marks instead of italics to refer to the sentence mentioned.) See also Gordon and Lakoff (1975: 92), Leech (1983: 85–88), and Horn (1989: 212; 1992: 261).

[14] Given the particular disjunction contained in clause (iii) of definition IV, I do not believe it matters whether *believes* or *knows* is used. There would be even fewer cases in which clause (iii) of definition I is satisfied if *know* replaced *believe* there.

Peter's utterance be contributing something required by the purpose of the conversation if Peter is so deluded as to think he is talking to little green men? Assuming the common knowledge and cooperative presumption conditions are also satisfied, the Generative Assumption implies that no matter what Peter is saying, he is implicating that he is not talking to little green men on Alpha Centauri, and definition IV implies that the implicature is conversational.

There is also a curious incoherence in definition IV. Clause (iii) is formulated the way it is because it was observed that S may conversationally implicate p even though the supposition that S believes p is not required to make his utterance consistent with the Cooperative Principle. But if S implicates p without believing p, then his utterance violates the Maxim of Quality, and so is not consistent with the Cooperative Principle!

3.8 QUANTITY IMPLICATURES: OTHER POSSIBILITIES

There are ways for determinacy and calculability to fail when a speaker says, "Some died" even though he knows everyone died. The general could even say it, thereby implicating that not all died, in an attempt to mislead his audience. That he has implicated something he knows to be false would put him in violation of the Maxim of Quality, of course. But we are concerned with the determinants of that implicature. We are trying to ascertain whether we can deduce that the general believes that not all died (or fails to believe that all died) from what he said together with the Maxim of Quantity and potential contextual determinants of implicature. We cannot use an assumption about what he has implicated in the process either of determining what he has implicated or of deriving his implicature from Gricean principles. Yet without using an assumption about what he has implicated, we cannot determine whether he believes that not all died. For it is not antecedently true that his utterance of "Some died" would be inconsistent with the Cooperative Principle unless the general believes not all died. Another possibility is that the general is dispensing information on a "need to know" basis and has uttered

"Some died" rather than "All died" because he thought his audience only needed to know that some died. Of course, when the general actually is dispensing information on a need to know basis, he will not be implicating that not all died when he says that some died. But that is irrelevant to the point I am trying to make. We want to know whether the determinacy of S's belief p is necessary for S to implicate p. Therefore when the general implicates that not all died by saying, "Some died," we need to ascertain whether his believing that not all died is required by the Cooperative Principle given that he said, "Some died." The fact that, compatibly with his utterance, the general could have thought his addressee did not need to know whether all died, suffices to show that such a belief is not required. Determinacy and calculability fail because nothing other than his implicature rules out the possibility that he is obeying the Maxim of Quantity by dispensing information on a need to know basis.

For a very different case, with broader implications, suppose S is asked, "Did anyone die?" S would be fully cooperative if he answered, "Yes." Recall that he would not thereby implicate that not all died or that he did not know whether all died. Now suppose S actually answers by saying, "Some did," implicating that not all did. Because he could have achieved the accepted purpose of the conversation by answering simply, "Yes," there is no sense in which he must believe that not all died in order to conform to the cooperative principle. Nothing in the accepted purpose of the conversation requires S to provide more information than he gave explicitly. His implicature was supererogatory. Example (2) in Chapter 2, repeated here as (6), was used to show that if (6)(a) could be derived from Gricean Principles, then the denial of (6)(b) should also be derivable. That showed indirectly that quantity implicatures could not really be derived from or explained by Gricean principles.

(6) "Did anyone die?"
     (a) Some did ⊐ −(All died).
     (b) Yes ⊅ −(All died).

Now we are showing directly that determinacy fails by observing that the very fact that "yes" is a fully cooperative response falsifies the key premise in the schema whereby Gricean theory purports to work out implicature (6)(a).

The Cooperative Principle does not imply that speakers must provide any information beyond what is required by the accepted purpose of the conversation. Hence the Maxim of Quantity is formulated as saying "Be as informative *as required,*" not "Be as informative *as possible.*"[15] If the Maxim of Quantity were formulated more stringently, then conformity to the Cooperative Principle would not require conformity to the maxim. Nor would general rationality. As M. Green (1995: 101) observes, providing more information than required has costs as well as benefits, with no balance generally prevailing. Moreover, the maxim would be false. Suppose H asks S who won the game. S would satisfy all conversational norms by answering truthfully, "The Yankees." S is under no obligation here to be as informative as possible. He need not add, "The score was 9 to 7, and the game was won in the 11th inning when Strawberry hit a two-run home run to right field," even though this is relevant, interesting, and maybe even useful information. Based on the ethnological studies of Keenan and Ochs, furthermore, sociolinguists have concluded that Malagasy speakers often withhold information in culturally accepted ways we find alien.[16] Finally, Gricean theory would predict countless nonexistent implicatures if the Cooperative Principle were understood to imply being as informative as possible. Strengthened in this way, the Working-out Schema would, if valid in the usual cases, predict falsely that in answering simply "Yes," S implicated that he did not know whether or not everyone died. And from the fact that S did not give the score, we would be able to infer erroneously that he did not know it or that the score was not 9 to 7. The theory would credit Malagasy speakers with implicatures they did not intend.

---

[15] Compare M. Green (1995), who appropriately dubs the latter the "Principle of Volubility." Green cites passages from Strawson, Grice, Levinson, Harnish, Horn, and Hirschberg endorsing what he calls volubility.

[16] See, for example, Keenan (1975), Fasold (1990: 53–62, 138), Kasher (1982: 35–36), and G. M. Green (1989: 96).

Grice (1975: 26) goes so far as to argue for a submaxim requiring that S *not* make his contribution more informative than required.[17] Although Grice concedes that providing excess information might merely waste time rather than transgress the Cooperative Principle, he justifies the submaxim by saying (i) the additional information is liable to be confusing and misleading, and (ii) provision of the additional information will violate the Maxim of Relation. The baseball example shows that this justification is unsound on both counts. So does the acceptability of answering "Nearly everyone" to "Did anyone die?" Furthermore, this submaxim would make vast tracts of ordinary conversation uncooperative. Consider, for another example, the well-known case in which A asks B whether she owns a Mercedes-Benz, and B answers that she does not own any expensive car, thereby implicating that she does not own a Mercedes. In this case, her explicature is supererogatory.

Let us return to the notion of a *Horn scale*.

A linguistic **scale** consists of a set of linguistic alternates, or contrastive expressions of the same grammatical category, which can be arranged in a linear order by degree of *informativeness* or semantic strength. Such a scale will have the general form of an ordered set (indicated by angled brackets) of linguistic expressions or *scalar predicates,* $e_1, e_2, e_3, \ldots e_n$, as in:

(117) $\langle e_1, e_2, e_3, \ldots e_n \rangle$

where if we substitute e_1 or e_2 etc., in a sentential frame A we obtain well-formed sentences $A(e_1)$, $A(e_2)$, etc.; and where $A(e_1)$ entails $A(e_2)$, $A(e_2)$ entails $A(e_3)$, etc, but not vice versa. For example, take the English quantifiers *all* and *some*. These form an implicational scale $\langle all, some \rangle$, because any sentence like (118) *entails* (119) (i.e., whenever (118) is true (119) is true also) but not vice versa:

(118) All of the boys went to the party
(119) Some of the boys went to the party.

Now, given any such scale, there is a general predictive rule for deriving a set of Quantity implicatures, namely if a speaker asserts that a lower or weaker point (i.e., a rightwards item in the ordered set of alternatives) on

---

[17] "Quantity-2" is also affirmed by Berg (1991: 419) and Matsumoto (1995).

a scale obtains, then he implicates that a higher point (leftwards in the ordered set) does *not* obtain. Thus if one asserts (119) one conversationally implicates that not all the boys went to the party; this is so even though it is quite compatible with the truth of (119) that (118) is also true, as shown by the non-contradictoriness of (120):

(120)   Some of the boys went to the party, in fact all

We may formulate this generally as a rule for deriving **scalar implicatures** from scalar predicates:

(121)   *Scalar implicatures:* Given any scale of the form $<e_1, e_2, e_3, \ldots,$ $e_n>$, if a speaker asserts $A(e_2)$, then he implicates $\sim A(e_1)$, if he asserts $A(e_3)$, then he implicates $\sim A(e_2)$ and $\sim A(e_1)$, and in general, if he asserts $A(e_n)$, then he implicates $\sim(A(e_{n-1}))$, $\sim(A(e_{n-2}))$ and so on, up to $\sim(A(e_1))$

(Levinson 1983: 133).[18]

Levinson's example can easily be extended: <*all, nearly all, most, many, a few, some*>. As his example indicates, the concept of a Horn scale is not limited to "predicates" in any sense. Note too that a series of expressions form a scale only relative to a specified range of sentence frames. "S failed to prove that *all* S are P," for example, does not entail "S failed to prove that *some* S are P." And the latter does not implicate the denial of the former.

Scales are useful for *summarizing* the generalized quantity implicatures of a language. The question for us to address is whether the implicatures so summarized can be *derived* from the Maxim of Quantity. The answer is no. For the maxim says, "Contribute as much information as is *required by the conversation.*" Yet what is required by the conversation will vary from context to context, speaker to speaker, topic to topic, and so on. It is not *generally* true, as we have seen, that the purposes of a conversation *require* the speaker to contribute the *maximum* amount of pertinent information. Hence the maxim does not entail the false principle that the speaker should generally make the strongest possible statement. To be as informative as required is not necessarily to be as informative

[18] See also Horn (1972; 1989: esp. §4.4), Gazdar (1979), Levinson (1987b: 69–71), Fasold (1990: 126–129), Hirschberg (1991), Rooth (1992, 82–83), and Van Kuppevelt (1996: §3.3).

as possible. Consequently, the Maxim of Quantity does not entail that a speaker should in general contribute the information that all S are P, or the information that not all S are P, if he possessed it. Nor does the maxim specify *how* the speaker should contribute the information. That is, the maxim does not entail that the speaker should implicate not all S are P rather than assert it.

Looking back at the Working-out Schema for sentence implicature in Chapter 1, the premise to examine is P3: *Users of Σ in G-contexts could not be observing the Cooperative Principle (including the Maxim of Quantity) unless they believed p.* We cannot say in general that users of "Some S are P" could not be observing the Cooperative Principle or the Maxim of Quantity unless they believed not all S are P. There are many types of contexts, of course, in which such a generalization would hold. But there are also contexts of many types in which users of the sentence could be observing the Maxim of Quantity without believing not all S are P. Here is a sample: (i) The conversational goal is to establish the truth of proposition q. The participants have just established "If some S are P, then q." (ii) The speaker has just said, "I do not mean to imply that not all S are P, but it is true that. . . ." (iii) The logic teacher has asked the speaker to state as many true propositions of the form "Some S are P" as possible. (iv) The IRS auditor asks, "Were any of these expenses reimbursable?" expecting a simple "Yes" or "No" answer.[19] (v) The general is dispensing information on a need to know basis. (vi) The speaker does not know whether all S are P. The class of such contexts is neither closed nor small. The premises of the Working-out Schema put us in no position, then, to draw the conclusion that the *sentence* "Some S are P" implicates that not all S are P.

Using the line of argument developed at length in Chapter 2, we can also give something of a reductio argument against the thesis that the quantity implicatures summarized by any given scale are derivable from the Maxim of Quantity. For many scales

---

[19] Matsumoto (1995) shows in detail that whether S implicates "not-p" rather than "I don't know whether p" in answering wh-questions depends on whether S explicitly provides as much information as expected or less.

can be specified on which asserting a lower point does not implicate denying all higher points. Consider: *100%, 99.999%,
99.998%, . . . , 1.001%, 1%.* If the implicatures summarized by
Levinson's scale or its extension were derivable from the Maxim
of Quantity, then we should be able to derive the principle that
asserting a lower point on the percentage scale implicates the
denial of all higher points. That is, let $A(e)$ be the sentence frame
"At least _____ of all S are P"; then asserting $A(e_i)$ should implicate $-A(e_{i-j})$ for all j between 1 and $i - 1$. This rule fails for most i
and j. For example, "At least 1% of S is P" does not implicate "It is
not the case that at least 2.738% of S is P," or "It is not the case
that at least 30.230% of S is P."

In section 2.1, we observed that if Gricean theory can account
for the fact that "S believes p" implicates "S does not know p,"
then it should predict wrongly that "S knows p" implicates "S does
not regret p." Matsumoto attempts to account for the difference
using Grice's second Quantity Maxim, prohibiting the provision
of more information than is necessary:

> Consider the choice between *know* and *regret*. These verbs differ not only
> in terms of their lexical presuppositions, but also in terms of the
> absence/presence of an assertion about the emotional state of the
> subject. . . . [Hence] the use of *regret* in place of *know* in B's utterance
> ["They know that there was an accident"] would convey more informa-
> tion than is required in this context, so the Quantity-2 Condition is not
> satisfied and an implicature is not produced.
>
> On the other hand, *know* and *believe* do not differ regarding the
> absence/presence of any additional assertion. Rather, the difference
> between them lies in the absence/presence of a presupposition and in the
> degree of some scalar notion (i.e., confidence) that is asserted. These dif-
> ferences in the information conveyed by *know* but not by *believe* cannot
> be dismissed as more than is necessary in exchanges in which implicature
> is produced. . . . Thus the additional strength of the statement with *know*
> (rather than *believe*) cannot be dismissed as more than is required in these
> contexts. Therefore the Quantity-2 Condition is satisfied, and an implica-
> ture is produced. (Matsumoto 1995: 37)

Despite its recency, Matsumoto's derivation is no more rigorous
than Levinson's. First, "S knows p" does assert more than "S

believes p," as hundreds of books and articles on the analysis of knowledge attest. In addition to the fact that S believes p, "S knows p" entails that "p" is true and that S is justified in believing p. "S knows p" also entails "S is certain that p," but even this "scalar" difference means that "S knows p" asserts more than "S believes p." Second, it is not generally true that contexts require the extra information expressed by "know" rather than "believe." Nor is it generally true that contexts do not require the extra information expressed by "regret" rather than "know." Grice's quantity maxims provide no insight into the difference between *<know, believe>* and *<regret, know>*.

Hirschberg (1991, Ch. VI) and Rooth (1992: 82–83) observed that stress ("focus") has the function of selecting a particular Horn scale when more than one is associated with the uttered sentence. Imagine S and H talking about the supply of beer. Contrast the following:

(7) (a) *Some* bottles are cool.
　　 (b) Some bottles are *cool*.

(7)(a) has the implicature Horn and Levinson considered: "Not all are cool." (7)(b) has a very different implicature: "Some are cool but not cold."[20] Whereas S might use (7)(a) to warn H to watch out for some warm bottles, he would use (7)(b) to warn H not to get her hopes up. The stress determines whether the scale *<all, some>* is relevant rather than *<cold, cool>*. My point is that because stress does not influence the *information* that is *explicitly* conveyed by a sentence, Grice's Maxim of Quantity cannot possibly predict or generate the implicature of either (7)(a) or (7)(b).

3.9 TAUTOLOGY IMPLICATURES

We observed in section 2.2 that although Grice claimed tautologies have the implicatures they do because their utterance flouts the Maxim of Quantity, he never showed how the implicatures are to be calculated. Harnish (1976: 332) and Levinson (1983: 111)

---

[20] Only in some contexts do I hear the implicature "None are cold."

conceded that it is unclear how the implicatures of tautologies are to be calculated. Ward and Hirschberg (1991: 511) attempt to show how the implicatures can be calculated, but their working-out schema assigns tautologies an implicature they do not possess (see fn. 12 of Ch. 2). The evidence presented in section 2.2 makes it clear, I believe, that tautology implicatures are not calculable. *If* a speaker who uttered "War is war" could not be observing the Cooperative Principle unless he believed it is the nature of war that terrible things happen, then the same should be true for speakers who utter "A war's a war," "Wars will be wars," "War is a state of armed conflict between groups," "War either is or is not war," and *La guerre est la guerre*. But the same thing is not true.

Let us consider the matter more directly. Return to Sarah, who utters "A war's a war" in response to Ted's argument that intervention in Bosnia would put us in a situation more like the Korean war than the Vietnam war. Suppose Sarah implicates what the sentence implicates, namely, that one war is as bad as another. Is the supposition that Sarah believes one war is as bad as another required to make her utterance consistent with the Cooperative Principle? It is, by the Quality Maxim, if we take her implicature as a background constraint. But we are looking for what makes it true that she is implicating that one war is as bad as another, so we cannot use that implicature as a background constraint. We must not engage in ex post facto reasoning. Is there anything in the tautological meaning of the sentence Sarah utters, the context, or the purpose of the conversation, which antecedently implies that Sarah must believe one war is as bad as another if she is being cooperative? Certainly not. Sarah would be conforming to the Cooperative Principle just as well if she were using "A war's a war" to express any of the following beliefs: "War is glorious, that is all that matters"; "This conversation is uninformative"; "You are stating the obvious"; "What you are saying is certain beyond all possible doubt"; "Your argument is worthy of Aristotle"; "Clausewitz could not have put it better"; and so on. Sarah also could have been using the sentence ironically, to express the belief that one war is not as bad as another, and thereby to commend Ted and ridicule those who maintain there was no significant difference between Korea and Vietnam. Levinson suggested that the Maxim of Relation would play a crucial role in the derivation. Any of these beliefs would be as relevant to the argument about Bosnia as the belief that one war is as bad as another.

3.10 CONJUNCTION IMPLICATURES

Grice and his followers claim that the sequential interpretation of conjunctions like "John took off his trousers and went to bed" can be derived from the Maxim of Manner, specifically, from the sub-maxim enjoining speakers to be orderly. The evidence presented in section 2.3 makes it clear that such implicatures are not calculable. If a speaker who uttered that sentence could not be observing the Cooperative Principle unless he believed the event described by the first conjunct preceded that described by the second, then the same should hold for speakers who utter sentences like these: "John flipped the switch and turned on the light"; "John was in the kitchen and he was baking bread"; "John slipped – the road was icy"; "Jack married Jill and Ted married Alice"; "John both took off his trousers and went to bed"; and even "(John took off his trousers) • (John went to bed)." But the same does not hold. Furthermore, the injunction to be orderly does not specify that one should select temporal rather than other sorts of orderings, or forward rather than reverse temporal orderings.

More directly, imagine S uses "John took off his trousers and went to bed" with its normal sequential implication. If the supposition that S believes John took off his trousers before going to bed is required for his utterance to be consistent with the Cooperative Principle, then the supposition must be required for S's utterance to "contribute what is required by the accepted purpose of the conversation." Let us suppose the accepted purpose is to describe what John did last night. S's utterance would contribute to that purpose only if S believed that John did both things and had no opinion about the order in which he did them. S's utterance would contribute to that purpose if he believed John got into bed first. Indeed, S might have expected H to reason that if John had taken his trousers off first, he, S, would have said so. Less plausibly, but still possible, S's utterance might have been a lame attempt at metaphor; he may have been expressing the belief that John undertook whatever task he was engaged in with determination, using "He rolled up his sleeves and went to work" as a model. Finally, he might have been using the sentence ironically, to imply that John stayed up fully clothed all night.

We observed in section 2.3 that other conjunctions have different implicatures, which suggests that the account of the sequential interpretation in terms of the Maxim of Manner was not genuinely explanatory. Posner (1980) attributed other sorts of implicatures to other maxims. For example, he attributed the colocational implication of "Annie is in the kitchen and she is making doughnuts" to the Maxim of Quantity:

> If someone explicitly states that Annie is in the kitchen and then adds *without specifying another place* that she is making doughnuts, then he is guilty of *suppressing relevant information* if he thereby wants to convey that the doughnuts are being made outside of the kitchen. This would be a violation of maxim I/1 ["Make your contribution as informative as is required"]. (Posner 1980: 191)

But the speaker would be just as guilty of suppressing relevant information if he adds that Annie is making doughnuts without specifying *the same place.* Thus Posner gives us no more reason to conclude that the speaker implicates "Annie is making doughnuts in the kitchen" than that he is implicating "Annie is making doughnuts elsewhere."[21] Moreover, if the speaker is guilty of suppressing relevant information in the doughnut case, then we should be able to conclude that "John brushed his teeth and went to bed" implies that John went to bed where he brushed his teeth (normally, the bathroom). Finally, the Maxim of Quantity says that speakers should contribute as much information as is *required* by the accepted purpose of the conversation, not that they should provide all relevant information. It is difficult to imagine conversational purposes that would require the information that two

---

[21] Compare Kroch (1972), Kempson (1975: 152–156), and Atlas and Levinson (1981: 47), mentioned in a similar connection in section 2.3.

actions were performed in the same place, but not the information that they were performed in different places.[22]

Schmerling also observed that many conjunctions have other implicatures, and that it is hard to give a precise catalog of all the possibilities. She used the term "priority" to vaguely denote the general relationship involved, and attributed the implicatures to a conversational principle different from Grice's:

> The fundamentally different character of the types of sentences treated in the previous section [e.g., *I've got to try and find that screw*] from that of those treated in this section suggests very strongly that a rule of conversation is responsible for the asymmetry of the latter: In conversation, we first lay a groundwork for what we are going to say next. This is, of course, a very general principle, and like Grice's other principles, it is not limited to conversation. (Schmerling 1975: 229)

First, "laying a groundwork" does not necessarily give rise to relations of priority. For example, before we can use the phrase "John's wife" we often have to lay a groundwork by stating that John has a wife. Similarly, before telling you that I climbed it, I may lay a groundwork by stating that Mt. Everest is the tallest mountain in the world, located in the Himalayas, and so on. So it is not clear how, from Schmerling's groundwork principle, any implicature of priority can be derived. Second, the "groundwork" is sometimes presented second, not first, as in "John slipped; the road was icy" and "John set a record and jumped 20 feet." Third, no reason is given why the groundwork principle should not apply just as well to conjunctions like "Paris is in France and Berlin is in Germany"

---

[22] Posner similarly attributes the broadly causal interpretation of "The window was open and there was a draft" to the Maxim of Relation. "If someone explicitly states that a window is open and then adds *without specifying another source* that there is a draft, then he is guilty of *communicating irrelevant information* if he does not want to convey that the draft is coming from that window. This would be a violation of maxim III [Relation]" (Posner 1980: 191). But Posner here simply assumes that "The window was open and there was a draft" communicates the information that the draft came from the window, which is the very fact we are trying to explain. Without that assumption, we cannot conclude that he is guilty of communicating irrelevant information if he does not want to convey that the draft is coming from the window.

and "John both took off his trousers and got into bed," which do not implicate any relation of priority.

3.11 CONFLICTING PRINCIPLES

When the Gricean maxims conflict, we are ordinarily unable to determine what is required for conformity to the Cooperative Principle. I believe that properly understood, the Quantity, Quality, and Relation Maxims are consistent. But the Maxim of Manner often clashes with the other three. In the case of irony, for example, Manner clashes with Quality. When S says, "It is a fine day!" we cannot interpret S as meaning what he said because on that interpretation S would be violating the Maxim of Quality. But we cannot interpret S as meaning the opposite of what he said, because on that interpretation, S would be violating the Maxim of Manner. It is hardly perspicuous to use a sentence to mean the opposite of what the sentence means. Indeed, it is hard to see how any implicatures can be worked out on the basis of the maxims, because it would always be more perspicuous to "explicate" a proposition rather than implicate it.

As we have seen, Griceans believe that quantity implicatures can be worked out from the Maxim of Quantity, whereas sequential conjunctions can be worked out from the Maxim of Manner, specifically, the submaxim, "Be orderly." I have argued that the implicatures cannot be derived from these principles. But let us suppose there is another pair of principles from which the two sets of implicatures can be derived. These rules, whatever they are, would produce conflicting results in the case of conjunctions, as we observed in section 2.3. By the "order" rule, "p and q" would implicate "p before q." But by the "quantity" rule, "p and q" would implicate "−(p before q)." The "order" rule would also produce clashes with the Maxim of Relation. For there are surely contexts in which the order of events is irrelevant, where the only relevant matter is that all the events occurred. Such a context can be created by the hearer saying, "Relate the principal events, but don't give away the order in which they occurred; I want to see if I can figure that out."

The Gricean maxims also clash with what we might call the *Principle of Style,* which further specifies how we should convey information.

Principle of Style: Be stylish, so be beautiful, distinctive, entertaining, and interesting.

Because both Manner and Style deal with the way we convey information, they might well be considered submaxims of a more general principle. Pursuing style at the expense of other goals writers pursue, poets have traditionally deviated from the Gricean maxims, and twentieth-century poets have often abandoned the principle of politeness as well. A clear and simple prose style used to give "just the facts, please," can be boring, tedious, and dull. We liven up our writing with figures of speech and other devices. Irony is an example. As we have seen, it often produces violations of the Maxim of Quality (at the level of what is said) as well as the Maxim of Manner. We often "embellish" a narration to make it more interesting (violating Quality) and delete boring or ugly details even when they are important (violating Quantity).

The Gricean maxims often clash with the *Principle of Politeness,* broadly construed. Leech (1983) has developed this point most fully.[23]

Principle of Politeness: Be polite, so be tactful, generous, praising, modest, agreeable, and sympathetic.

Speakers often withhold information that would be offensive or disappointing to the hearer, violating the Maxim of Quantity, and frequently exaggerate in order to please or flatter, violating the Maxim of Quality. Leech suggests that the Principle of Politeness is thus involved in the explanation of the figures of speech known

---

[23] See also Davison (1975), Lakoff (1977), Brown and Levinson (1978, 1987), Bird (1979: 143), Holdcroft (1979: 140), Horn (1989: 360), Fasold (1990: 159–166), and Matsumoto (1995: §2.4). Holdcroft makes the related observation that "M. Quant. would seem often to be overridden by considerations of a prudential or even moral kind."

as litotes and hyperbole. Brown and Levinson (1978: 116) similarly observe that people often speak elliptically, thereby promoting a sense of solidarity – but violating the Maxim of Manner. People pick "safe topics" (e.g., the weather) to stress agreement and communicate an interest in maintaining good relations – but violating the Maxim of Relation. Euphemisms avoid mentioning the unmentionable, but in the process violate Manner and Quantity.

Let us consider the following case in detail:

(8) S knows full well that all S are P;
     Up to this point S has been observing both the Cooperative Princi-
        ple and the Politeness Principle, and would like to continue
        observing both if possible;
     It would be impolite for S to assert, "All S are P";
     The purpose of the conversation is to determine whether "q" is true,
        something that could be inferred from the fact that all S are P;
     S asserts, "Some S are P."

Knowing all this, we are in no position to determine whether S did or did not implicate "All S are P" using conversational principles. For the Cooperative Principle and the Politeness Principle conflict: the former requires S to contribute the information that all S are P; the latter requires him to withhold it. Nor can we determine whether S implicated "All S are P" using the Working-out Schema. For without knowing what S implicated, we cannot determine whether he is still obeying the Cooperative Principle. In addition, there is no basis for us to say that S could not be observing the Cooperative Principle unless he believed that all S are P – or not all S are P, for that matter. Hence the Working-out Schema cannot be used because the second and third premises are inaccessible. Determinacy and calculability fail, therefore, when the Politeness Principle and the Cooperative Principle clash.

Brown and Levinson thought the conflict between politeness and the Gricean maxims was actually essential to implicature:

[Grice's] Maxims define for us the basic set of assumptions underlying every talk exchange. But this does not imply that utterances in general, or even reasonably frequently, must meet these conditions, as critics of Grice have sometimes thought. Indeed, the majority of natural conversations do not proceed in such a brusque fashion at all. The whole thrust of this paper is that one powerful and pervasive motive for *not* talking Maxim-wise is the desire to give some attention to face. (No doubt many other motives exist as well; the wish to avoid responsibility emerged as one in our field-work.) Politeness is then a major source of deviation from such rational efficiency, and is communicated precisely by that deviation. But even in such departures from the Maxims, they remain in operation at a deeper level. It is only because they are still assumed to be in operation that addressees are forced to do the inferential work that establishes the underlying intended message and the (polite or other) source of the departure – in short, to find an implicature, i.e. an inference generated by precisely this assumption. (Brown and Levinson 1978: 100)[24]

The notion of a principle being "in operation at a deeper level" when speakers are not doing what the principle says to do requires some explication. Take "white lies" as a concrete case. The speaker willfully disobeys the Maxim of Quality ("tell the truth") in order to be polite; the hearer may realize this and prefer it. In what sense does the Maxim of Quality remain "in operation"? Perhaps what Brown and Levinson have in mind is that the speaker still feels that he should ideally obey the maxim and that his violation of the maxim is therefore a cost, something he is willing to do only because the benefits outweigh it. But if it is the "operation" of conversational principles that is important in implicature, then determinacy and calculability must be abandoned. Both depend on the premise that S implicates p only if S has to believe p given that he *is* observing the Cooperative Principle.

Brown and Levinson might propose to redefine determinacy, making it the requirement that S implicates p only if S has to believe p given that the Cooperative Principle is "operative." This formulation of the determinacy condition, and the new Calculability Assumption it produces, is no less plausible than Grice's formulation. But the two conditions are significantly different, which may be obscured by the formulation of Grice's maxims as impera-

[24] Compare Brown and Levinson (1987: 4–5), G. M. Green (1989: 96), and Thomason (1990: 331–333). Contrast Bird (1979: 144).

tives. We've observed before that there are several forms of Grice's conversational principles:

Maxim of Quality: "Tell the truth."

> **Normative:** People *ought to* tell the truth.
> **Behavioral:** People *do* tell the truth.
> **Motivational:** People *want to* tell the truth.
> **Cognitive:** People *believe they ought to* tell the truth.

Whereas Grice appears to define determinacy and calculability in terms of the behavioral principle corresponding to the maxim, the Brown and Levinson formulation relies on cognitive and motivational principles.

On the formulation of determinacy we might impute to Brown and Levinson, S implicates what he has to believe given that he has the beliefs and desires attributed to people in general by the motivational and cognitive versions of the Cooperative Principle and associated maxims. This determinacy condition fails as badly as Grice's. The Politeness Principle may be operative as well as the Cooperative Principle, the Maxim of Manner as well as the other three maxims. If we are given only (i) that the cooperation and politeness principles were both "operative" at the cognitive and motivational levels, and (ii) that the Principle of Politeness requires fibbing and the Cooperative Principle requires not fibbing, we cannot determine whether the speaker will tell a white lie or not. It would not even help to add (iii) that the speaker does not believe what he is going to say. For we still could not determine whether the speaker will tell a white lie or speak ironically. We would need to know, in addition, and among other things, whether the speaker values honesty more or less than politeness in situations of this kind. Given vast individual and cultural differences,[25] it is doubtful that any general principle of comparative valuation would be valid. Brown and Levinson claim,

---

[25] Wierzbicka explores cultural differences in all the articles cited in the reference list.

[A]ny rational agent will tend to choose the same genus of strategy under the same conditions – that is, make the same moves as any other would make under the circumstances. This is by virtue of the fact that the particular strategies intrinsically afford certain payoffs or advantages, and the relevant circumstances are those in which one of these payoffs would be more advantageous than any others. (Brown and Levinson 1978: 76)

But the complexity of the payoff matrices Brown and Levinson go on to describe makes it completely implausible that all people tend to make the same choices, even if they are rational.

It is possible for determinacy to fail dramatically when the Cooperative Principle and the Politeness Principle clash for reasons that have nothing to do with the clash. For there might be different ways for the clash to arise and different ways for it to be resolved. For an example of the former possibility, let us suppose that Mary is writing a letter of recommendation for her daughter Jane. Mary is a famous philosopher; Jane just is applying for her first position. Mary truthfully writes, "Jane is not a bad philosopher." Without further information, we cannot tell whether Mary is using litotes, implying that Jane is really quite good, or damning with faint praise, and implying that Jane is not very good. Both could be viewed as resulting from a clash of politeness and quantity. The former interpretation would suggest that Mary is trying to convey a positive recommendation of her daughter without being too immodest. The latter interpretation would suggest that Mary is trying to convey a negative recommendation of her daughter without damning her daughter. This example is like the previous case in that we cannot use conversational principles or the Working-out Schema to figure out what the speaker has implicated. But this example differs in that it is not the conflict of the quantity and politeness principles that is the obstacle. The problem in this case is more elementary: we simply do not know how Mary assesses her daughter's philosophical ability. The problem is serious nonetheless because that is what letters of recommendation are supposed to tell us. As a result of our ignorance, we are in no position to affirm premise P3 of the Working-out Schema, according to which Mary could not be observing or operating with the Cooperative Principle unless she believes p, whether p is "Jane is quite good" or "Jane is not very good" – at least not before we know what Mary has implied.

That determinacy can fail because there are different ways to resolve conflicting principles can be seen by observing that Mary could also have proceeded more directly. If she had a positive assessment of her daughter, she could have obeyed the Cooperative Principle while making a concession to Politeness by saying, "I hate to sound immodest, but I genuinely believe that Jane is an excellent philosopher." If she had a negative assessment, she could have done the same by saying, "I hate to criticize my own daughter, but the sad truth is that she is not a very good philosopher at all." Because it does not – and could not – specify the way in which information is to be provided, the Maxim of Quantity does not tell us whether a speaker will implicate the required information or explicitly assert it.

3.12 "RELEVANCE" THEORY

Sperber and Wilson properly criticize the Gricean framework for failing to resolve the clashes of its maxims. They remark, "In our framework, with its single principle, there is no possibility of clashes" (Wilson and Sperber 1986: 389).

We have proposed a definition of relevance and suggested what factors might be involved in assessments of degrees of relevance. We have also argued that all Grice's maxims can be replaced by a single principle of relevance – that the speaker tries to be as relevant as possible in the circumstances – which, when suitably elaborated, can handle the full range of data that Grice's maxims were designed to explain. (Wilson and Sperber 1986: 381)

The problem with the Gricean framework is not simply its multiplicity of principles. That problem could be eliminated by omitting the maxims and putting forward only the Cooperative Principle. In fact, only the Cooperative Principle appears in definition I and the Generative Assumption. The problem is that any principle general enough to hold in all cases of implicature will be too general to yield specific predictions. For example, the rule that one should "contribute what is required by the accepted purpose of the conversation" does not enable us to predict that "Some died" implicates "Not all died" or that "John put on his trousers and went to bed" does not implicate "John did not put on his trousers before going to bed." For we cannot say that, in general, the information represented by the first implicature is required by the accepted purpose of the conversation, whereas the information represented by the second is not. Both sentences can be used in too many kinds of conversations, with widely differing purposes, participants, and contexts.

Sperber and Wilson's principle has the same difficulty. Exposition is difficult because formulation of the theory varies significantly from presentation to presentation. And many interlocking technical terms require considerable clarification. I do not believe the details of the principle affect the point I wish to make, so I work here with the relatively accessible formulation found in Wilson and Sperber (1986: 381–382).[26] Their *"Principle of Relevance,"* as we have seen, states that "the speaker tries to be as relevant as possible in the circumstances" (381). "The relevance of a proposition increases with the number of contextual implications it yields and decreases as the amount of processing needed to obtain them increases" (382). The "contextual implications" of a proposition are propositions that can be deduced, by a restricted set of rules, from it together with the set of "contextual assumptions," and that cannot be deduced from it or the contextual assumptions alone (381). "Contextual assumptions" are items of background knowledge relevant to the conversation, including "the propositions that have most recently been processed," others logically and conceptually related to them, and input information from the perceptual environment (381–382). These remarks suggest that a speaker examines alternative propositions, evaluates the number of contextual implications per unit cost for each, and

[26] See also Sperber and Wilson (1986a: 46–51, 118–171; 1986b; 1987: 702–704), Kempson (1986), Carston (1987), Recanati (1987), and Blakemore (1987a: 54–71; 1992: 24–37). For wide-ranging criticism of the theory, along with replies from Sperber and Wilson, see *Behavioral and Brain Sciences,* **10,** 1987, 697–754. See also Levinson's (1989) judicious and synoptic review.

chooses to convey that proposition with the highest ratio. Putting this in the style of Grice's principles yields the following:

Principle of Relevance (or Communicative Efficiency): Make your contribution be the one with the maximum ratio of contextual implications to processing cost.

The Sperber and Wilson principle is thus a *communicative efficiency* rule, an application of cost-benefit analysis. The intuitive idea is that speakers try to provide as much new information (or misinformation) for the processing cost as possible.[27]

Sperber and Wilson's use of "relevance" to mean "communicative efficiency" or "information to cost ratio" is highly technical and takes some getting used to. Their usage is not completely unrelated to the ordinary sense of "relevant," however, because contributing something relevant to the conversation in the ordinary sense would seem to be necessary for maximizing the ratio of contextual implications to processing cost. The number of contextual implications, and thus the ratio of contextual implications to cost, would presumably be zero for a completely irrelevant proposition. Thus Grice's Maxim of Relation is implied by the Principle of Relevance, it seems, but does not exhaust it. The Principle of Relevance also seems to imply that part of the Maxim of Manner which urges speakers to avoid unclarity, ambiguity, prolixity, and disorderliness. All of these defects of formulation can be avoided and would thus seem to unnecessarily increase processing costs. A more perspicuous formulation would convey the same proposition, with all the same contextual implications but lower processing cost.

The Principle of Relevance does not imply any of Grice's other

---

[27] Some formulations suggest that Sperber and Wilson are saying that speakers should maximize contextual effects and minimize cost; but this formulation simply conjoins two principles that can and usually do conflict. In yet other formulations, Sperber and Wilson define the principle of relevance as the thesis that there is a *presumption* the speaker is communicating something maximally or optimally relevant (see, e.g., Sperber and Wilson 1987: 704); on this take, the principle is more akin to Grice's cooperative presumption than to his Cooperative Principle, and is discussed in section 4.2.

principles, however. Cooperative Principle: nothing guarantees that the contribution with the greatest number of contextual implications per cost must be the contribution required by the accepted purpose of the conversation.[28] Maxim of Quality: nothing in the Principle of Relevance requires that the conveyed proposition or any of its contextual implications be true or justified. Maxim of Quantity: because the conveyed proposition need not be true, it might be misinformation rather than information. In addition, the contribution that is just as informative as required need not have the greatest ratio of contextual implications to processing costs. Some more, or less, informative proposition might be proportionately less costly to process. Furthermore, the Principle of Relevance fails to imply the Maxim of Manner to the extent that brevity involves sacrificing content and not just eliminating unnecessary verbiage, and to the extent that orderliness involves conveying information about order. A lengthier formulation will presumably require more processing, but may yield proportionately more information. A more orderly presentation might increase both contextual implications and processing costs while reducing their ratio. The Principle of Relevance may not imply the Maxim of Manner at all. For the processing minimized by perspicuity is that of determining the proposition conveyed from the words uttered, whereas Sperber and Wilson indicate in many places that the processing relevant to "relevance" is that of obtaining contextual implications from the proposition conveyed.[29] If the Principle of Rele-

---

[28] Compare Clark (1987), Morgan and Green (1987), Sperber and Wilson (1987: 746), Levinson (1989: 467), and M. Green (1995).

[29] Compare Wilson and Sperber (1986: 382) and Sperber and Wilson (1986a: 124–125; 1987: 703–704). Contrast Sperber and Wilson (1987: 747) where, in response to Cutler (1987), they say, "The level of effort which affects the relevance of an utterance is not just that of the inferential process which takes as input the output of the decoding process; it is that of the whole processing of the utterance, including decoding." Furthermore, Sperber and Wilson's "presumption of relevance" incorporates two claims: the presumption that the proposition conveyed has an adequate ratio of contextual effects to processing cost; and the presumption that the "stimulus" used to communicate that proposition is "the most relevant one the communicator could have used to communicate it" (1987: 704). I do not believe the sense of the last quoted phrase fits any of the authors' definitions; it involves a very different notion of "communicative efficiency."

vance can "handle the full range of data that Grice's maxims were designed to explain," as Wilson and Sperber claim, it is because Grice's theory fails, not because their principle subsumes Grice's principles.

The Principle of Relevance also seems to conflict with the Principle of Politeness.[30] When I hear my child's squawking on the violin, I should hurt him by saying the maximally relevant "Your performance was terrible" rather than the more noble "Your performance needs more work."

Unlike Grice's principles, the Principle of Relevance is not something speakers can *try* to follow or hearers can *use* to interpret utterances. Nor can theorists use it to predict or explain implicatures. For starters, even Sperber and Wilson do not know all the rules of the restricted deductive system in terms of which "contextual implications" are defined. They have sketched some of the general characteristics of the system, suggested a few rules, and left the rest for further research (Sperber and Wilson 1986a: 83–108). However, without knowing the full system, we cannot count all the contextual implications of propositions. We cannot even be sure the implications are countable. Using ordinary rules of deduction, every proposition has an infinitely large set of contextual implications, and the indicated ratios are undefined. The rules Sperber and Wilson have suggested appear to have sufficient power to yield the same result. For example, let P = "The table is 36 inches long" and let {C} contain both "The keyboard is 18 inches long" and "If the table is 36 inches long and the keyboard is 18 then the table is at least r inches longer than the keyboard, for every real number r between 36 and 18." Then assuming the "deductive device" contains *modus ponens* and universal instantiation (or syllogistic rules), P contextually implies every proposition of the form "The table is at least r inches longer than the keyboard" where r is a real number between 36 and 18.[31]

---

[30] Compare Matsumoto (1995: 55).

[31] See also Seuren (1987: 733), Hinkelman (1987), and Levinson (1989: 457). Sperber and Wilson (1987: 741) missed Hinkelman's point because she let {C} contain "Any woman is a citizen *if* her mother is," which generates no regress,

Moreover, Sperber and Wilson's formulations seem to rule out certain familiar implicatures. Consider a typical relevance implicature. If Mary asks *Is the wallet in the car?* Jane might respond, *Well, the wallet is in the suitcase and the suitcase is in the car,* thereby implicating that yes, the wallet is in the car. But "The wallet is in the car" can be deduced from "The wallet is in the suitcase and the suitcase is in the car" all by itself, and thus does not count as a contextual implication. The "containment rule" by which this implication follows is suggested by Sperber and Wilson (1986a: 105) as a plausible candidate for their deductive system. "The wallet is in the car" would appear, therefore, to be ruled out as an implicature. The theory also would seem to predict that a speaker cannot possibly implicate a contextual assumption because it has zero contextual effects.[32]

These problems of technical detail could perhaps be avoided by finding a slightly different way to operationalize "quantity of new information." But even if we focus on the intuitive idea that speakers are to maximize the amount of new information per unit of processing cost, the Principle of Relevance does not enable us to predict what a speaker believes or implicates. For no one in the world knows how to measure either quantity of information or processing cost with nearly enough precision to calculate the requisite ratios. And sentences can be used with the same implicatures in too wide a variety of contexts to make it plausible that any such ratio correlates with what is implicated. Thus determinacy and cal-

rather than "Any woman is a citizen *only if* her mother is," which does. Sperber and Wilson (1986a: 99) explicitly mention *modus ponens,* and their analysis of the "Mercedes" example (1986a: 194; 1987: 705) relies on instantiation. They also observe that implications obtained using one set of premises and rules can be obtained using a weaker set of rules and stronger premises (1987: 99).

[32] Another difficulty arises when Sperber and Wilson replace "contextual implications" in the Principle of Relevance with the broader category of "contextual effects," which includes "strengthenings and contradictions" as well as "contextual implications" (see Wilson and Sperber 1986: 384–390; Sperber and Wilson 1986a: 108–137, 142–151; 1987: 702, 741). Contradictions have zero contextual implications (Wilson and Sperber 1986: 385). Because Sperber and Wilson provide no means of commensurating the different types of contextual effects, ratios of contextual effects to processing costs are undefined.

culability fail even when Grice's Cooperative Principle and associated maxims are replaced by the single Principle of Relevance (cf. Levinson 1989: 465–467).

Take a typical quantity implicature. I got up before my logic class after an exam last semester and said, "Some got an A," implicating "Not all did." I did not implicate any of the following: "Less than 25% got an A," "Some got a D," "More people got an A on this exam than on the last one," "I am pleased but not overwhelmed with the results," and so on. The Principle of Relevance provides no reason to predict that I said "Some got an A" and implicated "Not all got an A" rather than saying, "Not all got an A" and implicating "Some did." It provides no reason to predict that I implicated "Not all got an A" rather than any of the other propositions listed. At the level of sentence implicature, we cannot say that, in general, the speaker who utters, "Some died" must be implicating "Not all died" for his utterance to have the maximal ratio of contextual effects to processing costs, whereas the speaker who utters, "John took off his trousers and went to bed" need not be implicating "John did not take off his trousers before going to bed" for his utterance to have the maximal ratio of contextual effects to processing costs. Nothing in the principle suggests that "War is war" normally has one implicature and "A war's a war" another, rather than vice versa.

One who is antecedently convinced of the principle can always insist that because a certain proposition is implicated, it must have the maximal relevance ratio. But the possibility of such ex post facto reasoning does not confer any more predictive power on the Principle of Relevance than it would on the Cooperative Principle. Furthermore, such a stance would seem to imply that I could not have continued the conversation by explicitly asserting any of the other propositions. But I could well have done so. "Some got an A. But less than 25% did" would have been a completely natural thing to say in the context, as would "Some got an A, some got a D." None of my purposes compelled me to say what I did rather than any of the more expansive statements. The spirit just did not move me to say more. However, if the fact that I implicated q rather than r could be derived from my saying p together with conversational principles, it is hard to see how it could have been completely open for me to have said "p and r."

In more official statements, Sperber and Wilson formulate the Principle of Relevance not in terms of "*maximal* relevance," but "*optimal* relevance." "An ostensive stimulus is optimally relevant to an addressee if and only if it has enough contextual effects to be worth his attention and puts him to no unjustified processing effort in accessing them" (1987: 743). Being qualitative rather than quantitative, this principle avoids the measurement problem. But for the same reason, all hopes of determinacy and calculability vanish. For optimal relevance, so defined, does not pick out a unique contribution to the conversation. Countless propositions will be informative enough to be worth the processing, but only a few will be implicated. In my classroom example, all of the possible implicatures mentioned would be informative enough to be worth the effort involved in processing them. For calculability to hold, we need to be able to work out which of all the possible implicatures were actually implicated. We cannot if optimal relevance is our only guide. An analogous problem would arise for utilitarians who said only that the right action is the one with "adequate" utility. The principle of utility would not then be strong enough to provide guidance even in the simple case in which an investor needs to choose between two vehicles with guaranteed rates of return of 20% and 30%, respectively. Both are more than adequate. Sperber and Wilson go on to say, "The first hypothesis tested and found consistent with the principle of relevance is the only hypothesis consistent with the principle of relevance" (1987: 704, 743; see also Blakemore 1992: 73). But this is groundless on either formulation of the principle of relevance and would in any event make what the speaker implicates too heavily dependent on the vagaries of the hearer's thought processes (see section 4.4).

A further problem is that the body of contextual assumptions or background information is indeterminate. Consider case (1) in section 3.5. Which of all the things Diane knows, or Carl knows, or they both know, is to be included in the relevant set? Without knowing that, we cannot calculate relevance ratios because we cannot count contextual implications or determine which information is new. Sperber and Wilson hold that the set of contextual assumptions from which contextual implications are to be deduced is not fixed by the context of utterance, and that the hearer must choose. "On this approach, the implicatures of an utterance are those contextual assumptions and implications which the hearer has to recover in order to satisfy himself that the speaker has observed the principle of relevance" (383).[33] But then the principle of relevance will be impossible to follow because there will not be a unique ratio to maximize. The speaker cannot choose to contribute that proposition with the maximum ratio of contextual effects to processing cost, if the speaker does not know which body of contextual assumptions the proposition is to be combined with to deduce implications. If S is considering two propositions P and P′ and two sets of assumptions {C} and {C′}, it is quite possible that r(P) > r(P′) relative to {C} while r(P′) > r(P) relative to {C′}. Furthermore, r(P) relative to {C} may equal r(P′) relative to {C′}. The speaker's task would be like telling an aeronautical engineer to choose the wing design that will maximize the ratio of speed to fuel economy without telling her what kind of engine will be supplied. The hearer's task is also impossible. She cannot choose the set of contextual assumptions required if the speaker has observed the principle of relevance until she knows what propositions the speaker has asserted or implicated. But to determine what the speaker has contributed, the hearer must use the set of contextual assumptions and the principle of relevance.

Note that if the sorts of derivations which advocates of relevance theory have advanced were valid, many failures of differentiation would arise. For example, the fact that "The park is some distance from my house" normally implicates "The park is a long way from my house" is accounted for by saying that because the proposition explicitly said is trivial and thus has few contextual

[33] See also Wilson and Sperber (1986: 390), Sperber and Wilson (1986a: 132, 142; 1987: 698, 703–705), Kempson (1986: 90), and Blakemore (1992: 31–32, 71–74, 124–125). Contrast Wilks (1987) and Levinson (1989: 459).

effects, the hearer will "recover" the more informative pro-position.[34] But aside from the fact that any number of propositions are more informative than the one implicated, the same procedure could be used even when the speaker asserted the trivial proposi-tion without implicating anything stronger. We should also expect all tautological sentences to have implicatures, when only a few do. The relevance theoretic treatment of conjunction implicatures has a similar problem, resembling as it does that of Levinson (see section 2.3).

3.13 MODAL IMPLICATURES

R. Lakoff observed a problem for Gricean theory that has received relatively little attention.[35] Consider the following sentence forms:

(9)　(a)　I must tell you that I love you.
　　　(b)　I may tell you that I love you.
　　　(c)　Must I tell you that I love you?
　　　(d)　May I tell you that I love you?

Lakoff observed that whereas (9)(a) and (9)(d) are *performative,* (9)(b) and (9)(c) are not. That is, a speaker who says (9)(a) has thereby told you that he loves you; a speaker who says (9)(c) has not thereby told you that he loves you. Why should the fact that one sentence is indicative and the other interrogative make such a difference? Why should (9)(d) be performative when addressed to Kathy when "May I tell Kathy that I love her" is not, even when I am speaking to Kathy? Gricean theory seems to provide no insight into the differences among these sentences. Leech's Princi-ple of Politeness (section 3.11) and Sperber and Wilson's Principle of Relevance (section 3.12) provide no more insight into the phe-nomena than Grice's Cooperative Principle.

We are concerned with implicature rather than performative-ness, but the same problem arises. Consider the pattern of implica-tures recorded in (10) and (11):

---

[34] See Carston (1987: 714) and Blakemore (1992: 60, 77–83).
[35] See Gordon and Lakoff (1975: 102–103) and Davison (1975).

(10) (a) I must tell you how much I love you ⊐ I love you a lot.
      (b) I will tell you how much I love you ⊐ I love you a lot.
      (c) I may tell you how much I love you ⊅ I love you a lot.

(11) (a) Must I tell you how much I love you? ⊐ I love you a lot.
      (b) Will I tell you how much I love you? ⊅ I love you a lot.
      (c) May I tell you how much I love you? ⊐ I love you a lot.

First, there seems to be nothing in the meaning of "I must tell you how much I love you" that, together with the Cooperative Principle and associated maxims, enables us to predict that speakers using it normally implicate "I love you a *lot*" rather than "I love you a *little*." Both would be perfectly good answers to the question "How much do I love you?" Indeed, speakers can use "I must tell you how much I love you" ironically with the opposite implication. "I love you a lot" and "I love you a little" are equally informative, and either might be the truth. One will be relevant to any conversation the other one is. Perspicuity would seem to rule against using the modal sentences with any implicature. That is, it would be easiest on the understanding if "I must tell you how much I love you" were used to mean "How much do I love you? I must tell you," which is what it literally means. Finally, Leech would correctly observe that it is more polite and tactful to convey the idea that you love someone a lot rather than a little. But the same implicature is present when tact is not an issue, as with "I must tell you how heavy that rock is," or when tact pulls in the other direction, as with "I must tell you how ugly you are."

Second, nothing in the meaning of the modal auxiliaries enables the Gricean to predict that "I must tell you" and "I will tell you" implicate "I love you a lot," whereas "I may tell you" does not, nor why the interrogative transformation preserves the implicature of "I must tell you" while switching the implicatures of "I will" and "I may."[36] For the determinacy and calculability condi-

---

[36] Gordon and Lakoff (1975: 102–103) noted that "may" would ordinarily be interpreted deontically in (11)(c) and nondeontically in (10)(c). But it is also possible to interpret the "may" deontically in (10)(c), in which case "I may tell you how much I love you" means the same as "I am permitted to tell you how much I love you." Neither implicates that I love you a lot.

tions to be satisfied in the case of (11)(c), it must be true that *the speaker could not be observing the Cooperative Principle when asking, "May I tell you how much I love you?" unless he believes that he loves you a lot.* However, without taking into account the known implicature of the sentence, the fact that S has asked, "May I tell you how much I love you?" together with the fact that S is contributing what is required to a typical conversation, gives us no reason to conclude that S must believe that he loves you a lot, and gives us no more reason to conclude this than would have been provided had S instead stated, "I may tell you how much I love you." The Gricean might suggest that the key premise of the Working-out Schema can be inferred from a conjunction, namely, *the speaker would not ask whether he may tell you unless he wanted to, and would not want to unless he believed that he loves you a lot.* Generally, people do not ask whether they may do something unless they want to do it. But this need not be true in every context in which a speaker uses "May I tell you how much I love you?" to implicate that he loves you a lot. The context may not enable us to rule out the possibility that the speaker has not yet made up his mind whether to tell you, but won't waste any further time deliberating if he cannot.[37] More commonly, the second conjunct will fail: the reasons why the speaker may want to tell you how much he loves you even though he does not believe that he loves you a lot are too familiar to detail.

It might not be strictly accurate to use the term *implicate* in set (11). It was stipulated that "implicature" denotes *the act of meaning or implying something by saying something else.* If "say" is interpreted broadly, to include asking and ordering as well as stating, then the definition does fit the positive cases in (11). For someone who asks, "May I tell you how much I love you?" would normally

---

[37] The Maxim of Quality may seem to provide the first conjunct when the sentence uttered is "I must tell you." For that maxim would rule that S could not utter the sentence without believing he must tell you. And it is plausible that if someone believes he must do something, then he must want to do it. But this latter principle is the controversial thesis of motivational internalism, which seems falsified by cases of akrasia. Furthermore, the Maxim of Quantity is no help with "May I tell you?"

thereby imply that he loved you a lot, and to ask, "May I tell you how much I love you?" is not to say that I love you a lot. Furthermore, the implication is as cancelable in the interrogative case as in the declarative. Thus none of the sentences in (12) imply that the speaker loves you a lot.

(12)   May I tell you how much I love you? –You might not like what I
       tell you.
       May I tell you how much I love you? – It's more than a little but
       less than a lot.
       May I tell you how much I love you, and do so with a fair degree
       of precision?
       I must tell you how much I love you, because the sergeant
       ordered me to.
       I must tell you how much I love you, but I don't want to lie.
       I must tell you how much I love you, but I don't really know.

However, when Grice (1975: 25–26) clarified his favored sense of "say," he focused on saying *that* something is the case. We might interpret Grice here to have stipulated that in the definition of implicature, "saying something else" means *stating* it. In that case, asking, "May I tell you how much I love you?" to imply that I love you a lot counts as an indirect speech act, but not an implicature.

For our current theoretical purposes, however, it does not matter whether ⊐ is taken to represent implicature narrowly defined or broadly defined. For Griceans have also applied their theory to indirect speech acts.[38] And for consistency, they should. Nothing in Gricean theory makes the differences between the two definitions significant. If the theory provides adequate explanations of implicatures narrowly defined, it should also explain the broader class. For example, if general psychosocial principles can explain and predict the act of implying p by stating q, they should also be able to account for the act of implying p by asking whether q. Similarly, conformity with the Cooperative Principle may require S to believe p whether his utterance was a statement, a question, or a request. Refusing to classify an implication as an implicature

[38] See Gordon and Lakoff (1975), Sadock (1978: 369), Searle (1975: 266), Posner (1980: 175 ff.), Levinson (1983: 165, Ch. 5), and Leech (1983: 24–25).

does not eliminate the problem of explaining how the implication arises and is understood. It would count strongly against Gricean theory if it maintained that implications similar to implicatures have completely different explanations than implicatures do.

Besides, similar problems arise even when we restrict ourselves to implicatures narrowly construed. Consider the following:

(13) (a) I have to tell you how much I love you ⊐ I love you a lot.
      (b) I don't have to tell you how much I love you ⊐ I love you a lot.
      (c) I can't tell you how much I love you ⊐ I love you a lot.
      (d) I need not tell you how much I love you ⊐ I love you a lot.

It is hard to see how *S could not be observing the Cooperative Principle unless he believes he loves you a lot* could be just as true when S says, "I have to tell you" as when S says its contradictory, "I don't have to tell you" or its contrary, "I can't tell you." And it is hard to see how the same claim could be false when S says the same things indirectly. Compare (13) with (14), and (10) and (11) with (15):

(14) (a) Given "You have to tell me how much you love me":
           I agree ⊅ I love you a lot.
      (b) Given "You don't have to tell me how much you love me":
           I know ⊅ I love you a lot.
      (c) Given "You can't tell me how much you love me?":
           No ⊅ I love you a lot.
(15) Given "Tell me how much you love me":
      (a) I must ⊅ I love you a lot.
      (b) Must I? ⊅ I love you a lot.
      (c) May I? ⊅ I love you a lot.

That is, if A says, "You have to tell me how much you love me," and B replies, "I agree," B has affirmed that he has to tell you how much he loves you. But he has not implicated that he loves you a lot. How in Gricean theory could affirming something by saying, "I agree" not implicate what affirming the very same thing by saying "I have to tell you . . ." implicates?

A final set of problems arises by noting that modal questions like (9)(c) with emphasis on *must* are equivocal at the level of implicature. In addition to implying "I love you a lot," they have a further implicature, as indicated in (16).

(16)   *Must* I (Do I *have* to) tell you how much I love you?
    (a)   ⊐ I don't want to tell you; *or*
    (b)   ⊐ I don't need to tell you because you should already know;
        or
    (c)   ⊐ Perhaps you don't know.

This presents several problems for Gricean theory: (i) Why are the interpretations exclusive? The speaker of (16) might implicate that he does not want to tell you how much he loves you, *or* he might suggest that perhaps you don't know. But a speaker would not ordinarily implicate both things, even though a speaker could perfectly well be averse to telling while believing that you might not know; (ii) Why, if (16) implicates one or the other of these three propositions, does it not also implicate their disjunction (cf. section 3.4)? (iii) Why does switching the emphasis from "must" to "tell" disambiguate the utterance, leaving only the (b) implicature?

(17)   Must I *tell* you how much I love you?
    (a)   ⊅ I don't want to tell you;
    (b)   ⊐ I don't need to tell you because you should already know;
    (c)   ⊅ Perhaps you don't know.

Similarly, "I don't *have* to tell you" is ambiguous between "It is optional whether I tell you" and "You already know," whereas "I don't have to *tell* you" unambiguously implicates "You already know"; (iv) Why does switching from "tell" to other verbs eliminate the (b) implicature?

(18)   Do I *have* to practice?
    (a)   ⊐ I don't want to practice.
    (b)   ⊅ I don't need to practice because I am already good
        enough.
    (c)   ⊐ Perhaps I am already good enough?

(v) Finally, the very fact that there are three possible interpretations of (16) (and two of (18)) ipso facto undermines the determinacy requirement: there is no one of the three implicated propositions that a speaker must believe or implicate if he is using (16) cooperatively. The Gricean might observe that different contexts will naturally select different interpretations. However, the relevant contextual factors will not be the *jointly* accepted purpose of the conversation (section 4.1) or any items of common knowledge, but the intentions of the speaker. Suppose Mary says to John, "Tell me how much you love me," and John replies, "Do I *have* to?" The fact that Mary asked for information may rule out the (c) interpretation, but nothing in the objective circumstances of the utterance need rule in either the (a) interpretation or the (b) interpretation. Thus Mary may have to ask, "How am I supposed to take that remark?"

4

Presumption and mutual knowledge

According to Gricean theory, conversational implicatures depend on what people presume or know about the speaker. For S to implicate p, others must presume that S is observing the Cooperative Principle, and they must know or at least believe that observance of the Cooperative Principle requires S to believe p. I argue here that these clauses in the Theoretical Definition are fundamentally misguided. They are the product of two mistakes: the assimilation of speaker meaning to communication, and of implicature to inference. What a speaker means or implies is determined by what the speaker intends. But one person's intentions do not depend on what others presume, believe, or infer. Conversational principles do play a role in the recognition of implicatures. But implicatures need not be recognized, and their recognition does not depend on any specialized reasoning process. The Cooperative Principle and associated maxims play no role in the generation of implicatures, and they play the same indirect and nonessential role in implicature recognition that known tendencies play in inductive inference generally.

4.1 THE COOPERATIVE PRESUMPTION CONDITION

The Theoretical Definition specifies that S conversationally implicates something only if S is presumed to be observing the Cooperative Principle. The Generative Assumption holds further that a conversational implicature exists in part because the speaker is presumed to be observing the Cooperative Principle. This *cooperative presumption condition* is vague in some respects: it is not clear *who* it is that is supposed to presume that S is observing the Cooperative Principle. Is it the person S is addressing, or is it the entire class of people that hears or reads S's utterance? If either class contains more than one person, must all members share the presumption, or just some? I argue that no matter how the condition is understood, it fails. Conversational implicatures may exist when there is no presumption on anyone's part that the speaker is observing the Cooperative Principle.

The absence of a presumption should not be confused with the falsity of one. The cooperative presumption is false when S is presumed to be observing the Cooperative Principle but is not observing it. The speaker may fail to contribute what is required by the accepted purpose of the conversation even though he is trying to, as when he misunderstands a question put to him. Or the speaker may deliberately violate the principle, as when he lies or withholds information. For example, when a boy emerges from his room before his mother thinks he could have finished his homework for the night, she may ask whether he finished all of his work. Catching the reason for her concern, the boy may answer, "Some of it," implicating that he did not do all of it. Alternatively, the boy might answer, "Yeah, it was a breeze," implicating that he was able to get the homework done so fast because it was easy. Being totally brazen, he might even say, "I did my homework for the whole week!" In all three cases, he may be lying, having done none at all. If his mother believes he is observing the Cooperative Principle, she is mistaken. The fact that implicatures may exist even when the cooperative presumption is false shows three things: (i) *presumption* cannot be strengthened to *knowledge* in the cooperative presumption condition; hence (ii) the Generative Assumption of Gricean theory could not attribute the existence of particularized implicatures to the Cooperative Principle itself; hence (iii) the last clause in Grice's Razor, according to which conversational implicatures can be explained by independently motivated principles, is false for speaker implicature. The last two points were made in section 1.4.

In this section, I show that the cooperative presumption *condition* is false by showing a wide variety of cases in which S implicates something even though there is no presumption that S is observing the Cooperative Principle. We first look at cases in which the speaker is cooperating, but is not presumed to be. In this case, the speaker is conveying the truth, the whole truth, and nothing but the truth. But he is presumed to be lying, withholding information, or evading something. In example (1) of Chapter 1, Ann's bigotry may have led her to assume that Bob would try to deceive her, sending her to an out-of-the-way place to get mugged. Bob may have answered truthfully, "There's a station around the corner," implicating she could get gasoline there, whether he thought she would believe him or not. The existence of Bob's implicature does not depend in any way on what Ann believes about his veracity. Consider another example, in which the audience does not know what to presume about the speaker.

(1) GEORGE: I was out drinking with the guys.
     KAREN: Are you lying to me?
     GEORGE: I've never lied to my Juliet, and never will.

Karen is not presuming that George is observing the Cooperative Principle. On the contrary, she is questioning his observance of the Maxim of Quality. Nevertheless, George implicated something after Karen raised the issue, and what he implicated is that he is not lying.

The cooperative presumption condition also fails when H correctly presumes that S is not observing the Cooperative Principle.

(2) KAREN: Were you with Jennifer last night?
     GEORGE: I was out drinking with the guys.

In (2), George implicated that he was not with Jennifer last night. He may have implicated this even if Karen knows he is lying, having seen George and Jennifer together.

(3) MRS. SMITH (accusingly):   Did you eat all the chocolates?
     BILLY (defensively):   I ate *some.*

In (3), Billy implicated that he did not eat all the chocolates. He did so even if his mother knows full well he ate all of them and punishes him for trying to mislead her.

(4) ALICE: Do you like my new dress?
     BRETT: I like all your dresses.

In (4), Brett implicated that he does like her new dress. Nevertheless, Alice may realize that he is just being polite.

The cooperative presumption condition may fail because the conversation has no accepted purpose, as when S is changing the subject, insulting his audience, engaging in idle chitchat, talking at cross-purposes, arguing with H, or explaining why he is unwilling to give H the requested information.[1] A less obvious example is presented in (5).

(5) STUDENT: I demand to know why you marked this problem
              wrong.
     TEACHER: I'm sorry, but I am late for class.[2]

The teacher's purpose in this conversation was to explain why he could not fulfill the student's purpose. As Sterelny (1982: 189) noted, "pointedly *refusing* to obey the CP [Cooperative Principle] can generate implicature-like phenomena, for instance, abruptly and determinedly changing the subject of a conversation." George may have responded to Karen's inquisition in (2) with "I believe I saw you with Clark last Friday," implicating that she is in no position to question his fidelity. George might even have responded with a remark completely irrelevant to Karen's inquiry, such as "I blew out a tire today." The deliberate or unwitting irrelevance of his remark does not prevent him from having implicated that he did not blow them all out.

In support of the cooperative presumption condition, Griceans

---

[1] Compare Bird (1979: 144), Grice (1989: 369–370), and Thomason (1990: 356). After observing that implicatures are possible even in situations that can only be described as hostile and uncooperative, Thomason suggested that cooperation is better viewed as sharing a "plan of the conversation": "Sharing a plan of the conversation may involve shared goals, but these have to do with discourse rather than with the subject at hand" (1990: 356). But even in a mild case like (5), it is hard to see the speaker and hearer as sharing any plan for the conversation. The student clearly plans to get an answer; the teacher plans not to give one. Grice's (1989: 369–370) response to the problem seems to completely miss the point.

[2] Compare Smith and Wilson (1979: 174) and Leech (1983: 95). Leech uses examples like this one to "illustrate how an apparent breach of the CP is shown, at a deeper level of interpretation involving the PP, to be no such thing: in this way, the CP is redeemed from difficulty by the PP" (1983: 81). However, the examples show that in many cases, being polite requires *not* contributing what is required by the accepted purpose of the conversation, so that the Politeness Principle conflicts with the Cooperative Principle rather than rescuing it.

point to the absence of quantity implicatures when an uncoopera-tive witness is being cross-examined. If the prosecutor asks a defendant whether he has visited some of the cities in which the murders were committed, and the defendant answers, "Yes," he will not be taken to have implicated that he did not visit all of them. The hostile witness may nevertheless use many *other* types of implicature. For example, the defendant may have implicated that the answer is "Yes" by saying, "I've visited most major European cities." Alternatively, he may have snapped that his visa expired, implicating that the answer is "No."

Any attempt to reduce failures of the cooperative presumption condition by weakening what it takes for a conversation to have an accepted purpose will just increase failures of the determinacy condition. For example, if the Cooperative Principle were only to require that the speaker contribute something that furthers at least one aim common to both speaker and hearer, then the Coopera-tive Principle would be too weak to support the maxims.[3]

The cooperative presumption condition may even fail because there is no audience to presume anything about the speaker. Grice's (1989: 369) claim that "genuine monologues are free from speaker's implication" is patently false. When talking to his recently departed wife, for example, a speaker may use irony, metaphor, and other figures of speech, conjunction implicatures, tautology impli-catures, relevance implicatures – the whole gamut.[4]

4.2 THE PRESUMPTION OF RELEVANCE

Because Sperber and Wilson replace the Cooperative Principle with their Principle of Relevance, the analogue of the cooperative presumption in their theory is the "presumption of relevance," the presumption that the speaker's contribution has the maximal or

---

[3] Compare Bird (1979: 144), Kasher (1982: 39), and Thomason (1990: 356).
[4] William Lycan questioned whether talking to one's deceased wife is a "genuine monologue." It certainly fits the dictionary definition: "a prolonged talk or dis-course by a single speaker" (*Webster's Unabridged Encyclopedic Dictionary*). And even if such solo speech should not for some technical reason count as a monologue, it nonetheless may be perfectly meaningful.

optimal amount of new information per unit processing cost. Indeed, they often use "the principle of relevance" to denote "the thesis that every act of ostensive communication communicates the presumption of its own optimal relevance" (1987: 704).[5] This presumption is no more necessary than Grice's. As observed earlier, the speaker may assert or implicate an item of common knowledge. Because this is not new information, the efficiency ratio is zero. The hearer may well presume that the speaker has nothing at all worth saying, that he is withholding information, conducting a disinformation campaign, or filibustering. The presumption might be that the speaker is trying not to maximize how much the hearer knows, but simply to maximize how likely the hearer is to succeed in some practical endeavor, or to be amused or entertained. It would be naive for us or the hearer to suppose that the speaker is always so altruistic that he will be concerned exclusively with the amount of effort the hearer will expend deducing implications, and not at all with the amount of effort he the speaker will expend conveying the propositions, or the cost to himself in money or reputation if he divulges the information. Even if we assume altruism, the speaker may well be more concerned with costs to the hearer other than processing effort. The speaker might be more concerned with the psychological pain his information will cost the hearer, seeking to minimize that while conveying as much information as possible. None of these alternative presumptions would prevent the speaker from using a full range of implicatures.

Sperber and Wilson say, "the presumption of relevance is rooted

---

[5] See also Blakemore: "the principle of relevance entitles the hearer to expect that she can obtain adequate contextual effects for no unjustifiable effort" (1992: 58); "the hearer will assume that the speaker has produced an utterance that is worthy of her attention. That is, she will assume that the speaker has been relevant" (1992: 81); "the very act of communication gives hearers a guarantee that they will be able to derive adequate contextual effects" (1987b: 713). The meaning of all this is called into doubt by statements like the following, however: "hearers do not always actually accept that the presumption carried by an act of communication is true. The speaker's previous record as a bore or a baffler may lead the hearer to doubt his ability to succeed in being relevant." (1992: 37). Sperber and Wilson also say that the presumption need not be accepted as true (1986a: 158–159; 1987: 704).

... in general and independently motivated hypotheses about cognition. . . . It is backed by a theory of cognition from which it follows that by the very act of requesting the hearer's attention, the speaker communicates (truly or falsely) that the utterance is relevant enough to be worth the hearer's attention" (1987: 745). But the theory of cognition in question is simply that people automatically turn their attention to information that seems "likely to bring about the greatest improvement of knowledge at the smallest processing cost" (1987: 700). This theory seems patently false: most people seem much more interested in enjoyment, for example, than in knowledge. Surely high school teachers would have a lot easier time getting students to concentrate on their studies and avoid the temptations of sex, drugs, alcohol, sports, television, and so on, if it were true.[6] More importantly, a theory of what the hearer attends to entails nothing about what a speaker is or is presumed to be contributing to the conversation.

4.3 MUTUAL KNOWLEDGE

According to the mutual knowledge condition of the Gricean definition, S conversationally implicates p only if S knows or at least believes that H is able to determine that the supposition S believes p

---

[6] Compare Berg (1991: 419). Sperber responded to this objection by claiming that "the less motivated a person is to attend to something, the greater the effort and thus the lower the relevance" (personal communication). The possible effect of motivation on processing must be considered, of course. But it is dubious that the effect is always responsible when people attend to stimuli unlikely to increase their knowledge significantly. As a test, we could play two messages simultaneously to experimental subjects, one to each ear, in the style of Cherry (1953). Let one message be a description of some very important scientific or historical fact unknown to the subjects. Let the other be an extremely erotic passage from a new novel. Pretest the messages on separate groups similar to the subjects to be sure the messages are judged equally easy to process. I would be amazed if all the subjects, or even a large majority, attended to the nonfiction message. The fact that the other message is fiction, and new, minimizes the possible effect of interests on background knowledge, and thereby on the number of contextual implications (Sperber and Wilson 1986b: 544). (Incidentally, the "contextual implications" of a fictional proposition would not appear to measure its information content, which is null; but that won't stop people from attending to it.)

is required to make S's utterance consistent with the Cooperative Principle. Grice's condition also required S to believe that H believes S believes H is able to determine this, and others have gone further in requiring S to have every higher-order belief in this series. But even the lowest-order part of the condition is false and groundless.

We reviewed a broad array of cases in Chapter 3 where determinacy failed. These cases also suffice to show that S need not believe that H is able to work out his implicature. It would be contrary to the spirit of Gricean theory, which seeks to ground implicatures in rational conversational practices, to require the speaker to believe the hearer can do something that cannot be done. My coming to believe that it is impossible for anyone to derive implicatures from the Cooperative Principle has certainly not reduced my ability to implicate things.

We reviewed a variety of cases in section 4.1 where H does not presume that S is observing the Cooperative Principle. The same cases show that S need not believe H is able to derive his implicatures or beliefs from the Cooperative Principle. It is most striking in this connection that implicatures may exist with no accepted purpose to the conversation, and no audience at all.

We can even imagine cases in which the speaker implicates that the hearer is incapable of working out any implicatures! Suppose Maggie and Mark are discussing the Gricean theory of implicature; Rick tries to join in, saying he does not see how a certain implicature can be worked out. If Mark thinks sufficiently little of Rick's intellectual abilities, he might well try to insult Rick without him noticing, by saying, "No one with a subamphibian brain can work out implicatures." Then Mark implicated that Rick cannot work out implicatures. We could hardly conclude that Mark must believe Rick can work out that implicature.

Given that speaker implication is a special case of speaker meaning, some sort of mutual knowledge condition would be required in the definition of conversational implicature if the Gricean definition of speaker meaning were correct. But satisfaction of the mutual knowledge condition of Grice's definition of conversational implicature does not ensure satisfaction of the mutual knowledge condition on Grice's definition of speaker meaning. And the latter is false anyway, for the same sorts of reasons.[7]

4.4 MEANING VERSUS COMMUNICATION

The cooperative presumption and mutual knowledge conditions are completely misplaced in the Theoretical Definition and the Generative Assumption. What S implicates cannot be due even in part to what others presume or know about S. To implicate something is to mean or imply it in a certain way. And as Grice (1957, 1969) correctly observed, to mean or imply something is to have certain intentions. But S's intentions do not depend on what anyone else presumes.[8] The *satisfaction* of our intentions often depends on what others are doing or thinking. The mere *possession* of those intentions does not. My having certain intentions cannot be *constituted* or *generated* by any fact about you.

I believe that inclusion of the cooperative presumption condition in the generative principle is a particular instance of a general tendency in the Gricean literature to confuse *speaker meaning* with *communication*.[9] Indeed, Levinson (1983: 101) identifies a theory of the former with a theory of the latter. According to Searle,

The problem posed by indirect speech acts is the problem of how it is possible for the speaker to say one thing and mean that but also to mean something else. And since meaning consists in part in the intention to produce understanding in the hearer, a large part of that problem is that of how it is possible for the hearer to understand the indirect speech act when the sentences he hears and understands means something else. . . . The hypothesis I wish to defend is simply this: In indirect speech acts the speaker communicates to the hearer more than he actually says by way of relying on their mutually shared background information, both linguistic and nonlinguistic, together with the general powers of rationality and

---

[7] See Davis (1992a) and *Meaning, Expression, and Thought* (forthcoming: Ch. 3, §8.6) for substantiation of this point, and for references to the voluminous literature on speaker meaning.

[8] Compare Walker (1975: 157), Horn (1989: 232), and Hirschberg (1991: 17–23).

[9] See Davis (1992a) and *Meaning, Expression, and Thought* (forthcoming: Chs. 3 and 4).

inference on the part of the hearer. To be more specific, the apparatus necessary to explain the indirect part of indirect speech acts includes a theory of speech acts, certain general principles of cooperative conversation . . . , and mutually shared factual background information of the speaker and the hearer, together with an ability on the part of the hearer to make inferences. (Searle 1975: 266)[10]

What H presumes about S is an important factor determining whether S communicates with H. In order for S to communicate with H, it is not enough for S to mean or imply something. H must also understand S, which involves recognizing what S means or implies. Because H has no direct access to what S means, H must infer it from what she sees and hears. To the extent that H uses the Cooperative Principle as a premise in such inferences, the cooperative presumption may have enabled S to communicate with her. But H's presumption does not make it possible for S to mean or imply something.

Even if meaning did consist in the intention to produce understanding, as Searle maintains, it would not follow that implicatures depend on what the hearer presumes about the speaker. For the intention to produce understanding does not depend on what the hearer presumes either. The most that would follow is that S *intends* H to presume he is being cooperative. A parallel point can be made concerning Sperber and Wilson. In defense of their principle of the presumption of relevance, they say the following:

Unless the communicator is merely pretending to communicate, it is in her interest to be understood, and therefore to make it as easy as possible for the addressee to understand her. An addressee who doubts that the communicator has chosen the most relevant stimulus compatible with her communicative and informative intentions – a hearer, say, who believes that he is being addressed with deliberate and unnecessary obscurity – might doubt that genuine communication was intended, and might justifiably refuse to make the processing effort required. All this is mutually manifest; it is therefore mutually manifest that the communica-

---

[10] See also Searle (1975: 267; 1982: 532), Harnish (1976: 333) (who defines "S conversationally implicates that q to H"), Hugly and Sayward (1979: 20), Bach (1994b: 11), and Schiffrin (1994: 191).

tor *intends* it to be manifest to the addressee that she has chosen the most relevant stimulus capable of fulfilling her intentions. (Sperber and Wilson 1986a: 157; emphasis added)

This line of reasoning might justify the conclusion that S *intends* H to presume that he is being maximally or optimally relevant, but not the conclusion that H *does* presume S is being relevant.

Searle's thesis that meaning involves intending to produce understanding is also false. People have on many occasions spoken to their pets, their babies, and the dead. Many people have deliberately cursed at others in a language their audience is known not to understand. People write diaries, scribble notes to solve problems, and mutter under their breath. Such speakers are not trying to communicate with anyone, and they do not intend anyone to presume they are obeying the Cooperative Principle. Yet they certainly mean something. They may be pretending to communicate, but they are not pretending to implicate.

4.5 IMPLICATURE AND INFERENCE

The central role of calculability and the Working-out Schema in Grice's theory has led some to think that an implicature is an inference.

If a speaker wants to do an FTA [face threatening act], and chooses to do it indirectly, he must give H some hints and hope that H picks up on them and thereby interprets what S really means (intends) to say. The basic way to do this is to invite conversational implicatures by violating, in some way, the Gricean Maxims of efficient communication. (Brown and Levinson 1978: 218)

There is no straightforward distinction between "what is implicated" and "what is said"! Matters of indexicality aside, pragmatic inference is constitutive of both. (Atlas 1989: 148; emphasis deleted)

Our discussion will also focus on the concept of implicature: an inference that arises when language users process both semantic (i.e. logical) meanings and conversational principles. (Schiffrin 1994: 193)[11]

---

[11] See also Van Kuppevelt (1996: *passim*).

To implicate is to say something with certain intentions. If H understands a speaker who has implicated p, then H has made a certain inference. But H's inferring that S has implicated p cannot be identified with S's implicating p. That we often "invite" hearers to make certain inferences from what we say does not mean that hearers visit implicatures on us by accepting our invitation. To assume that S's implicature is somehow constituted by or dependent on H's inference is to make the same mistake that was embodied in the cooperative presumption.

Searle makes the erroneous connection in a more subtle way:

> If we can figure out the principles according to which hearers understand metaphorical utterances, we shall be a long way toward understanding how it is possible for speakers to make metaphorical utterances, because for communication to be possible, speaker and hearer must share a common set of principles. (Searle 1982: 532)

> In order that the speaker can communicate using metaphorical utterances, ironical utterances, and indirect speech acts, there must be some principles according to which he is able to mean more than, or something different from, what he says, whereby the hearer, using his knowledge of them, can understand what the speaker means. The relation between the sentence meaning and the metaphorical utterance meaning is systematic rather than random or ad hoc. (Searle 1982: 520)

People can, and often do, produce metaphors no one else understands, and thereby fail to communicate. Ironic utterances are frequently mistaken for literal utterances. Even literal utterances may fail to be understood: immigrants often say things in a language their audience does not understand, secret codes are designed to prevent communication, and students often write too poorly to get their point across. Consequently, the principles according to which hearers understand utterances, if there are any, cannot be part of what *makes it possible* for speakers to produce them and mean things by them.

In general, *contextual clues* must be distinguished from *contextual determinants*. Clues provide evidence for the truth of a proposition, but do not make it true. Consider the following dialogues:

(6) A: Let's stop and get some money for groceries.
     B: The bank was flooded yesterday, so it may not be open.

(7) A: Let's stop and have a picnic by the river.
     B: The bank was flooded yesterday, so it may not be open.

Because the word *bank* is highly ambiguous, we cannot simply "decode" B's utterance to figure out what B meant. The fact that A had just mentioned money is a good clue that B meant "commercial bank" rather than "riverbank" in (6). In (7), the fact that A had just mentioned the river is a good clue that B meant "riverbank." But neither of these clues in any way *determines* what B meant. In (6), B could have been referring to the riverbank. If he were, we would characterize his remark as irrelevant. If B engaged in such "non sequiturs" frequently, we would think there was something wrong with him. If we suspected he was deliberately trying to mislead us, we would probably be annoyed. The nasty ambiguity of "determine" may obscure the distinction I am drawing. We use contextual clues to "determine" (i.e., figure out) what B means or implicates. But the contextual clues we use do not themselves "determine" (i.e., make true) what B means or implicates.

This case stands in marked contrast to "token–reflexive" indexicals. If someone said "Today is very hot" on August 9, using "Today" with its standard temporal meaning, then the date of the utterance makes it true that "Today" referred to August 9. The date is not merely a clue, but a determinant, of what the indexical refers to. Other indexicals are more complex. If S says, "That ball is red," looking directly at one of many balls on the floor, then (a) the fact that S is looking at a certain ball is a contextual clue that he is referring to it, and (b) the fact that he is referring to the ball he is looking at makes it true that the phrase "that ball" refers to it on this occasion.

Being a species of speaker meaning and implication, implicature is more like the bank example than either of the indexical cases. When S says, "Some died," the context may provide clues as to whether S implicated that not all died. But none of the contextual clues are completely reliable, let alone determinative. Contextual clues help us recognize implicatures, but do not generate them. When we wish to be understood, we make sure there are abundant clues as to what we are implicating. But we could always choose to implicate something else, or nothing at all. And we need not wish to be understood. There is one respect, though, in which all three cases are alike: to properly interpret the speaker's utterance, we need evidence as to his intentions (cf. Morgan 1978: 244). This is true even in the token-reflexive case, for before we decide on a referent for "Today," we need to know that S was using it with its standard indexical sense, and not as the name of his girlfriend.

4.6 THE RECOGNITION OF IMPLICATURE

Although the existence of conversational implicatures does not depend in any way on the assumption that the speaker is observing the Cooperative Principle, conversational principles may play a role in the recognition of implicatures. Indeed, the Cooperative Principle and associated maxims seem to play the same indirect role in implicature recognition that known tendencies play in inductive inference generally. Because speakers in general tend to observe the Cooperative Principle, and hearers know this in a vague and tacit sort of way, hearers tend to assume that particular speakers are cooperating, in the absence of evidence to the contrary. If the principle is used explicitly, the inference is a standard application of the statistical syllogism. If the hearer then determines that the hypothesis that S is implicating p fits better with the assumption that S is being cooperative than the hypothesis that he is not, the hearer may conclude S is implicating p, by hypothetical induction. Further support for the hypothesis may be provided by the recollection that S and other speakers have implicated similar things in similar circumstances before. The existence of an applicable implicature convention would be especially powerful evidence (Chs. 5 and 6). The hypothesis may receive final confirmation after the fact from S's testimony that he did indeed implicate p.

To say that the recognition of implicatures is an inferential process is not to say that it involves any *specialized* reasoning process.

I should also mention that an important feature of a conversational implication is that in order to understand what has been implicated the audience must draw an inference, and the audience must go through a characteristic and more or less complex pattern of reasoning in order to calculate what implication has been made. (Martinich 1984: 509)[12]

Meaning and implication are not directly observable phenomena. Hence Martinich is correct in saying that to understand what has been implicated, the audience must make an inference. It does not follow, and is not true, that the audience must use the Gricean Working-out Schema or any other "characteristic" pattern of reasoning. This point can be underscored by several observations.

First, the Cooperative Principle and associated maxims may play the same limited role in figuring out what S *said*.[13] Knowledge of what the words S uttered mean is not sufficient here either. We also need to know the intended referents of the pronouns S used and the intended senses of the ambiguous terms S used. To determine what B intended in (6), it will be helpful to know whether B is trying to be cooperative. We might imagine A reasoning as follows: "We are having a conversation about money; B would be saying something false or irrelevant unless he is using the word 'bank' to mean 'commercial bank' rather than 'riverbank'; so he must be saying that the commercial bank was flooded." Cutler (1987: 715–716) argues that similar inferences are used to figure out even what words S has uttered. The role of conversational principles in the understanding of implicatures is therefore not unique.

Second, conversational principles together with what S said can help us infer a broad range of mental states, not just the beliefs the speaker expressed or the intentions by virtue of which he means or implicates things. For example, in dialogue (1) of Chapter 1, Bob responded to Ann's query as to where she can get gasoline by saying, "There's a station around the corner." Using the Cooperative

---

[12] Compare Brown and Levinson (1978: 63, 216–217) and G. M. Green (1989: 115–118). Contrast Morgan (1978: 244–245, 250).

[13] See Atlas (1979: 275–279; 1989: esp. 146), Wilson and Sperber (1981: 1986), Kempson (1986), Carston (1987: 713–714; 1988), G. M. Green (1989: 115), Levinson (1989: 468), Blakemore (1987a: 24–26; 1992: Chs. 4–5), Crimmins (1992: 151), Bach (1994a), and Schiffrin (1994: §3.2).

Principle and associated maxims, we can infer from Bob's response that he believes all of the following propositions: his response contributes what is required to the conversation; his response is relevant to where Ann can get gasoline; gasoline can be obtained in stations; something around the corner is not too far away; Ann understands English; and so on. Yet Bob did not mean or imply any of these things by uttering, "There's a station around the corner." Similarly, we can infer that Bob wanted to help Ann and hoped his response would be helpful. But in uttering, "There's a station around the corner," Bob was not expressing that desire or hope. One of the standard problems in defining expression, meaning, and related notions is to distinguish the mental states the speaker expressed from the broader class of mental states the speaker manifested. Conversational principles are just as helpful in determinations of the broader class.

Third, when the hearer has reason to believe the speaker is being uncooperative, she should apply her general knowledge of how speakers behave in uncooperative situations. If H knows S is being cross-examined as a hostile witness and realizes such witnesses tend to divulge as little information as possible, H may conclude that S is not using any quantity implicatures. The fact that lying under oath is perjury, whereas misleading the court is not a criminal offense, will lead her to be on the lookout for other sorts of implicatures. G. M. Green (1989: 115) said that unless S is being cooperative, what he means will not be rationally inferable. But uncooperative behavior is no less predictable or rule governed. Indeed, whole professions are devoted to the rational prediction of extremely uncooperative behavior, as military strategists and tacticians illustrate.

Fourth, H need not use *any* general conversational principles to figure out what S implicated (or said). As Sterelny (1982: 191–193) observed, knowledge of the speaker is what is critical, not knowledge of particular general tendencies or principles of rational behavior. H might well know that S is being cooperative on a particular occasion without inferring that fact from the inductive generalization that speakers tend to be cooperative, just as I can know that my Scirocco pulls to the left without knowing that Sciroccos in general do.[14] H might even have reason to believe that S is being cooperative despite being in a situation in which speakers are typically uncooperative. If H knows S is trying to cooperate despite being under cross-examination, then H will have to consider seriously the possibility that S is using quantity implicatures. Conversely, if H has reason to believe S is being uncooperative despite being in a situation in which people do typically cooperate, H should suspect that S is not using quantity implicatures.

Finally, H might conclude that S implicated something without even considering whether S was being cooperative. For example, H might infer that S implicated "Not all died" directly from the fact that S said, "Some died" together with the fact that speakers who assert propositions of the form "Some S are P" generally or conventionally implicate "Not all S are P." H may confirm this conclusion by asking S what he implied and may buttress it further by recalling that S had previously promised to imply that not everyone died. There are many ways hearers can figure out what speakers implicated. The idea that reliance on the Gricean Working-out Schema is the only way we could figure out what speakers implicate is a fundamental mistake.

The role of the speaker's own testimony in establishing what he implicated has, to my knowledge, been almost completely ignored. This is especially remarkable because implicature is stipulated to be a form of speaker meaning or implication, which is widely and correctly taken to depend on the speaker's intentions, traditionally thought to be known primarily through introspection and first-person reports. Consider an actual example. I was playing tennis on a hot, humid, partly cloudy, typical Washington summer afternoon, sweating profusely. There is always a threat of a late afternoon thun-

---

[14] The Gricean could avoid Sterelny's objection by revising the definition of conversational implicature, referring to S's being cooperative instead of to S's observing the Cooperative Principle. This would produce Theoretical Definition V: S conversationally implicates p iff (i) S implicates p; (ii) S is presumed to be doing what is required by the accepted purpose of conversation; (iii) S must believe p in order to be contributing what is required by the accepted purpose of the conversation; (iv) S believes H is able to determine that (iii) is true. This revision would not avoid the other objections, however.

derstorm, a perennial subject of concern among tennis players. I noticed that the drops of sweat on my side of the court were almost as numerous as if it were beginning to rain. So I joked, "There's rain on the court here. How's your side?" My opponent took me literally and said there was no rain on his side, just some drops of sweat. I then had to explain that that's what I was implying, as a commentary on the dreadful heat and humidity. He then understood. My opponent recognized my implicature by an inferential process. On that occasion his inference was after the fact and based on my explanation of what I meant, a form of first-person testimony. Now the next time we are playing, and the Washington weather is producing a similar pattern of drops on my side of the court, I might be tempted to make the same comment. This time, however, my opponent's recollection of what I implicated last time should enable him to infer what I mean from what I say, at least in part by an argument from analogy. Alternatively, his recollection of what I meant might someday lead him to say "There's rain on the court here . . . ," expecting me to infer what he meant by analogy from my own precedent. Or he might try the metaphor out on one of his other opponents, possibly having to explain what he meant. In this way an implicature practice could arise and flourish without conversational principles playing any role in the inferring of what is implicated.

The question *How is it possible for hearers to understand implicatures?* is a fascinating one for cognitive scientists. It seems reasonably tractable because we have a general idea of how people recognize the intentions of others. I have just argued that conversational principles play an inessential, indirect, and nonunique role in figuring out what speakers are implicating. But even if I am wrong, Gricean claims about the origin and explanation of implicatures would not be saved. For the question *How is it possible for speakers to implicate certain things?* is different and not nearly as tractable. We have little idea of the conditions by virtue of which people have beliefs, desires, thoughts, or intentions. It seems extremely unlikely that any principles which enable H to understand S are also principles that enable S to mean or implicate things. Indeed, it is hard to imagine what sorts of principles could enable S to have the intentions that constitute implicating.

5

The existence of implicature conventions

According to Grice's Razor, it is more economical to postulate conversational implicatures than senses, conventional implicatures, or semantic presuppositions. For conversational implicatures can be derived from general psychosocial principles, whereas things like senses require specific linguistic conventions. We have seen that the first premise here must be rejected. Conversational implicatures cannot be derived from the Cooperative Principle, the Maxims of Quantity, Quality, Relation, and Manner, or the Principles of Style, Politeness, or Efficiency. This holds for both sentence implicatures and speaker implicatures.

The evidence we have reviewed also suffices to show that in addition to the conventions assigning meanings and presuppositions to particular words and sentences, there are many *conversational implicature conventions,*[1] conventional ways of conversationally implicating things. Because a complete explanation of the data involving conversational implicatures requires the postulation of implicature conventions, the theoretical complexity introduced by the postulation of conversational implicatures is of the same order of magnitude as that introduced by senses or conventional implicatures.

The claim that certain conversational implicatures are conventional has at least the air of self-contradiction. For Grice used the term *conventional implicature* to denote a class of implicatures distinct

---

[1] Compare Searle (1975: 274), G. M. Green (1975; 1989: 107), Morgan (1978), Kates (1980: 126), Horn (1989: 29, 344, 347–349), Wierzbicka (1987), Adler (1987: 711), Russell (1987: 731), and Fasold (1990: 155–157). Compare and contrast Grice (1978: 53–54), Bach and Harnish (1979: 202–208), Walker (1975, 1976), Nunberg (1981: 216–218), Sterelny (1982: 190), Leech (1983: 24, 26, 29–30), and Sperber and Wilson (1987: 750).

from the conversational. When Sadock gives Grice's six characteristics of conversational implicatures, he writes,

Conversational implicata are not part of the meaning of the uttered forms. They are NONCONVENTIONAL. (Sadock 1978: 284)

We will see that being conventional does not entail being part of the meaning of implicature-bearing sentences, and that the distinction Grice marked with the terms "conversational" and "conventional" is valid even though convention is involved in both.

5.1 CONVENTIONS

By "convention," I mean an *arbitrary social custom or practice*. More explicitly, a convention is *a regularity in the voluntary action of a group that is socially useful, self-perpetuating, and arbitrary*.[2] To be socially useful is to serve a mutual interest, something that people want not only for themselves but for others or for society as a whole. Linguistic conventions are socially useful because they serve a mutual interest in *communication*. That is the sociobiological function of language. Because people wish to communicate, they need to coordinate their actions. Speakers need to use a language their audience will understand, which is normally the language their audience uses. It is not nearly as important which language speakers and hearers use as long as it is the same language.

Conventions are self-perpetuating in special ways. Given the mutual interest, the fact that people have conformed to the regularity in the past gives people a good reason to continue conforming. Previous conformity thus serves as a *precedent*. Sometimes the precedent works directly: the fact that Americans have driven on the right before gives me an excellent reason to drive on the right now. Sometimes, the precedent is indirect. Steering wheels are conventionally installed on the left side of cars made in America.

---

[2] This is a modification of Lewis's (1969, 1975) theory. See also Ziff (1960: 22–26, 57–58), Grice (1968: 233), Schiffer (1972: Ch.V), Burge (1975), Bennett (1976: Ch. 7), Grandy (1977), and Blackburn (1984: 82–92, 118–122). I explain my theory more fully in *Meaning, Expression, and Thought* (sections 8.4–8.6).

This is done in part because people drive on the right, it being easier to drive on the right when steering from the left. Yet for the same reason, the practice of driving on the right has flourished in part because steering wheels have been installed on the left. Moreover, steering wheels are installed on the left principally because drivers in America are used to having them on the left, and plants are equipped to produce cars with left-sided steering. Yet people are so habituated, and plants so equipped, because steering wheels were installed on the left before. So indirectly, steering wheels are installed on the left today because they were installed on the left in the past. In the linguistic case, the precedent works both directly and indirectly. The very fact that people in America have used English before gives Americans a good reason to use English now: a community with one language is easier to communicate in than one with many languages. More importantly, however, the fact that Americans have used English before gives Americans a good reason to expect that their current audience will understand English now. This leads Americans to continue using English. In both ways, the fact that others before me have used the word "true" to mean "true" gives me a good reason to do so now, assuming I wish to communicate.

Lewis and his followers placed exclusive emphasis on precedence as the mechanism of self-perpetuation. But four other mechanisms are at least as powerful. (i) The regular use of a word or sentence to express an idea leads to a mental *association* between the expression and the idea, so that thoughts of the expression tend to call up the idea, and vice versa. The more frequent the pairing, the stronger the association. (ii) Regular action leads to a *habit* in each individual, which is reinforced by subsequent actions done out of that habit. Language involes two sets of reinforcing habits. That speakers regularly use e to mean μ leads hearers to automatically hear e as meaning μ; the more frequent the usage, the more automatic the understanding. That audiences automatically hear e as meaning μ normally gives speakers a good reason to use e to mean μ – the more automatic the understanding the better the reason for use. The fact that an individual habitually conforms in a flexible, creative, and purposive manner to such a complex set of regularities implies in turn that the individual has some sort of knowledge or internal representation of the regularities, as Chomsky stressed. (iii) Because adult Americans use English, American children learn English. They learn it natively at home, and they are taught it in school. Adults who join the group pick up the convention from old members. The use of English is thus a *tradition*. (iv) Finally, because they are traditional means to social ends, linguistic conventions are reinforced by *social pressure*. Despite their characteristic arbitrariness, the c ᴧ.ventions of a group are *generally accepted norms*. They are widely viewed by members at both an intuitive and an intellectual level to be right and proper.[3] Violations of the rules are generally considered mistakes, and speakers are criticized for them, or corrected. Children are praised and otherwise rewarded for learning to speak and write properly. Sometimes the penalties for nonconformity are stiff, as when the conventions are enacted as laws. Sometimes the penalty is merely an utterance that "sounds odd." All five mechanisms – precedent, association, habit, tradition, and normative pressure – are self-reinforcing and capable of sustaining the regularities for generations.

Some conventions get started, or are reinforced, by an *agreement* to act in a common manner. Indeed, in a second sense, the word "convention" denotes an international agreement, and in a third denotes formal meetings designed to secure agreements. But in the sense we are concerned with (customary practice), most conventions, like linguistic conventions, did not result from agreements. It is hard to even imagine the first language arising by agreement. How could people agree to such a thing without using a common language? In the inimitable words of Bertrand Russell, "We can hardly suppose a parliament of hitherto speechless elders meeting together and agreeing to call a cow a cow and a wolf a wolf."[4] Linguistic conventions do occasionally arise from agreements, as when

---

[3] Compare Ziff (1960: 30–31), Kripke (1982: 89–95), and Blackburn (1984: 83). See also Rosenberg (1974: 43–45).

[4] Russell (1921: 190). See also Quine (1936), Alston (1964a: 57), Lewis (1969: 83–88), Bennett (1976: 206–210), Grice (1982), Blackburn (1984: 119), and Suppes (1986: 113).

scientific congresses succeed in standardizing terminology. But other origins are much more common, as when a stipulative definition catches on (Edward Kasner coined "googol"; his readers used it because he did, and so on) or a metaphor dies. In some cases, agreements evolve into conventions that undermine the purpose of the agreement, as when brand names become generic names. The statement that a regularity is conventional entails that it maintains itself in certain ways, but claims nothing about how it originated. It follows that conventions need not be laws: they need not be codified or reinforced by legal sanctions.

Conventions are arbitrary in that there is another possible regularity in action that could have served the same common interest and would have perpetuated itself in the same ways if only it had gotten started. The American interest in communication would have been served equally well by Spanish. If Americans spoke Spanish, that would give Americans a good reason to continue speaking Spanish. American children would learn Spanish because adults use it. And Americans would criticize each other for speaking Spanish incorrectly. Sometimes the arbitrariness of conventions is obscured by the fact that they are not arbitrary *given* the existence of other conventions. For example, given that people drive on the right in America, it is not arbitrary that steering wheels are placed on the left. Steering from the left makes it significantly easier to drive on the right. But the placement of steering wheels is nevertheless arbitrary in the relevant, absolute sense. For both practices could be altered in tandem, and with sufficient time for retooling would serve the same social interest equally well, and perpetuate itself as surely. In the linguistic case, the practice of using English in America is not arbitrary *given* that Americans conventionally interpret other Americans as speaking English. But both practices could be altered, and, with sufficient time for reeducation, would serve the purpose of communication equally well and perpetuate themselves in the same way.

Some features of a language have no alternative. The fact that expressions are perceivable is an obvious example. If the Chomskyan thesis of an innate language acquisition device is correct, there will be many unobvious examples. The necessary features of language are not restrictive enough, however, to make only one language humanly usable, as the thousands of languages spoken on earth today prove. There is nothing in the nature of the human mind, the word "hood," or the idea of an engine covering by virtue of which the word expresses the idea. Hence "hood" could just as well mean "car top," and the idea of an engine covering could just as well be expressed by "bonnet," as in British English. The arbitrariness of symbols stands in marked contrast to the statistical or causal character of indexes and the representational character of icons.[5]

A regularity in action is *a common way of doing things.* "Dog" is regularly used in America to mean "dog," to express the idea of a dog, to talk about dogs, and so on. The use of "dog" to express the idea of a dog is both a common way of using the word and a common way of expressing the idea. A regularity in action may also be described as a *rule.* If W is the common way of doing A, then W is "the way A is done." When the regularity is a convention, it is more than a de facto rule. It is a de jure rule "in force" in the community:[6] a norm to which members seek to conform, and believe they ought to. S's reason for doing A in way W will typically be: "That's the way A is done."

Somewhat paradoxically, there may be a common way of doing something uncommon. Using the word "googol" to express the idea of 10^{100} is both a common way of using that word and a common way of expressing that idea. But Americans seldom use the word "googol" or express the idea of 10^{100}. How common a way W of doing A is, is determined by the *relative* frequency of W *given* A, not the absolute frequency of W. In some cases, such as driving on the right, a regularity will be socially useful only if it is the only common way of doing things. But in other cases, such as language, the common interest may be served by several common ways of doing things. The general interest in communication is served quite

[5] Compare Pierce (1931–35: vol. II), Alston (1964a: Ch. 3), Bennett (1976: 14, 149), and Anttila (1989: 12).
[6] Compare Alston (1964b: 57–58) and Lewis (1969: 100–107). Contrast Ziff (1960: 34–38).

well even though "plane" and "airplane" are both commonly used to express the idea of an airplane, and even though "plane" is commonly used to express both the idea of an airplane and that of a certain tool. Consequently, it is not the case that, by convention, people use "plane" *only when* they mean "airplane," nor *whenever* they mean "airplane."[7] As these examples illustrate, conventional regularities need not be perfect: a common way of doing things need not be universal or unique. It is conventional to drive on the right even though people occasionally drive on the left, and it is conventional to use "plane" to mean "airplane" even though people often use it to mean "tool used to plane wood." The existence of ambiguity and synonymy is not problematic for the thesis that word meanings are conventional.

Bach and Harnish (1979: 108–110) define conventions as "count-as rules," actions, which, if done in certain situations, count as doing something else.[8] The rule whereby baseball players score a run by crossing home plate is such a rule because crossing home plate counts as scoring in certain circumstances. Similarly, saying "I promise" counts as promising in certain circumstances. However, the notion of a count-as rule does not fit two of the paradigm examples of conventions Bach and Harnish cite. "Money is a conventional means of exchange," they say. Furthermore, "It is a commonplace, however unexplicated, that language is a system of conventional means for communicating." We regularly buy food by giving the grocer money. But giving the grocer money does not count as buying food. What counts as buying food is giving the grocer money in exchange for food. But the connection between buying food and giving the grocer money in exchange for food is not conventional in any sense, for the latter necessarily entails the former. Similarly, we often communicate by uttering sentences, but uttering sentences never counts as communicating. What

---

7 Compare Grice (1968: 232–233), Yu (1979: 282–285), Loar (1981: 256), Schiffer (1987a: 250–251), and Avramides (1989: 68). Contrast Schiffer (1972: 128–129, 136, 154, 156), Fodor (1975: 78), Bennett (1976: 213), Bach and Harnish (1979: 108–110, 189–190), and Chierchia and McConnell-Ginet (1990: 153).

8 Compare Strawson (1964: 292).

counts as communicating is uttering sentences with certain intentions that are recognized by an audience. This connection holds by virtue of the nature of communication, not any arbitrary convention. Because I wish to show that implicature practices are conventional in the same sense languages are, I have not defined conventions as count-as rules. Only some linguistic conventions are count-as rules.

Lewis and his followers argued that for an action to be conventional, it must be *"common"* or *"mutual" knowledge* that the action is regular, socially useful, self-perpetuating, and arbitrary.[9] Some features of a conventional action are undeniably common knowledge in the ordinary sense of this term. It is generally known, for example, that people use the word "red" to mean "red." But Lewis and his followers give "mutual knowledge" a highly technical sense: it is "mutually" known that p, according to one definition, iff everyone knows that p, everyone knows that everyone knows that p, everyone knows that everyone knows that everyone knows that p, and so on. Given that "mutual" knowledge of one proposition requires knowledge of an infinite sequence of ever more complex propositions, it is doubtful that mutual knowledge is humanly possible. That issue is academic, however, because *linguistic conventions need not be universally known.* In that event, even the *first-order* condition of mutual knowledge is unsatisfied.

Not everyone knows, for example, that people regularly use the word "googol" to mean 10^{100}. Indeed, the percentage of English speakers who know anything about the word "googol" is quite small. Because few people know what "googol" means, *no one* knows that *everyone* knows that people use "googol" to mean 10^{100}, no one knows that everyone knows that everyone knows this, and so on. This holds for "implicit" or "potential" knowledge as well as actual, explicit knowledge. There is nothing special about the word "googol" here. No one knows every word of a natural

9 Lewis (1969: 52–68, 152–159; 1975: 6), Schiffer (1972: 30, 131, 148–155; 1987a: 249–261), Bennett (1976: 179–180, 190–192), Loar (1976a: 353), and Hungerland and Vick (1981: 50, 137–144). Bach and Harnish (1979: 108–110, 189–190) impose a parallel requirement.

language like English, and relatively few words are known by every speaker of English. Those who have a large vocabulary are usually intelligent enough to realize that most people do not.

Similarly, satisfaction of the arbitrariness clause may fail to be mutual knowledge.[10] Speakers of English need not realize, for example, that word order is arbitrary. They may mistakenly think English word order is "natural" and that any other order would be unintelligible. I myself still find it hard to accept that reading from left to right is not somehow the natural way to read. Lyons (1971: 4) reports that ancient Greek grammarians actually believed there was a necessary connection between the meaning of a word and its form. I am arguing, of course, that implicature practices are conventional and arbitrary despite the fact that most scholars believe they are natural, being deducible from general psychosocial principles.

We now turn to showing that there are conversational implicature conventions. To do so, we show there are regularities in implicating that are socially useful, self-perpetuating, and arbitrary.

5.2 QUANTITY IMPLICATURES

We have noted that sentences of the form "Some S are P" (with stress on "some") implicate that not all S are P. This implies a specific regularity in action: speakers commonly use "Some S are P" to implicate that not all S are P. The regularity is socially useful, contributing as it does to communication. Speakers who implicate not all S are P communicate the thought that not all S are P. The regularity is self-perpetuating: the fact that speakers before us have used "Some S are P" to implicate "Not all S are P" gives us a good reason to do so ourselves; moreover, the habit of using the sentence to express the thought, and the association between the two, are both reinforced each time "Some S are P" is used to implicate "Not all S are P"; finally, the practice is transmitted from one generation to the next as language is learned. Last but not least, the regularity is arbi-

---

[10] This was observed by Burge (1975), Grandy (1977), and Blackburn (1984: 121).

140

trary. We could have used "Some S are P" to implicate "Perhaps all S are P" or "It is an open question whether all S are P." Or we could have used "Some S are P" with no implicature at all about stronger propositions, the way we use "At least 99% of all S are P." (We could also switch the function of stress and its absence, so that the latter rather than the former normally triggers the standard quantity implicature.) These alternative regularities would have contributed sufficiently to the common goal of communication, enough to perpetuate themselves if they had gotten started.

The regularity in question is not perfect. As the cross-examination case illustrates, we do not always use "Some S are P" to implicate that not all S are P. But the same goes for the conventions assigning meanings to words. It is conventional to use "vixen" to mean "female fox." But although this usage is common, it is not universal. If we always used "vixen" to mean "female fox," the word would not have other meanings. Similarly, the precedent that keeps us using "Some S are P" to implicate not all S are P is not as powerful a reason for continuing the practice as the precedent that keeps us driving on the right. But again, the same goes for the conventions assigning meanings to words.

It may seem that the regularity in implicature is not arbitrary because the proposition implicated by "Some S are P" depends on the meaning of the sentence and is logically related to the proposition assigned to the sentence by semantic conventions. But to say that a regularity is arbitrary is only to say there could have been alternative regularities, which would have served the same purposes and perpetuated themselves in the same way if they had gotten started. Grice thought the implicature could actually be calculated from the meaning of the sentence. The arbitrariness of implicature practice makes this untenable. Put positively, the failure of determinacy (Chapter 3) supports the arbitrariness and conventionality of implicature practice.

We may concede that implicature conventions are not always *as* arbitrary as semantic conventions. Whereas it would make no difference at all if *mose* were used to mean "at least one" rather than *some,* it would be less "natural" to use "An S could be a P" to implicate that not all S are P, and "All S are P" could not be so used. However, in other quantity implicatures the arbitrariness is stark, as in (2) through (5) of Chapter 2. There seems to be nothing in the meaning difference between "could have solved" and "was able to solve," for example, that makes it more natural for the former to implicate "did not solve" and the latter to implicate "did solve" than vice versa. More importantly, the degree to which linguistic practices are arbitrary is not important for our purpose, which is to deny that theoretical economy in any way favors the postulation of conversational implicatures over senses or conventional implicatures.

Lycan objected to the claim that there are implicature conventions on the grounds that implicature regularities are not socially useful "per se."[11] Although implicature regularities do serve the purpose of communication, a social good, their being *implicature* regularities does not make them any more useful for this purpose than alternative regularities, such as explicit statement regularities. As noted before (sections 1.4, 3.8), I can communicate the same thoughts to my students whether I *state*, "Some students passed" and *implicate* "Not all passed" or rather *state*, "Not all passed" and *implicate* "Some passed." I observe in Chapter 6 that implicature conventions serve other social purposes, such as politeness, efficiency, and style. But it would be risky to claim that every implicature convention must serve one of these other purposes, or that explicit statement regularities could not possibly achieve the same ends.

The reply to Lycan's objection is that conventional regularities do not need to be socially useful "per se." It is enough that they be socially useful. Indeed, the arbitrariness clause in the definition of convention would seem to make it *impossible* for a conventional regularity to be useful "per se." A regularity is arbitrary only if some other regularity *could* serve the same purpose. The fact that I can communicate the same thoughts to my students whether I state, "Some students passed" and implicate "Not all passed" or state the latter and implicate the former shows that the quantity implicature regularity is arbitrary in a fundamental way. The same point holds for narrowly semantic conventions. It is conventional

[11] Personal communication.

142

to write the three-letter sequence *man* to mean "man," and this regularity is useful in that it enables us to communicate. But this regularity is not socially useful "per se." We could just as well write other letter sequences to express the same idea. Alternatively, we could use sound sequences or touch sequences rather than writing. In other words, the fact that what can be done by implication can usually if not always be done explicitly supports the conventionality thesis rather than undermining it.

The convention of using "Some S are P" to mean not all S are P is an instance of a more general regularity, that of using a weaker statement to implicate the denial of a stronger statement. Although far from universal, as we observed in section 2.1, this practice is very common and does have social utility. The practice nevertheless lacks one of the characteristics of a convention because the general regularity of quantity implicature depends on the specific quantity implicature conventions. The general regularity holds because we use "Some S are P" to implicate "Not all S are P," "Possibly p" to implicate "Not necessarily p," "N is warm" to implicate "N is not hot," and so on. The fact that we damn with faint praise and praise with faint damns also contributes to the general regularity. Horn scales may be viewed as formal tools for summarizing the conventional, lexical basis of the general regularity.[12]

When we use "Some S are P" to implicate not all S are P, we do so because that particular sentence form has been used that way before, not because weaker statements are generally used to implicate the denial of stronger statements. The general quantity implicature regularity is therefore not self-perpetuating in the way characteristic of semantic conventions. Consequently it would be *un*conventional if we used "Some presidents died" to

---

[12] For references, see footnote 18 of Chapter 3. Hirschberg complains, "Gazdar does not suggest how these scales may be derived or how they may be identified from utterances. In effect, he is forced to assume that they are just 'given' to us" (1991: 69–70). Given that the quantity implicatures are governed by specific conventions and not derivable in the Gricean fashion at all, I would say that Gazdar was forced by the evidence to make the proper assumption even though it conflicted with his theoretical predispositions.

implicate "Not all presidents were assassinated" or "It is not the case that at least 45 percent of all presidents were assassinated." That people have often used weaker statements to implicate the denial of stronger statements would not be a good reason for us to use "Some presidents died" in either way. And such uses of the sentence would not be the exercise of any habit or competence transmitted from generation to generation. Note that we cannot even properly use "Some *died*" to suggest doubt if someone claims that all presidents were assassinated the way we can naturally use "*Some* were assassinated." However, the fact that the general practice of using weaker statements to implicate the denial of stronger statements depends as it does on particular conventions is sufficient to show that the general practice cannot be explained in terms of general psychosocial principles or canons of rationality.

5.3 TAUTOLOGY IMPLICATURES

Sentences of the form "An N's an N" implicate that *one N is as good (or bad) as another*. Hence there is a regularity in action: speakers commonly use "An N's an N" to implicate that one N is as good as another. The regularity is socially useful (serving the purpose of communication) and self-perpetuating (past conformity breeds future conformity). The regularity is also arbitrary. We could have used "An N's an N" to implicate that *an N is C,* where C is a contextually salient characteristic of Ns, which is what we conventionally use the related forms "N is N" and "That's N" to implicate. Compare (8) and (9) of Chapter 2 (and see Fraser 1988). We could have used "An N's an N" to implicate what we would normally use "Ns will be Ns" to implicate. We could have used "An N's an N" to implicate that there is something uniquely good about an N, which is how the Poles use *co X to X* (Wierzbicka 1987: 102). We could have used "An N's an N" to implicate that the answer to the previous question is obviously "Yes," the way we often use "Is the pope Catholic?" Alternatively, we could have used "An N's an N" without any implicature, the way we use "No tables are nontables."

5.4 CONJUNCTION IMPLICATURES

We commonly use "e and f" to implicate "e before f," when e and f are sentences describing events. We also commonly use "e and f" to implicate the stronger "f because e." These practices are socially useful (fostering communication), self-perpetuating (past conformity breeds future conformity), and arbitrary. We could have used "e and f" to mean "–(e before f)," "f before e," or "e because f"; or we could have used it without any such implicatures.

5.5 DISJUNCTION IMPLICATURES

It is well known that English utterances of the form "p or q" are sometimes interpreted and intended *inclusively,* allowing the possibility that both alternatives are true, and sometimes *exclusively,* excluding the possibility that both are true. In his attempt to defend the thesis that English connectives have the same meaning as certain connectives of propositional logic, Grice argued that "or" is unambiguous and has the same sense as *v,* so that the inclusive interpretation is its sole meaning. Grice and his followers argued that the exclusive interpretation results from a quantity implicature.[13] Persuasive evidence supports the Gricean hypothesis: "or" never has the exclusive interpretation when embedded in certain compounds, as in "It is not the case that p or q"; the implication can be canceled by adding "or both"; someone who says, "I am going to France or Germany this summer," implying that he is not going to both countries, did not actually say that he is not going to both countries; and so on. Given such powerful evidence, I assume Grice is right about the exclusive interpretation resulting from a quantity implicature.

But Griceans have also applied Grice's Razor to the case, claiming that the implicature hypothesis is more economical theoretically than the ambiguity hypothesis because the exclusive implica-

---

[13] See Grice (1978: 44–50; 1989: 8–9), Kempson (1975: 146), McCawley (1978: 245), Gazdar (1979: 78–83), Levinson (1983: 136–140), Leech (1983: 88), Bach (1987: 77; 1994a: 13), Fasold (1990: 137–138), and Horn (1992: 261).

ture could be derived from the Maxim of Quantity, a general principle of conversation, whereas senses require the postulation of language-specific conventions. This economy claim is untenable. If the proposition that "p or q" implicates −(p&q) could be derived from the Maxim of Quantity, then it should also be derivable that "p or q or both," "p and/or q," and even "p v q" have the same implication. But these forms are completely unambiguous. And why wouldn't the same reasoning lead to the conclusion that "p or q" implicates both −p and −q?

Furthermore, speakers often use "p or q" with an epistemic implication, implying *I don't know which*. This implication cannot be derived from the Maxim of Quantity, at least not in the same way the exclusive interpretation is. And when used with the epistemic interpretation, the exclusive interpretation need not be present. Suppose I am asked, "Where is Kathy going this summer?" If I respond "France, or Germany, or some other European country," implying that I do not know which, then I do not imply that Kathy will not visit both France and some other European country.

Disjunctions are often used with a different sort of nonepistemic exclusive interpretation. Sometimes "or" implies *or else,* as when a teacher says, "You will take the final or fail the course." Here, there is no implication that the student won't both take the final and fail the course. That is, the teacher is not implying that merely taking the exam will be enough to pass the course. Instead, the teacher would most likely be issuing a warning or threat, implying that *not* taking the exam will guarantee failing the course. The contrast is that between "Not taking the exam excludes the possibility of not failing" and "Taking the exam excludes the possibility of failing." Furthermore, disjunctions are often used with a different sort of inclusive interpretation. Sometimes "or" implies *or equivalently.* Thus I might earlier have said, "The hearer uses abduction, or inference to the best explanation, to infer that S is implicating p." If the implicature of *not both p and q* could be derived from "p or q" using the Maxim of Quantity, how could "p or q" ever imply "p or else q" or "p or equivalently q"? For that matter, what maxims can the "or-else" or "or-equivalently" interpretations be derived from? Ball suggests the Maxim of Manner for the latter:

The receiver of (17) [*Gelatin's power to displace moisture is due to its "bloom,"* *or strength*] can reason as follows: if I (the receiver) am a member of the intended audience, and if I haven't missed some prior explanation, then the writer cannot have meant (17) to be understood as a descriptive disjunction, because the first disjunct is so obscure that I cannot process it (this sense of "bloom" is not in my lexicon). To be "mannerly," the writer needs to explain this new sense of "bloom." If I assume that *or* is being used here to offer an alternative, more familiar term, then all is well. The writer is asserting that gelatin's power to displace moisture is due to a property which I know as strength, but which is appropriately called "bloom" in the sub-language of cooking. (Ball 1986: 9)

But I could perfectly well say, "The length of the field is 300 feet, or 100 yards," implying that the two alternatives are equivalent, even though the first alternative is not at all obscure. And a philosopher might well say, "God is the absolutely simple unity encompassing within his manifoldness everything in the supremely noumenal world, or he is nothing," implying that the two alternatives are mutually exclusive, even though the first alternative is so obscure that members of the intended audience cannot process it.

Because the fact that "p or q" implicates $-(p\&q)$ cannot be derived from the Maxim of Quantity, it represents a specific quantity implicature convention. The same goes for the other disjunction implicatures. Implicature conventions differ from narrowly semantic conventions, but the postulation of one is no simpler theoretically than the postulation of the other. Whether the exclusive interpretation is treated as a quantity implicature or a second sense, it is a matter of convention.

5.6 MODAL IMPLICATURES

As we observed in section 3.13, we commonly use "I must tell you how much N Vs" to implicate "N Vs a lot," while using "I may tell you how much N Vs" with no such implicature. The determinacy and calculability requirements fail because these practices are arbitrary. We could just as well have used "I may tell you how much N Vs" to implicate "N Vs a lot," while using "I must tell you how much N Vs" with no such implicature. Or we could have used "I must tell you how much I love you" to implicate "I love you a little" or "I love you moderately." These practices would have perpetuated themselves and served the same purposes if they had gotten started.

5.7 FIGURES OF SPEECH

The implicature conventions we have focused on so far are defined in part by the use of a particular sentence form: "Some S are P," "N is N," "p and q," "p or q," and "I must tell you H." Hence these conventions governing speaker implication all create sentence implicatures. The fact that it is conventional for *speakers* to use "Some S are P" to implicate "Not all S are P" makes it true that *sentences* of the form "Some S are P" implicate "Not all S are P." Other implicature conventions lack this feature. One briefly mentioned in section 5.2 is damning with faint praise. Figures of speech provide additional examples.

Consider irony. We frequently use a sentence p to implicate not-p, especially when we use a certain tone of voice. This practice is definitely not the norm, but it is a common enough way of using sentences. The use of p to implicate not-p is socially useful, again enabling communication. It is also self-perpetuating: the fact that others have used sentences ironically gives us a reason to do the same, and the practice is handed down from generation to generation. Finally, the practice is highly arbitrary: we could just as well use p on occasion to implicate that it is wonderful that p, or that it is possible that p. Or we could use p to implicate the converse of p, or some other transformation of p (cf. Sperber and Wilson 1981: 161), or nothing at all. Because irony can be used with any sentence, the existence of a convention to use sentences ironically does not give rise to any sentence implicatures. It is not true that "It is a fine day" implicates "It is not a fine day," even on a particular occasion in which the speaker used the former to mean the latter.

It is also conventional to use sentences metaphorically, hyperbolically, meiotically, and so on. All these figures of speech represent

148

common and self-perpetuating ways of using sentences that enable us to communicate. They are arbitrary in the sense that the goal of communication does not require their use. Other ways of using sentences would enable us to communicate about as well, and they would perpetuate themselves in the same way.

5.8 RELEVANCE IMPLICATURES

In case (1) of Chapter 1, Bob answered Ann's question indirectly, by making a statement closely related to the implicated information. Ann asked where she could get gasoline; Bob implicated that she could get gasoline at the station around the corner; he implicated this by saying there is a station around the corner, a proposition implied by what Bob implicated. In another case, H asked whether S drives a Mercedes, and S implicated that he does not by saying he does not drive any expensive car; in this case, the answer S implicated was implied by what S said. Both cases illustrate a common practice: *implicating requested information by making a statement closely related to it by implication.* This practice is clearly useful (enabling us to communicate requested information) and self-perpetuating (we communicate this way in part because others have done so before). The arbitrariness of the practice is somewhat obscured by its utility. But there are alternative regularities. Indeed, we sometimes answer questions ironically, and most often answer directly. It could have been customary to answer "Is it the case that p?" with either "It is good that p" or "It is bad that p," depending on how one evaluates the requested information.

The relevance implicature convention does not give rise to any *sentence* implicatures. For the regularity is not defined by the use of a particular sentence form. In this respect, the convention resembles damning with faint praise and differs from the paradigm quantity implicatures.

Case (1) of Chapter 3 is slightly different. Carl said he was sick and Diane responded that a flying saucer is nearby. Carl did not request any information. Nevertheless, Diane may have implicated something relevant to what Carl said, such as that he could get help on the flying saucer that is nearby. She implicated this by making a statement closely related by implication to the proposition she implicated. Thus the first cases of Chapters 1 and 3 are both instances of a more general practice: *implicating something relevant to the preceding speech act of one's interlocutor by making a statement closely related by implication to the proposition implicated.* This practice can be followed in some cases by following others, such as a quantity implicature convention. Thus in case (3) of Chapter 4, Mrs. Smith asked, "Did you eat all the chocolates?" and Billy answered, "I ate *some,*" implicating that he did not eat all of the chocolates. Or if H observes that civilians might be killed, S might respond, "War is war," implicating that it is the nature of war for terrible things to happen. The general relevance implicature practice can even be followed by violating the Cooperative Principle, as in case (5) of Chapter 4, where the student demanded to know why a question was marked wrong, and the professor responded that he was late for class.

It should not be inferred, however, that these other implicature practices can all be subsumed under the relevance implicature convention. Indeed, one can use the other conventions to implicate something irrelevant to the previous speech act. For example, in case (1) of Chapter 1, Bob could have said, "We'll go to dinner and take in a show tonight," implicating that they would go to dinner before taking in a show, even though what he said and implied is completely irrelevant to Ann's query about gasoline. Bob might have contributed something irrelevant for a variety of reasons: inattention, rudeness, psychosis, or simple brashness.

Whether the general relevance implicature convention can be stated more precisely, or generalized further, is an open question. Even if the practice cannot be described more precisely, it can be effective as long as members of the community generally share a common sense of what is or is not relevant to a given speech act. Nearly everyone would count "You can get help on the flying saucer" as relevant to "I am sick." Nearly everyone would count "Alpha Centauri is far away" as irrelevant to "I am sick" in real-life contexts. Hence someone who responded to "I am sick" with "Alpha Centauri is over three light-years away" would be departing from conversational norms. Whether the general practice counts as a convention may also be debatable. But there are alternatives: instead of implicating something relevant to the preceding speech act, we could state it directly; and instead of implicating a relevant proposition by asserting a proposition related to it by implication, we could use irony to express our attitude. Furthermore, the practice does seem self-perpetuating. We habitually engage in the practice and pass it on to our children. The fact that others have followed the practice before gives us a good reason to do so, and a good reason to expect that others will recognize we are doing so. To be sure, this reason is not decisive: because there are several common ways of answering questions, for example, precedence does not favor one over the other. But this is common with linguistic conventions. There are several common ways of referring to the number two, for example, by using "two," "2," "II," and so on. All are conventional ways of referring to the number.

5.9 CLOSE-BUT IMPLICATURES

In case (6) of section 2.1, B implicated that no student got an A by affirming that some got Bs. She was following a common practice: *implicating the denial of one statement by affirming another that is close in content but not the same.* The practice is as useful and self-perpetuating as the relevance implicature convention. And it is definitely arbitrary. We could just as well have developed the practice of implicating that the statement denied itself rather than its denial. We could have used "Some got Bs" to implicate "Some got As" rather than "None got As." The close-but implicature practice does not generally generate sentence implicatures because it is not defined by the use of a particular sentence form. An exception, of course, is the subclass of quantity implicatures. The quantity implicature convention can be viewed as setting the precedent for the whole class. That is, we can view the close-but implicature convention as resulting from the spread or generalization of the quantity implicature convention.

Note that although "I have a cat" does not implicate "I do not have a Siamese cat," the former would normally be used to implicate the latter in response to the question "Do you have a Siamese cat?"[14] The sentence "I have a cat" does not implicate that I do not have a Siamese because it is not conventional to use it with that implication. Indeed, it may never have been so used. Nevertheless, if it were so used, that usage would be an example of the regularity constituting the close-but implicature convention.

5.10 MANNER IMPLICATURES

The terms "quantity implicature" and "relevance implicature" have standardly been used to connote that the implicatures they denote comply with and are thus generated by the Maxims of Quantity or Relation. I have argued that this usage is based on a misconception. The term "manner implicature," in contrast, has customarily been used to denote those that *flout* the Maxim of Manner. Grice (1975: 37) provided a well-known example, in which the submaxim "be brief " is flouted. The speaker says "Miss X produced a series of sounds that corresponded closely with the score of 'Home Sweet Home,'" and thereby implicates that Miss X's performance was defective. Although not as common as the other practices we have examined, Grice's example is nonetheless conventional. I might denigrate your house by referring to it as a large hollow assemblage of wood and bricks, your car by referring to it as a boxlike machine with wheels capable of consuming gasoline, and so on. In general, we commonly implicate that an object or action is poor of its kind by providing an unusual and long description. The practice enables us to communicate, and it is self-perpetuating. It is arbitrary in that there are other ways of achieving the same goal. The critic could just come out and say that the performance was terrible, or, if humor was essential, could engage in parody, or use a metaphor.

[14] Hirschberg (1991: 156–157); Matsumoto (1995: 29, 55–56). Both misinterpret the example, concluding there is no genuine distinction between particularized and generalized implicatures.

5.11 INTERROGATIVE AND IMPERATIVE IMPLICATURES

Morgan (1978: 252) noted two conventions in which the implication is generated by asking a question rather than making a statement. The first is to *challenge the wisdom of a proposed course of action by questioning the mental health of the suggester.* Thus if someone suggests paying $100 an acre for real estate near a toxic waste dump, one might reply, "Are you crazy?" or "Have you lost your mind?" or "Are you out of your gourd?" The other is to *answer a yes/no question and communicate that the answer is obvious by asking another question whose answer is patently obvious.* Thus if someone asks whether I am going to play tennis today, I might answer "Does the pope pray?" or "Does it rain in Seattle?" Because, as Morgan observed, these conventions do not specify the use of any particular sentence or sentence form, no sentence implicatures exist as a result of the conventions. The arbitrariness of the conventions may seem doubtful given such an obvious connection between the question asked and the statement implicated. But there are clearly other ways of accomplishing the same ends. These are common only because they are transmitted as traditions from generation to generation.

There are also implicature conventions in which the implication is generated by issuing a directive rather than making a statement. For example, it is customary to communicate that an indicated possibility is unlikely to occur anytime soon by telling one's interlocutor not to do something that would have undesirable consequences if the possibility did not eventuate in a timely fashion. Thus if Kathy says, "Alan might come to visit," I might answer, "Don't get your hopes up" or "Don't hold your breath" or "Don't break out the champagne yet."

On a narrow reading of the definition of implicature (sections 1.1, 3.13), the acts of implying that we are examining in this section do not count as implicatures precisely because they are generated by questions or commands rather than statements. To implicate p is to mean or imply p *by saying something else.* On a narrow reading, "saying" denotes *stating.* On a broad reading, "saying" includes asking and ordering as well as stating. It does not matter for our purposes which reading is used in the definition. If Gricean theory applies to implicatures narrowly construed, it should also apply to implicatures broadly construed. Nothing in Gricean theory turns on the fact that the speaker implicates something by stating as opposed to questioning or ordering something else.

Of course, if we did adopt the narrow definition, then the existence of conventions governing the act of implying something by asking a question or issuing an order would not in and of itself prove the existence of implicature conventions. But given their many similarities, the existence of such implicature-*like* conventions would make the existence of implicature conventions proper more plausible by analogy.

6

The nature of implicature conventions

I have argued that sentence implicatures exist not because conversational implicatures are derivable from conversational principles, but on the contrary because there are conventional ways of conversationally implicating things. Implicature practices are arbitrary to some extent rather than completely determinate. Because the Gricean paradigm is incompatible with their existence, conversational implicature conventions have scarcely been noticed let alone studied in depth. In this chapter, we begin examining the distinctive nature of implicature conventions. We compare and contrast them with more familiar linguistic conventions. I suggest that instead of generating conversational implicatures in any way, the conversational principles of Grice and his followers tell us why implicature practices are socially useful. Although the implicatures of a sentence are not derivable from its meaning, I try to explain why they invariably do bear some relation to its meaning that makes them seem fitting or appropriate. I conclude with an alternative speculation about how some implicature practices came to be nearly universal, a surprising but not unprecedented feature given that they are conventional. We should look to historical rather than theoretical linguistics for the explanation.

6.1 FIRST-ORDER VERSUS SECOND-ORDER SEMANTIC CONVENTIONS

Let us say that the conventions giving words, phrases, and sentences their meanings are *first-order* semantic rules: they assign meanings and implications directly to sound sequences or letter strings. Then conversational implicature conventions are *second-order* semantic rules: they assign additional implications to linguistic forms only insofar as they have specified meanings by virtue of the first-order semantic rules. "Some cats are white" implicates that not all cats are white because it means that one or more cats are white. The convention underlying the implicature is to use sentences meaning "Some S are P" to implicate that not all S are P. That is, it is conventional to use sentences of this form with their literal meaning ("At least one S is P") to implicate something further that is not meant by the sentence. The dependence of the implicature on the meaning shows up clearly when there is an ambiguity. Thus "Some females are vixens" can be used to implicate that not all females are female foxes only when it is used to mean "Some females are female foxes." It can be used to implicate that not all females are shrewish women only when it is used to mean "Some females are shrewish women." In thinking implicatures could be *calculated* or *worked out* given sentence meanings, Grice appears to have misidentified the nature of the dependence of sentence implicature on sentence meaning. Implicatures are connected to meanings by convention, not by psychosocial principles.

In terms of the theory I favor, both first-order and second-order semantic rules are conventions for using linguistic forms to express thoughts or ideas. The first-order rules are conventions for using sentences to *directly* express certain thoughts. The second-order rules are conventions for *indirect* expression, rules for expressing further thoughts by expressing thoughts assigned by first-order rules.

The composition rules of a language are also secondary in a way because they assign meanings to word complexes on the basis of the meanings of the words in the complex. But composition rules are not second order in the sense I have in mind. The rule assigning the meaning "hater of dogs" to the phrase "dog hater" gives it this meaning because the component words "dog" and "hater" have certain meanings. But the rule does not assign that meaning to "dog hater" because of some *other* meaning the phrase *itself* has. In contrast, "Some cats are white" implicates "Not all cats are white" because the sentence itself means "One or more cats are white." The second-order rules allow the sentence to be used to express the thought "Not all cats are white" when it is used in accord with the first-order rule to express the thought "One or more cats are white."

As we noted in section 1.1, Grice drew an important distinction between "conventional" and "conversational" implicatures. The implication of contrast carried by *but* is a conventional implicature, whereas the implication of nonuniversality conveyed by *some* is conversational. The latter implicature is cancelable; the former is not. Grice's terminology suggests that conversational implicatures are by definition not a matter of convention. But as we have seen, that is a mistake. When talking about particularized implicatures – speaker implicatures – it is true that conversational implicatures need not be conventional. But generalized conversational implicatures – sentence implicatures – exist only because there are conversational implicature conventions. Sentences of the form "Some S are P" are conventionally used to implicate that not all S are P just as "p but q" is conventionally used to implicate that q is somehow surprising given p. The difference between "conventional" and "conversational" implicatures at the level of sentences lies in the *nature* of the conventions involved. Both are semantic conventions, but only the former are first-order conventions. The contrastive implication is part of the meaning of *but*. The nonuniversal implication is no part of the meaning of *some*.

First-order and second-order semantic rules both arise from conventions governing speaker meaning, which can be defined in terms of expression. Simplifying somewhat, the word "vixen" means "female fox" because it is conventional for speakers to use the former to mean the latter. That is, "vixen" means "female fox" because speakers conventionally use "vixen" to directly express the idea of a female fox.[1] "Dog hater" means "hater of dogs" rather than "hater that is a dog" because speakers conventionally use expressions of the form "N + hater" to mean "hater of Ns" rather than "hater that is N." Similarly, "Some S are P" implicates "Not all S are P" because speakers conventionally use the former to mean the latter in a certain way.

---

[1] I develop this idea in *Meaning, Expression, and Thought,* Part II.

Implicature conventions differ further from first-order semantic conventions in the type of speaker meaning involved. Implicature conventions are regularities in *"cognitive"* speaker meaning, as opposed to the *"cogitative"* type involved in the first-order semantic conventions.[2] The difference here is that between *meaning that p by uttering "e"* (cognitive speaker meaning) and *meaning "p" by the expression "e"* (cogitative). The two forms are logically independent even though they typically coincide. If S was speaking ironically, he may have meant "John is in debt" by the sentence "John is in hock" even though he meant that John is not in debt by uttering the sentence. S may have meant that Ted Kennedy is liberal by uttering "The handsomest senator is liberal" without meaning "Ted Kennedy is liberal" by that sentence. "Kicked the bucket" means "died" because people conventionally mean "died" by the expression. Phrases are not conventionally used to mean *that* anything is the case. "Some S are P" implicates that not all S are P because people conventionally mean that not all S are P by uttering the sentence. Speakers do not customarily mean "Not all S are P" by sentences of the form "Some S are P."

Implicature conventions are second order because they involve a regularity in *indirect meaning*. Idioms are first order because they involve a regularity in *direct meaning*. Suppose I use "Scott is a bug" metaphorically, to express the thought that Scott is repulsive and should be squashed. Then I mean "Scott is an insect-like invertebrate" (rather than "Scott is a hidden microphone") by the sentence I use, and thereby mean that Scott is repulsive. Thus I use the sentence with a certain cognitive meaning by using it with a particular cogitative meaning. This is true of implicatures generally. When implicatures become conventional, so does the indirection. When metaphors die and become idioms, in contrast, the indirection is lost. When we use "He kicked the bucket" with its idiomatic meaning, we mean "He died" directly. We are not using

[2] See Davis (1992a, 1992b) and my *Meaning, Expression, and Thought* (Ch. 1, §3.6, and §8.3) for explanations and references to the literature. The distinction was first noticed by Grice (1969: 148–150) and Schiffer (1972: 2–3, 110–111).

the sentence to mean "He performed the action of kicking on the bucket" or anything like it. Hence we are not expressing the idea that he expired by expressing the idea that he performed the action of kicking on the pail. We can of course still hear the literal meaning of the sentence as we use it, and this gives the idiom its color. But we are not using the sentence with its literal meaning at all. Second-order semantic conventions become first order, and generalized implicatures turn into senses, when speakers begin directly meaning, in the cogitative sense, what they formerly meant indirectly, in the cognitive sense.

Implicature conventions also differ from first-order semantic conventions in being *inessential to the language*. A change in the meaning of any English word constitutes a change in the English language. If "brown" came to mean "blue," an English word would have changed its meaning, and as a consequence English would have changed slightly. More relevantly, if the contrastive meaning of "but" were lost, and the word became completely interchangeable with "and," there would be a change in English. The same goes for idioms: if "kicked the bucket" no longer meant "died," English would be a little easier for foreigners to master. But if "Some S are P" lost its quantity implicature, and no longer implicated not all S are P, that change would not count as a change in English itself. It would be a change only in the *use* of English. Similarly, someone using English words with none of their conventional senses is not speaking English. But failure to use any implicature conventions does not result in not speaking English (cf. Sterelny 1982: 190).

We should not conclude, as Sadock does, that because implicature practices are inessential to the language, they must be nonconventional.

It is the grammar of a language that is the repository of the conventional aspects of language use. The nonconventional, while surely of interest to students of language, does not need to be, and indeed should not be, mentioned in the description of the language, which is the conventional sign system. Rather, the account of conversational implicature is best understood as a partial description of the USERS of the language, and hence truly deserves the name "pragmatics." (Sadock 1978: 367)

The term "grammar" has been used expansively in the last few decades, but on no standard usage would the grammar of English include the conversational implicature conventions we have described. The grammar of a language cannot therefore be the repository of *all* the conventional aspects of language use. First-order semantic conventions would be included, but not the second-order ones. Sadock is not alone in taking grammar to be the repository of all linguistic conventions.

Semantics, as a component part of grammar, is the specification of the rule-governed contribution that sentences of the language make to utterance interpretation, and pragmatics is the set of general language-independent principles which complete the picture, to determine how utterances are understood. (Kempson 1986: 89)

The rules governing tautology implicatures are not parts of the grammar, nor are they language independent.[3] Yet knowledge of these rules contributes substantially to utterance interpretation. First-order semantic rules are not the only semantic rules.

Lest it be considered suspiciously ad hoc to suggest that conversational implicature conventions are unique in being "nongrammatical," observe that *word formation rules* and *naming conventions* provide other examples.[4] "Sue" is a girl's name in English-speaking countries. It is conventionally given to girls rather than boys. That does not make "Sue is a man" ungrammatical in any way. And the sudden popularity of "Sue" as a boy's name would not constitute a change in the English language. Similarly, if "pepperfish" existed in English, we would expect it to denote a fish somehow associated with pepper. But if curiously it came to denote a yellow insect, there would be no infraction of grammar (cf. Nunberg 1981: 203). Note that naming conventions are secondary in an entirely different way than implicature conventions are. Naming conventions are rules for giving meanings to new words or new meanings to old words, and thus concern the creation or modification of first-

---

[3] Compare and contrast Wierzbicka (1991: §10.8).
[4] See Lehrer (1974, 1992a, 1992b) and Lehrer and Kittay (1992) for fascinating discussions of these conventions.

order semantic rules. They do not assign one content to an expression by virtue of its having another primary content, as implicature conventions do.

Morgan provided other examples of "conventions of use" that are not "conventions of language" to make plausible his claim that "an expression can be conventionalized and yet keep its literal meaning," an idea he found counterintuitive (1978: 250). He cited the Cebu custom of saying "Good morning" where we knock on a door, the Eskimo custom of opening conversations with "You are obviously doing such and such," and our custom of greeting someone by saying "How are you?" I call these practices *speech-act rituals*. Consider the ways we identify ourselves on the telephone. We say "This is N" or "N speaking" or even "N here." We could just as well answer by saying "You have reached N," "Here is N," "N is speaking," or "N this is," yet we don't. We say "Hello, my name is N" when we call someone we do not know, but not when we answer an unknown caller. We say "N speaking" when answering, though not when calling. We use "You have reached N" when recording a message on an answering machine, but not when answering a call in person. It would not be in any way ungrammatical to answer the phone "Hello, my name is N"; it is nevertheless not the appropriate way to answer a telephone. Speech-act rituals are like implicature conventions in that they involve the conventional use of a sentence with its literal meaning to say something and perform a further act. But the further act is not a "semantic act" – not the act of meaning or implying something. Conventions governing such acts are therefore not semantic conventions. Speech-act rituals, furthermore, are inessential to the language. The English language would not change if we began answering the phone "You have reached N" or used "N here" on our answering machines.

We see in section 6.3 that some semantic conventions governing "indirect speech acts" are "grammatical" and others are "nongrammatical." The latter constitute a class of second-order semantic rules distinct from implicature conventions.

The fact that implicature conventions are second order leads to the prediction that second language learners will at least sometimes be appreciably slower to master implicature conventions than the basic lexical conventions and composition rules, just as they are generally slower to acquire idioms. Specifically, native speakers of one language should be slower to learn the implicature conventions of another when the implicature conventions of the two languages are different. Thus French speakers should be slower to learn the tautology implicatures of English, but not the quantity implicatures. The tautology implicatures of the two languages differ, but the quantity implicatures are the same. Grice's theory makes rather different predictions. Given calculability, interlinguistic differences in implicatures should not exist, and could never be detected if they did.

6.2 IDIOMS

As noted, the conventions that generate sentence implicatures are much like the conventions that generate idioms. "Kicked the bucket" means "died" because speakers conventionally use the expression with that meaning. The idiomatic meaning is presumably related in some way to the meanings of the component words and would not have existed if those meanings had been sufficiently different. But the idiomatic meaning is not determined compositionally by the meanings of the component words. Hence idioms have to be learned expression by expression. Similarly, what a sentence implicates is not determined compositionally by the meanings of its component words. The implicature conventions that generate sentence implicatures have to be learned form by form. We do not have to learn separately that "Some students are philatelists" implicates "Not all students are philatelists," but we must learn that sentences of the form "Some S are P" implicate "Not all S are P."

Sentence implicatures also resemble idioms in being dependent in *some* way on the literal meanings of the sentences. Thus neither conventions are as arbitrary, generally, as the lexical rules of a language. But the nature of the dependence on literal meaning is different. "Born with a silver spoon in one's mouth" came to mean "born into a wealthy family" in part because of what "silver spoon" meant. If "silver spoon" had meant "wooden spoon," "born with a silver spoon in one's mouth" would never have acquired its idiomatic meaning. Whereas the dependence of idiomatic meaning on literal meaning is diachronic, the dependence of implicature on literal meaning is synchronic. "Some animals fly" implicates that not all animals fly because of its current literal meaning. If that changed, the implicature would go with it. But the idiomatic meaning of "kicked the bucket" does not depend on its current meaning. Assuming that the idiom began life as a metaphor, then its current idiomatic meaning resulted from what it literally meant in the past. Even though the literal meaning has not changed, its current literal meaning does not contribute to its idiomatic meaning. Metaphors are more like sentence implicatures in this respect than idioms are.

The *"nondetachability"* of sentence implicatures also distinguishes them from idioms.[5] Even though "struck the bucket with a foot" and "booted the pail" are synonymous with "kicked the bucket," they do not have anything like the idiomatic meaning of the third. But "Some animals move through the air on wings" has the same implicature as "Some animals fly." The relevant rule implies that any sentence meaning "Some animals fly" implicates that not all do. There may be exceptions to nondetachability even for sentence implicatures. We noted earlier, for example, that "John could have solved the problem" implies that John did not solve it, whereas "John was able to solve the problem" implies that John did solve it. Even clearer cases of detachment can be found interlinguistically. Wierzbicka's observation that the French translation of "War is war" does not have the same implicature is a case in point. It remains true that detachability is uncommon with implicatures, common with idioms.

Diachronically, it is plausible that implicature conventions devel-

---

[5] Grice (1975: 39; 1978: 43). As Grice and others have recognized, nondetachability fails for manner implicatures, which are generated not by what is said but by the way it is said. But like figures of speech and relevance implicatures, manner implicatures are particularized rather than generalized (see sections 5.7–5.9). That is, the term "manner implicature" classifies speaker implicatures rather than sentence implicatures. So the detachability of manner implicatures does not count against the general rule that the sentence implicatures are nondetachable.

oped in the same way idiom conventions did.[6] "Kicked the bucket" started life as a metaphor, and thus an implicature. Someone used it as a metaphor to implicate that someone died. The metaphor caught on and became conventional. Eventually, the metaphor died with overuse, and "kicked the bucket" came to mean "died" directly. "Went to the bathroom" started life as a euphemism, as individuals implicated that subjects were excreting. The usage caught on and the euphemism eventually "died" and became an idiom. Individual words acquire new meanings by the same process of metaphorical extension and lexicalization: consider the senses of "kill," "foot," and so on. It is plausible that the use of "Some S are P" to implicate "Not all S are P" similarly started life as a nonce implicature that caught on and spread, becoming conventional. This has not, to my knowledge, been historically attested. But then again, I do not expect anyone to have looked given the dominance of the Gricean paradigm, which predicts that the implicature has no such history. Moreover, the origins may be obscured by the mists of time (see section 6.6).

Lycan objected that on my account, implicature conventions could never get off the ground. For I have rejected the Calculability Principle. If nonce implicatures cannot be calculated, he asked, how could they ever catch on? A similar question could of course be asked about nonce metaphors. If hearers cannot calculate them, how could they ever catch on and become idioms? The answer is that there are many ways of coming to believe implicatures exist without using the particular method of inference known as the Working-out Schema. The main point of section 4.6 was that to say the recognition of implicatures is an inferential process is not to say it involves the use of any specialized reasoning process. I have denied the latter, but not the former. Any method of reasoning that enables us to infer another

---

[6] Compare Sadock (1974: 97–98), Cole (1975: §viii), Morgan (1978: 250), Brown and Levinson (1978: 221, 265–267), Cowie, Mackin, and McCaig (1983: xii), Cruse (1986: 44), Anttila (1989: 38, 137–146), and Cowie (1992: 3168).

person's intentions could in principle be used to discover what another person is implicating.

Suppose S is the first person who ever used "Some S is P" to implicate "Not all S is P." Whether he had good reason to or not, S may decide this was a good thing to have done. As a result, S may do it again and again. Now suppose H heard S say, "Some S is P" on some occasion before others realized what S was implicating. The hypothesis might pop into H's head that S was implying "Not all S is P." As is customary with the method of hypothetical induction, there may be no explanation as to how or why that idea came to H. H can use hypothetical induction to infer that S was implying "Not all S is P" as long as H comes to believe this hypothesis explains some aspect of S's behavior. Perhaps H observed that S tended to use "some" and "only some" interchangeably, and had an unusual resistance to saying "Some S is P" when it is well known that all S are P. We might also suppose that H confirms her hypothesis by asking S whether or not he was implying that not all S are P. With it now mutually acknowledged that S had used "Some S is P" with a certain implicature, H might use it with the same implicature on another occasion. S may infer H's implicature by an argument from analogy with his own case. In similar fashion, the practice may spread from S and H to the whole language community.[7] How implicature conventions actually arose is of course an open question. To respond to Lycan's objection, I only need to show that it is realistically possible for implicature conventions to arise even if nonce implicatures are not calculable.

Another interesting empirical question that could not arise given the Gricean paradigm is why certain common implicatures became implicature conventions rather than idioms, whereas others became idioms rather than implicature conventions. Why

---

[7] In the early stages of an implicature practice, people might not yet have enough evidence as to what people are implying to count as *knowing* what speakers are implicating, or as *recognizing* their implicatures. For a practice to spread, it is enough for people to *believe* a useful precedent has been set. Thus it might be that no one could really claim to *know* others had implicated "Not all S are P" before it was conventional to implicate this.

hasn't "Some S are P" come to mean "Some but not all S are P," the way "kicked the bucket" has come to mean "died"? Some initially plausible explanations do not work for all cases. For example, the frequency with which the sentence form is used without its implicature and the importance of such uses would seem to play some role in explaining quantity, conjunction, and disjunction implicatures. The relative paucity of literal use without the now idiomatic meaning would seem to be involved in why "kicked the bucket" and "went to the bathroom" became idioms. But tautologies are not used very frequently without one of their now conventional implicatures, and the forms involved in certain apparent speech act idioms (section 6.3) are used frequently without performing the indirect speech act. Perhaps the answer lies in the fact that English already contains "Only some S are P," which explicitly means that some but not all S are P and contrasts with "Some S are P." Adequate and detailed explanations of why implicature conventions arose rather than idioms will require systematic historico- and sociolinguistic research. Given the adventitious nature of conventions, there may well be no general explanation that works in every case.

6.3 INDIRECT SPEECH-ACT CONVENTIONS

The term *indirect speech act* is standardly used to denote any illocutionary act performed by uttering a sentence whose mood is primarily associated with a different illocutionary force. When we ask someone to drive us home by saying, "Is it possible for you to drive me home?" we have performed such an act. By using an interrogative sentence, we have *literally* asked a question. But in doing so, we have also made a request, an act primarily associated with the imperative mood. In contrast to the cases discussed in sections 3.13 and 5.11, the indirect speech act here is not declarative, and so does not count as an implicature. Nevertheless, because conversational implicatures resemble indirect speech acts in being conveyed by performing a distinct speech act, we should expect the two phenomena to have similar explanations. Indeed, Griceans have assumed that indirect speech acts are also generated by, and calculable from, conversational principles.[8] This assumption is erroneous, for all the reasons discussed in the case of implicatures. The indirect speech acts of speakers are too dependent on intention, and those of sentences too dependent on convention.

We find the same evidence of conventionality with indirect speech acts that we find in the case of sentence implicature,[9] such as cross-linguistic variation. Brown and Levinson (1978: 133) note that "Why don't you bathe at all?" in Tzeltal would be a polite suggestion rather than a reproach; "Why shouldn't we go to Kangayam?" in Tamil would be the equivalent of "Let's go!" rather than a serious question. Sadock (1974: 93) noted that "Think whether you should open the door" functions as a request to open the door in Swedish, as does "Are you ready to open the door?" in Hebrew and "May you try to open the door" in Greenlandic. Wierzbicka (1985) offers many more examples:

To say, "Why don't you close the window?" in English would implicate a mild suggestion. The equivalent in Polish would generate quite a different implicature, along the lines of "I can't see any excuse for your failure to have closed the window long before this!" On the other hand, "Won't you close the window?," translated into Polish, is not likely to be heard as a directive at all, but as a real question meaning something like "It seems you're not going to close the window. That's strange; I wonder why?" The question implies surprise on the lack of action. (Fasold 1990: 174, citing Wierzbicka 1985)

---

[8] Searle (1975: 266), Gordon and Lakoff (1975: 83), Sadock (1978: 369), Brown and Levinson (1978), Posner (1980: 175 ff.), Levinson (1983: 165, 270–274), Leech (1983: 24–25), and Bach (1994b: 14).

[9] Sadock (1972; 1974: 88–95), Searle (1975: 269, 273–276), Cole (1975: §x), G. M. Green (1975), Morgan (1978), Kates (1980: 126), Nunberg (1981), Leech (1983: 26), Horn (1984: 29; 1989: 344), Wierzbicka (1985), Fasold (1990: 155–156). Bach and Harnish (1979: Ch. 9, esp. 190) argue against indirect speech-act conventions, but their arguments are based on definitions of "convention" that bear little relation to the ordinary sense in which the meanings of words and driving on the right are conventional. Nunberg (1981: 218) makes a similar move, relying on an inessential condition in Lewis's definition. Compare Gordon and Lakoff (1975: 85, fn. 3), who speculate that their "conversational postulates" are universals, and Brown and Levinson (1978: esp. 181, 143), who note the evidence but insist the "underlying principles" are universal, derivable from universal face assumptions and rationality.

Referring to the Gricean literature, Wierzbicka concludes that "studies in speech acts have suffered from an astonishing ethnocentrism" (1985: 145).[10]

Intralinguistically, we sometimes find sentences that do not seem to differ relevantly in meaning, only one of which is standardly used to perform a given indirect speech act. "Do you have the ability to drive me home?," "Do you have everything necessary to drive me home?," and "Can you really drive me home?" would not ordinarily be used as requests. A particular speaker could use the first as a request in special circumstances, if he wished to be sarcastic, perhaps, or were addressing someone decrepit. But such usage is not the norm. It is hard to imagine the second or third as a request under any circumstances. Similarly, questions normally used as requests when asked nonperformatively are seldom if ever requests when asked performatively. It is hard to imagine a native speaker requesting a ride by saying, "I hereby ask you whether it is possible for you to drive me home." And when the same question is put metalinguistically, it is uninterpretable as a request. I cannot ask for a ride by saying, "Is 'It is possible for you to drive me home' true?"

Finally, there are some patently arbitrary elements in our practices. For example, Searle (1975: 277) notes that I can offer to help (i) by either stating that or asking whether I can help; (ii) by asking whether you want me to help, but not by stating that you want me to help; or (iii) by stating that I want to help but not by asking whether I want to help. However, the second and third

---

[10] Brown and Levinson claim, "It is not through any failure of universal face assumptions or rationality that certain close equivalents of English expressions fail to operate in a general way in some other language. On the contrary, it is precisely these principles together with the nuances of the language's semantics that on a finer-grain analysis predict the failure of equivalence" (1978: 181). They had earlier said "the lack of a highly idiomatic translation of 'Can you do A?' in Tamil, with the force of a request, is an instance of this, which we examine as an example in another context on pp. 180–1" (1978: 144). But unless I missed it, Brown and Levinson nowhere showed that the Tamil equivalent of "Can you do A?" could not be used as a request because of the nuances of that equivalent's semantics.

practices could perfectly well be reversed. Searle holds that the chief motivation for indirect speech acts is politeness. But it would be just as polite, if not more polite, for me to offer help by asking, "Do I want to help you?" as by stating "I want to help." And by flouting the interrogative analogue of the Maxim of Quality, I would be signaling indirection. The reversed practice sounds alien to our ears, but that is to be expected given that current practices are conventional. Indeed, the reversed practices sound just the way idioms of another language do, or the way that mistakes sound when made by foreigners learning our language and erroneously transferring features of their native tongue.

Some forms appear to have become idioms.[11] "Can you drive me home?" seems to be a direct request. We do not hear the speaker as asking a question about what the audience can do, and we do not infer that a request has been made from the fact that such a question was asked. Furthermore, the "Can you?" form has different distributional possibilities when used as a request. For example, the word "please," expressing a polite request, typically occurs in imperative sentences before the verb, as in "Please pass the salt." But it can also occur before the verb in certain interrogative sentences that are standardly used to make requests, as in "Can you please pass the salt?" It cannot occur in otherwise similar interrogatives: "Do you have the ability to please pass the salt?" is unacceptable. Furthermore, the ability to use "Can you?" to make a request is essential to the language. If "Can you VP?" could no longer be used conventionally to make a request, and thus became like "Do you have the ability to VP?," that would count as a change in English. There is a convention whereby one can request an action bearing a salient relation to the fact that p by stating that

---

[11] Sadock (1972; 1974: chs. 4–6, esp. 98) and Cole (1975). Compare and contrast Searle (1975: 274) and Brown and Levinson (1978: 274). Cole (1975: 274–276) presented evidence that the lexicalization of speech-act idioms is still in process. Note that nothing I have said commits me to the false view that speech-act idioms are synonymous with the performative that can be used to perform the same act, *pace* Levinson (1983: 268). Moreover, nothing requires me to hold that "speech-act idioms" are in every respect like the most commonly discussed idioms.

p, as when I ask you to get off my foot by saying "You are standing on my foot." The abandonment of this practice would count as a change in the use of English, but not a change in English itself. The same goes, I think, for the convention whereby "Is it possible for you to do A?" is used to request that you do A.[12]

Implicature conventions do not generate the same sort of distributional differences. There is a similar phenomenon with implicature, but it is not narrowly grammatical. For example, Horn (1989: 388) has noted that "metalinguistic negation" can be used to cancel implicatures, but only when they are conventionalized. Thus (1)(a) would be appropriate, but not (1)(b).

(1) (a) I didn't eat *some* of the cookies, I ate *all* of them.
   (b) I didn't *travel* to France, I *drove* there.

Similarly, (2)(a) and (2)(b) are acceptable, but not (2)(c).

(2) (a) I didn't break *a* finger, I broke *two*.
   (b) I didn't break *a* finger, I broke *his*.
   (c) I didn't break *a* finger, I broke *mine*.

Finally, implicature conventions determine the appropriateness of *too*. Thus (3)(b) unlike (3)(a) would be markedly inappropriate (unless the food was supposed to be uncooked).

(3) (a) The restaurant wasn't air conditioned, the waiters weren't polite, and the food was warm too.
   (b) The restaurant wasn't air conditioned, the waiters weren't polite, and the food was cooked too.

Note that the use of "too" in (3)(b) is inappropriate even though "The food was cooked" could on occasion be used derogatorily to imply that the food was not cooked well. None of these unacceptable sentences, however, is ungrammatical.

---

[12] As an argument that "Can you VP?" is not an idiom, Levinson (1983: 269) notes that the hearer can appropriately respond "Yes I can," suggesting that the utterance is also heard and taken as a request. But another interpretation is that the answer is idiomatic too, an interpretation confirmed by noting that "I think so," "Probably," "If I try real hard," and so on, would indicate the hearer had either misinterpreted the original utterance or was being facetious.

One distributional difference associated with what is usually thought to be a generalized implicature can be seen in (4).

(4) (a) John skillfully was able to solve the problem.
      (b) John skillfully could have solved the problem.

However, the fact that (4)(a) is grammatical, unlike (4)(b), suggests that the relevant interpretation of "was able to" is actually an idiomatic sense rather than a generalized implicature.

Of course, the fact that the Gricean theory of indirect speech acts must treat "Can you VP?" the same as "Is it possible for you to VP?" is a separate problem for the theory, related to its inability to differentiate idioms from implicatures (section 2.4; cf. Sadock 1974: 90 ff.). The former is a speech-act idiom, the latter a sentence form conventionally used with indirect force. The differentiation problem for Gricean theory is compounded because there is also a convention whereby sentences of one mood are used to perform related speech acts associated with different moods, where the identity of the related speech act is determined by relational properties of the sentence's meaning rather than its content or structure.[13] This practice is similar to the relevance implicature conventions discussed in section 5.8. For example, we commonly urge or order someone to do A (or hint that they should) by using a declarative sentence to describe a problem that could be solved by doing A. I might urge Kathy to close the window by saying, "It is cold in here." Although the general practice is conventional, it is not conventional for speakers to use "It is cold in here" to urge Kathy to close the window. Consequently the sentence itself cannot be characterized as an indirect request, or as having the force of an imperative. Similarly, it is conventional to implicate requested information by making a statement closely related by implication. Bob may employ this convention in using "There is a station around the corner" to inform Ann that she can get gasoline there. But the sentence he used does not itself implicate that Ann can get gasoline there. The three grades of conventional involvement

---

[13] Lycan (1984: 174–186) explores the similarities and differences among these three types of indirect speech acts at length.

found in implicatures thus have exact parallels in the three types of indirect speech acts.

6.4 THE ROLE OF CONVERSATIONAL PRINCIPLES

Morgan (1978) anticipated my point that implicature and indirect speech-act practices are conventional. But he found the idea paradoxical and counterintuitive. For he held with the Gricean that the implicatures and indirect speech acts are calculable. That is, given the context and what the speaker said, Morgan believed we could infer that the speaker performed the additional speech act using Grice's maxims, which are specifications of general psychosocial principles. But this makes the connection between what is said and what is implicated natural and therefore nonarbitrary, when arbitrariness is the hallmark of conventions.[14] Morgan thought the resolution of this paradox of claiming that implicature practices are both natural and conventional lay in Searle's (1975: 274) observation that there are "conventions of usage" which are not "conventions of language." Morgan also suggested that conventional implicatures are "short circuited": calculable but not calculated. The existence of the convention, on his view, enables us to recognize the implicature without actually working it out from Grice's maxims.

It is true that implicature conventions are not "calculated" and are not "conventions of language," in the senses Morgan had in mind. But these observations do not resolve Morgan's paradox, which lay in his claim that implicature practices are both conventional and nonarbitrary. Implicature practices are conventional whether they are conventions of language or conventions of usage. They are nonarbitrary whether they are calculated or merely calculable.

I have argued at length that conversational implicatures, whether sentence implicatures or speaker implicatures, cannot be explained by or predicted from the Cooperative Principle, the

---

[14] Brown and Levinson (1978: 90–91, 99, 138, 147) also appear to claim both conventionality and calculability. Compare and contrast Nunberg (1981: 201–202).

Maxims of Quantity, Quality, Relation, and Manner, or similar conversational principles. It may still be felt that these rules must be related in some way to implicature. Indeed, I believe they are related both externally and internally.

Externally, the existence of conversational implicature conventions contributes to the observance of the Gricean Rules. In general, following implicature conventions is one way of contributing what is required by the accepted purpose of a conversation (see section 1.4). In particular, the specific quantity implicature conventions represent ways of being as informative as required, as do the tautology and conjunction implicature conventions. The relevance implicature convention represents one way of being relevant, and the irony convention represents one way of being truthful. (It is also, of course, a way of being untruthful.) More interestingly, I believe the irony convention is also in part a way of being informative. As Grice (1978: 53–54) noted, the ironic expression of a proposition also communicates a certain attitude that is not communicated by the nonironic expression of the proposition.[15]

On this view, the flouting of a maxim, as in irony, does not serve to generate the implicature in any way. It is partly an aid to understanding, providing a blatant cue that one of the implicature conventions is being employed.[16] Flouting also has entertainment value, making our utterances more interesting.[17] Thus flouting Grice's rules contributes to fulfillment of the Principle of Style.

Internally, a practice counts as a convention only if it is socially useful. The practice must contribute to a collective goal (or goals), which is its social function. The fact that the practice fulfills that

---

[15] Compare R. Lakoff (1977: 81), Brown and Levinson (1978: 268; 1987: 28), Sperber and Wilson (1981), and Nunberg (1981: 204).

[16] Compare Fasold (1990: 134), who seems to infer that "Contradictions and tautologies lend themselves very well to analysis by Grice's principles" from his observation that "Since tautologies are, taken literally, intrinsically uninformative, they will always infringe the quantity maxim, inducing people to look for an implicature that will save their faith in the cooperative principle." See also Brown and Levinson (1978: 218) who, as we noted in section 4.5, speak of "inviting" implicatures by violating the maxims; and Levinson (1983: 274).

[17] Compare R. Lakoff (1977: 100) and Sainsbury (1984: 427).

function sustains it over time. We have relied so far on the obvious fact that the function of implicature practices is to promote communication, the function of linguistic conventions in general. We may now add that we have a common interest not just in communication, but in *cooperative, efficient, polite, and stylish communication.* Because the Gricean principles represent rules for cooperative communication, they partly define the function of implicature practices. Politeness principles do the same, as do principles of efficiency and style. It is often regarded as more polite to implicate something rather than assert it, and implicature generally involves expressing "two ideas for the price of one." Figures of speech are tools of the stylist. *Any* shared value might be reflected in implicature conventions. I am sure that the mutual interests sustaining implicature conventions are much broader than the terms "cooperation," "efficiency," "politeness," and "style" are capable of capturing.[18] Implicature conventions can be sustained by a collective interest in cooperation even though individuals on occasion use the conventions to be uncooperative. Similarly, lexical conventions can be sustained by our interest in communication even though people occasionally exploit them for noncommunicative purposes, such as private diaries. And the use of interrogatives to make requests may be sustained in English-speaking cultures by a common interest in politeness even though interrogatives are often used to make highly impolite requests. Wierzbicka (1985: 172) offers, "Why don't you shut up?" as an example.

To the extent that norms for polite, cooperative, efficient communication vary from culture to culture, so should implicature conventions.[19] Thus Wierzbicka (1985) offered the "heavy restrictions on the use of the imperative in English and the wide range of use of interrogative forms in performing acts other than questions" as "striking linguistic reflexes" of the Anglo-Saxon cultural

---

[18] Wierzbicka (1985) cites a range of cross-cultural evidence suggesting that the common interests sustaining indirect speech-act conventions are much deeper than mere politeness. See also Davison (1975: 146–158, 181), Levinson (1983: 280), and Wierzbicka (1991, 1994).

[19] See R. Lakoff (1977: 92), Kasher (1982: 35–36), and Leech (1983: 32, 80).

tradition, one that "places special emphasis on the rights and on the autonomy of every individual, which abhors interference in other people's affairs," and so on. She observed that languages such as Polish, used by speakers with opposed cultural traditions, have different conventions involving imperatives and interrogatives. The fact that Wierzbicka is fighting ethnocentrism with cultural stereotypes does not diminish her point. A common interest need not be universally shared to sustain a common practice.

Keenan (1975) observed that the norms for cooperative behavior differ in other cultures:

The difference in implicatures that would be made among the Malagasy of Madagascar and what would be the case in Western culture was so great that Elinor Ochs Keenan (1975/1983) concluded that Grice's first submaxim of quantity, "Make your contribution as informative as is required" did not apply. As we know, if a Malagasy villager who had gone to the market and returned to the village was asked "What's new at the market?" he or she could respond "There were many people there" (Ochs Keenan 1975: 264–5). In a sense, the maxim can be seen as violated, since the answer gives no information (there are always many people at the market), and the questioner would really like to know what had gone on at the market. In another sense, if we understand Grice's term "required" to mean "what is required of a person during a conversation in this culture," it is possible to claim that the quantity maxim *is* being fulfilled. . . . The point for our purposes here is that no implicature is generated. (Fasold 1990: 173–74)[20]

Malagasy speakers treat information they alone possess as a prized commodity, and it is accepted that they will be reluctant to share it. They also set a higher epistemic standard when applying the Maxim of Quality:

There is a clear tendency to avoid making a specific commitment to some future event. Thus, if a member of household X asks a member of household Y when the turning of the ancestral bones is to take place, he will likely get an answer such as "I am not certain" or "In a bit" or "Around September," but no precise date will be specified even if such a date has been set. Individuals do not wish to commit themselves publicly

[20] Compare Horn (1984: 16–17).

to a precise date until they are absolutely certain the event will take place at that time. They may suffer tremendous loss of face if the event does not take place as specified. They will be guilty of premature or faulty judgment. Consequently, those outside the family are told details of time and place only at the last moment. (Keenan 1975: 259)

The higher standard of certainty required would also lead Malagasy speakers to make a weaker claim when we would think they were in a position to make a stronger one. For both reasons, we would not expect it to be conventional in Madagascar for sentences meaning "p or q" to be used to implicate "I do not know which," as in English-speaking countries.

The suggestion that Gricean explanations are "functional explanations" is not novel. It does not seem to have been appreciated, however, that if conversational principles merely provide functional explanations of implicature practices, then the other distinctive tenets of Gricean theory must be abandoned, such as calculability, the Generative Assumption, and Grice's Razor.[21] We should no more expect specific implicature practices to be derivable from a specification of their function than we can expect American rules of the road to be derivable from the function of those conventions. The existence of alternative ways of cooperatively communicating – even when cultural norms are fixed – makes such a derivation impossible, just as the existence of alternative ways of avoiding collisions makes it impossible to work out which side of the street people drive on from the fact that they all seek to avoid collisions. The "Principle of Cooperative Driving" ("Do what is required to avoid collisions and allow traffic to flow freely") does play some role in the explanation of why Americans drive on the right, but only an indirect role: because the practice of steering to the right enabled drivers to drive cooperatively when it arose, the practice persisted and became a convention; because it is a convention, American drivers have learned to steer to the right; because of this habit they automatically steer to the right and the convention perpetuates itself. Similarly, because certain implicature practices

---

[21] See Brown and Levinson (1978: 261), Leech (1983: Ch. 3), and Schiffrin (1994: 352–353).

enabled speakers to converse cooperatively in the past, the practices persisted and were transmitted to us.

Here is another analogy. The Principle of Natural Selection provides remarkable insight into why species have the characteristics they do. If traits have survival value in the organism's environmental niche, we can view them as being selected naturally. The interaction between the trait and the environment provided selective pressure favoring the trait. This does not mean that the species' possession of the trait can be deduced from the Principle of Natural Selection, even when supplemented by a description of the species' niche. For as far as evolutionary explanations go, the original appearance of the trait is a random event. At some point there had to be a viable genetic mutation, an unpredictable and uncommon occurrence. Similarly, implicatures may become conventional because they serve the purposes of cooperation, efficiency, politeness, and style. But their original appearance is adventitious with respect to principles of conversation. It depends on the intentions of speakers. That is, it depends on how speakers exercise their freedom of the will, which in turn depends, inter alia, on what thoughts occur to them, and what they believe and desire. That implicatures and communication in general serve many purposes that sometimes conflict provides a further element of unpredictability.

Leech drew a distinction between "absolute" and "motivated" conventionality:

There is the absolute conventionality of the rule, for example, that in English the word designating the male of the human species is pronounced /mæn/. This one has to learn as a bare fact when learning English (either as a native or as a foreign learner), and no motivation can be found for it. . . . There is, however, the MOTIVATED CONVENTIONALITY of a rule for which some motivation is evident, but which overdetermines the choice of linguistic behaviour which would be predictable from that motivation. For such cases, two kinds of statement are required: the first states the rule as a matter of convention, and the second states that given that this rule exists, it is reasonable, on extralinguistic grounds, that it does so. (Leech 1983: 25–26)[22]

---

[22] See also Brown and Levinson (1978: 64, 99, 203–204, 260–262).

There is *a* motivation for the rule specifying that /mæn/ means "man," namely, it enables us to express the idea of a man and communicate. But this motivation does not make it more reasonable to use /mæn/ for that purpose than many other speech sounds. The fact that we are interested in efficient communication, coupled with the fact that we frequently wish to express the idea of a man, makes it much more reasonable to use a short, easily produced sound rather than a monstrous tongue twister for that purposes. So even lexical conventions are "motivated" to some extent.

Now consider a range of possible implicatures for "I lost an N."

(5) (a) I lost an N.
     (b) I lost my N.
     (c) I lost someone else's N.
     (d) Nothing.
     (e) I lost a red N.
     (f) I lost your N.
     (g) I have Alzheimer's disease.
     (h) I have black hair.

The actual implicature, of course, is "I lost *my* N." As noted earlier, we could just as well have used (5)(a) to implicate "I lost *someone else's* N," or nothing at all. All three rules are better motivated than many alternatives given the meaning of "I lost an N" and our interest in cooperative, polite, stylish, and efficient communication. Although we could conceivably use (5)(a) to implicate "I have Alzheimer's disease," this thought is not closely enough related to the thought expressed by (5)(a) in the vast majority of circumstances in which (5)(a) is used. "I have black hair" is almost completely unrelated in nearly every context. Similarly, although we could use (5)(a) to implicate "I lost *a red* N," the existence of such a convention would also severely restrict the contexts in which we could use (5)(a) to communicate with complete truthfulness. And although we could use (5)(a) to implicate "I lost *your* N," the impoliteness of using (5)(a) to implicate this thought would also restrict the usefulness of (5)(a).

Lexical and grammatical conventions are less "motivated" than implicature conventions because politeness, style, and cooperation do not discriminate among alternatives. Our desire for these ends provides no reason at all to use *man* rather than *homme* to mean "man," or to use *Adj* + *Noun* rather than *Noun* + *Adj* to mean "Noun that is Adj." Lexical and grammatical conventions are not completely unmotivated because some are more efficient than others. We will surely never find a language in which "Mpoiutleylteypokmpoijpy" means "is." But for every first-order semantic convention, hundreds and thousands of alternatives are equally efficient, and many more are efficient enough so that the advantages of following a convention outweigh possible gains in efficiency. Hence "social pressures" have more influence on second-order semantic conventions than first order. The reason is that second-order conventions assign implications to expressions that already have meanings. The pairing of an implication with one meaning rather than another may make a difference in politeness, style, cooperation, and efficiency (cf. section 6.5).

In none of the cases examined do the "motivations" take the form of *conclusive reasons* for the conventional practice, or even reasons sufficient to make it more reasonable than any alternative. The arbitrariness of conventions makes this impossible. We cannot therefore go along with Leech in his ensuing remarks:

> One case of such motivated conventionality is the following:
>
> [1] Good luck! = "I wish you good luck"
> [2] Bad luck! = "I regret your bad luck"
>
> The fact that [1] cannot mean "I regret your good luck" and [2] cannot mean "I wish you bad luck" follows from the PP, the principle which (as it applies to language) means that people on the whole prefer to express polite rather than impolite beliefs. (Leech 1983: 26)

Nothing of the sort *follows* from the Politeness Principle. The most that would follow is that *if* "Good luck!" were used to wish someone bad luck, then it would be used only in those comparatively uncommon cases in which either (i) the speaker wished to be impolite, or (ii) the speaker wished to be ironical.

The Politeness Principle may provide some insight into why English has such brief idioms as [1] or [2] and not a range of others we could think of. For as the Politeness Principle predicts, we express a desire for others to prosper and express regret on their misfortune more often than we express a desire for others to do poorly or express regret on their success. Hence the drive for efficiency would provide more pressure to have short locutions expressing the former sentiments. But this does not make the connection between [1] and [2] and their meanings nonarbitrary. The explanatory insight provided by the Politeness Principle is quite limited. We cannot even deduce that English would not have such idiomatic exclamations if their meanings were not polite. I can think of a number of extremely impolite idioms, such as *Kiss off!*

The common interest in efficiency could similarly help explain why horse breeders have more names for horses than dog breeders, without removing the arbitrariness of the particular word-meaning pairings found in the breeders' lexicons (and without endorsing the Sapir-Whorf hypothesis of linguistic determinism). It could also help explain observations such as Wierzbicka's (1995), concerning how Australian English's distinctive set of interjections (e.g., *G'day, mate!*), abbreviations (*maggies*), names (*Richo*), and swear words (*bugger*) are a reflection of characteristic Australian attitudes and values. Leech (1983: 25) makes the same point, citing the arbitrariness of grammatical rules despite the fact that pragmatic explanations can sometimes be given for why languages have the grammatical rules they do. As an example, he offers an efficiency explanation for the rule common to many languages whereby the subject of an imperative sentence can be deleted when it is *you*. As Nunberg put it, "there is a difference between being able to assign some rationale to a usage and explaining it pragmatically; the first, but not the second, is consistent with the usage's being conventional" (1981: 202). My point is that sentence implicatures are conventional and therefore cannot be "explained pragmatically."

Leech suggested that the Principle of Politeness complements the Gricean maxims, by enabling us to derive implicatures which violate the maxims. We observed earlier that without some meta-principles telling us when politeness principles apply and when cooperation principles apply, nothing can really be "derived" from a theory containing both sets of principles. But let us look at a sample "explanation." Brown and Levinson observe that whereas

"John is not an enemy" implicates "John is not a friend" in accordance with the Maxim of Quantity, "John is not a friend" does not similarly implicate "John is not an enemy." On the contrary, "John is not a friend" implicates that John *is* an enemy. The standard question is, why should the maxim "apply" in the one case but not in the other? Brown and Levinson attribute the difference to the Principle of Politeness:

Our explanation is that in implicating that someone is an enemy, or is evil or immoral, or has told a lie, one is performing an FTA [Face Threatening Act], namely criticizing. In saying that someone is *not* an enemy, immoral, evil, etc., one is not criticizing and not performing an FTA. There is a good social motive (avoiding responsibility, etc.) for saying much less than you mean when criticizing; this being mutual knowledge, the utterance "John's not a friend" can easily be used to implicate that he's not an enemy, whereas if you wanted to say that John is a friend, there would be no good motive for not saying it directly. Therefore, if you say that he's not an enemy, he's probably not a friend.

Apparent exceptions in fact support our argument. In just those circumstances where the fact that John is my friend could endanger my or your face (e.g., John has just been arrested as a Commie spy), if I say "John is not an enemy of mine" I could implicate that he *is* a friend. (Brown and Levinson 1978: 269)

They add that "The same asymmetry in implicature on scalar predicates holds for some Tamil examples, providing support for our interpretation of the phenomenon" (Brown and Levinson 1978: 309, fn. 92).

Brown and Levinson make an important observation, I believe. The conventions we have enable us to be polite, more polite than we would be using some alternative conventions. Our collective interest in politeness thus helps sustain our conventions. But Brown and Levinson's observation does not enable us to derive our implicature conventions from the Principle of Politeness, nor to explain why the conventions arose in the first place. First, nothing in the conversational principles we have looked at enables us to resolve the clash between politeness and informativeness. That is, the principles of Quantity and Politeness provide no basis for predicting that speakers will commonly be willing to sacrifice informativeness for politeness. Second, in other cases we commonly make the reverse sacrifice. If Brown and Levinson's explanation were valid, we should expect "Some of your work is acceptable" to implicate "All your work is acceptable" rather than its negation. Implicating that not all of your work is acceptable is an FTA, whereas implicating its contrary would not be. Third, Brown and Levinson's reasoning could just as well be used to derive opposite implicatures in the case at hand:

In saying that someone is *"neutral"* – that is, neither a friend nor an enemy, one is not criticizing and not performing an FTA. So if you wanted to say that John is neutral, there would be no good motive for not saying it directly. Therefore if you say that he's not an enemy, he's probably not neutral either, which means that he is a friend!

Furthermore, Brown and Levinson's reasoning would equally well lead us to predict that "John is not a friend" implicates that John is neutral.

While it may be less impolite to implicate that John is an enemy than to say it baldly, implicating it is still an FTA. Hence there is a good social motive to avoid implicating that people are our enemies. Therefore if you say that John's not a friend, he's probably neutral.[23]

Brown and Levinson set out to show that from "our two 'face wants,' repeated application of rational means–ends reasoning will bring us down to the choice of linguistic and kinesic detail, to the minutiae of message construction" (1978: 288). They set themselves an unattainable goal.

The fact that the demands of cooperation, politeness, style, and efficiency often clash presents no problem for the claim that implicature conventions are sustained by their contribution to these collective goals. Nor is the fact that there is no generally accepted method of prioritizing these demands for all occasions.

---

[23] It might be objected that "neutral" does not conventionally mean "neither friend nor foe," which is not lexicalized (cf. Brown and Levinson 1978: 270). But it is hard to see why these facts are relevant. Furthermore, we find the same implicature patterns with the conventional triad "allied," "enemy," and "neutral" said of countries.

When people wish to sacrifice communicative efficiency for politeness, they will use implicature conventions that promote politeness more than efficiency. When their preferences are reversed – perhaps the next minute – they will use other conventions, such as sarcasm. Brown and Levinson noted that indirect speech-act conventions "encode" compromises between goals:

> In this strategy a speaker is faced with opposing tensions: the desire to give H an "out" by being indirect, and the desire to go on record. In this case it is solved by the compromise of conventional indirectness, the use of phrases and sentences that have contextually unambiguous meanings (by virtue of conventionalization) which are different from their literal meanings. In this way the utterance goes on record, and the speaker indicates his desire to have gone off record (to have conveyed the same thing indirectly). Conventional indirectness *encodes* the class of wants, and so partially achieves them both. Note that there are degrees of conventionalization, and so degrees of compromise in one direction (off-recordness) or the other (on-recordness). (Brown and Levinson 1978: 137)

Perspicuity favors going on record; politeness often favors indirectness. When we ask someone for a ride by saying, "Is it possible for you to drive me home," we have partially satisfied both goals to a certain extent. That particular compromise often seems appropriate to speakers of English, so they perpetuate the convention. The common interest in perspicuity and politeness may sustain the convention in this way even though there is no way to deduce from the Maxim of Manner and Principle of Politeness that the encoded compromise is the correct balance for that situation, and even though speakers do not always believe it is.

6.5 THE PRINCIPLE OF ANTECEDENT RELATION

Although not calculable, conversational implicature conventions are distinctive in being significantly less arbitrary than the lexical and compositional rules of a language. Judging from all the conversational implicature conventions we have examined, there is always some antecedent relation between the literal sense of the implicating sentence and the proposition implicated, which is perceived by members of the language community and makes it "fitting," "appropriate," or "intelligible" for them to use the sentence to implicate the proposition. In the case of quantity implicatures, the implicated proposition is the denial of a stronger proposition. In the case of conjunction implicatures, the implicated propositions entail the conjunction. In the case of relevance implicatures, the implicated proposition is contextually implied by the expressed proposition. In the case of irony, the implicated proposition entails the denial of the expressed proposition. In the case of metaphors, there is a perceived similarity between the propositions. In the case of tautologies, both propositions are about the same subject and state facts taken to be well known and immutable. And so on. The same principle holds for indirect speech acts generally. When we make a request indirectly, we commonly do so by asserting or questioning what Searle (1975) called the "felicity conditions" of the request: "preparatory conditions" (Can H grant the request? Would H be willing to?), "sincerity conditions" (Does S want what he is requesting?), and "propositional conditions" (Will H do A?).[24]

These relations are "antecedent" in the sense that they existed before the conventional connection was established, indeed, before the sentence was ever used with that implication. Even though "nature" does not *give* the sentence its implicature, speakers must find it "natural" to use the sentence with that implicature. I know of no example in which a sentence implicates a proposition totally unrelated to the sense of the sentence. It would be most surprising to find "Grass is green" implicating "Saturn has rings." I call this vague empirical generalization the *Principle of Antecedent Relation.* The satisfaction of Grice's Calculability Assumption would be sufficient for satisfaction of the Principle of Antecedent Relation, but it is far from necessary. The latter is compatible with a significant degree of arbitrariness; the former is not.

If it is true, as seems plausible, that idioms started life as conversational implicatures, gradually becoming conventional, then we should expect the Principle of Antecedent Relation to hold for idioms too (cf. Sadock 1974: 98). This is certainly true for dead

---

[24] See also Sadock (1974: 98), Gordon and Lakoff (1975: 86), Brown and Levinson (1978: 137–147), Levinson (1983: 270–273), and Fasold (1990: 151–157).

metaphors ("fork in the road") and euphemisms ("went to the bathroom"). It also holds for those indirect speech-act forms that appear to be idioms ("Can you VP?"). The principle is further confirmed by the fact that the clearest cases of semantic ambiguity are those in which the two senses of a lexical item are "totally unrelated." Thus there is no plausibility in claiming that "John went to the bank" is univocal, with the other interpretations being implicatures.

I believe part of the explanation for the Principle of Antecedent Relation lies in (i) the fact that the function of implicature conventions and indirect speech acts generally is not just communication, but cooperative, efficient, polite, and stylish communication, coupled with (ii) the fact that implicature conventions are second-order semantic conventions, assigning implicatures not to simple sound or letter sequences, but to such sequences together with senses. Because there are more constraints on these practices, less variation is to be expected. Some will be more "natural" (i.e., fitting) than others, having a better "rationale" (Nunberg) and "motivation" (Leech). For example, the Maxim of Relation says to make one's contribution relevant to the accepted purpose of the conversation. When a sentence Σ expressing proposition E implicates I, speakers commonly use Σ to convey both E and I. If they are following the Maxim of Relation, both E and I must be relevant to the accepted purpose of the conversation. In order for this to hold for a wide variety of contexts, E and I must be related to each other in content. It is possible to imagine a context in which a speaker might say "Grass is green" and thereby implicate that Saturn has rings. This might be done, for example, among a group with the strange view that the colors of terrestrial objects were indications of heavenly phenomena. But to my knowledge, there has never been such a context. In my household, we could perfectly well use "It's Friday" to implicate "We're having pizza" because we typically have pizza on Friday. But even in my household, the second proposition is not relevant to the purposes of most conversations in which the first is. In the broader speech community, the two propositions are even less closely related. So it is unlikely that our practice would spread and become conventional. Note that whereas Grice's Maxim of Relation is concerned with the relationship between the speaker's contributions and the purpose of the conversation, the Principle of Antecedent Relation is concerned with the relationship between the literal sense of the implicating sentence and the implicated proposition.

I believe another part of the explanation for the Principle of Antecedent Relation lies in the fact that conversational implicature conventions are just that, conventions governing conversational implicatures. On my view, S means or implies I by uttering Σ only if S utters Σ with the intention of providing an indication that he believes I, where an indication is a natural sign (Davis 1992a). Because intention implies expectation, S must have some expectation that uttering Σ will provide an indication that he believes I. Unless S is psychotic, S will have such an expectation only if S perceives some connection in the context of utterance between I and the proposition E literally expressed by Σ. If S's usage is understood, and catches on, then other people must also see some connection between the two propositions, and do so in many contexts. Unless there is mass delusion, that perception must be accurate.

Still another part of the explanation, I believe, is that a conversational implicature is likely to become conventional only if speakers and hearers are liable to think the implicated proposition I as a result of thinking the proposition expressed by the implicating sentence. This means that the two propositions must be *associated* to some extent in the traditional psychological sense.

6.6 THE UNIVERSALITY OF IMPLICATURE CONVENTIONS

Implicature conventions are typically *interlinguistic*. Quantity implicatures, irony, and conjunction implicatures, for example, are common to many languages. In most languages, linguists report, the form meaning "Some S are P" is conventionally used to implicate that not all S are P (see Horn 1989). The fact that implicature practices are common to many languages is commonly cited as evidence that they are natural in some way rather than conventional.

Adler's [1987] proposed view of tropes as a matter of convention or social practice . . . is not explanatory: Why the same tropes in culture after culture? Why not a trope based on permutation of subject and object, or of the referents of "I" and "you"? (Sperber and Wilson 1987: 751)[25]

The fact that we have certain tropes and not others equally conceivable is to be expected on the conventionality thesis, given that conventions are fundamentally arbitrary. But the near universality of certain practices is surprising on the conventionality thesis, and does require explanation. Why is it that the word meaning "some" implicates "not all" in so many languages when no two of the languages use the same word to mean "some"?

Three things should be noted before attempting an explanation. First, some implicature conventions are unique to particular languages. Thus different languages have different tautology implicatures. Second, many uncontroversially conventional linguistic practices are common to many languages, and some are nearly universal. The most obvious are certain punctuation conventions. In every language I know of, "." is used to end indicative sentences, "?" interrogative sentences, and "!" imperative sentences. In speech, the corresponding intonation conventions are just as widespread. Stress has a similar function in many languages, if not all. In the area of grammar, Leech (1983: 25) noted that "in many languages it is possible (and in fact usual) to delete the subject of an imperative sentence: (You) come here!" On the basis of an extensive and representative sample of the world's languages, Greenberg concluded, "All languages have pronominal categories involving at least three persons and two numbers" (Hewitt 1994: 1501). Lexically, I believe all modern written languages use arabic numerals, and people around the world generally use the same names for people. Cruse (1986: 43) observed that "a high proportion of dead metaphors have similar (although not often identical) dead metaphor equivalents" in other languages. He cited *Ne pas réveiller le chat* [literally, the cat] *qui dort* as having the idiomatic meaning of "Let sleeping dogs lie."

---

[25] See also Brown and Levinson (1978: 60, 90–91, 203–204, 232, 288) and Levinson (1983: 270).

Third, the fact that lexical conventions tend to be unique to particular languages also requires explanation. Why should every language have a different word for dogs?

Language differentiation is typically explained in terms of the isolation of different parts of a parent language community, resulting in the separate evolution of conventions in the offspring. The fact that conventional regularities need not be followed 100 percent of the time allows conventions to evolve slowly over time. Commonalities between two languages are sometimes attributed to "borrowing," more often to inheritance from a common ancestor. Historico-comparative linguists have a rule that "If two or more languages share a feature which is unlikely to have occurred spontaneously in each of them, then this feature must have arisen once only, when these languages were one and the same" (Anttila 1989: 302). We might accordingly speculate that the most universal implicature conventions arose in the original language community and were sustained by their effectiveness even as the first-order semantic conventions slowly evolved into the thousands of languages found in the world today. The fact that implicature conventions are second order and promote the universal goal of cooperative, efficient, polite, and stylish communication would thus help explain why implicature conventions are common to different language communities. The factors leading to differentiation of lexical conventions would not necessarily affect them because implicature conventions can attach to the meanings expressed rather than the particular words expressing them, and the same meanings are often expressed widely.

Linguists have offered genetic explanations for other linguistic universals. For example, Payne (1994) presents data from Greenberg suggesting that nearly all languages with V-final word order also have tense-aspect auxiliaries following the main verb rather than preceding it. Payne comments,

[T]he most significant type of explanation can be found at a diachronic level: Greenbergian universals tend to hold because language categories develop historically in fixed patterns: for example, the category of adposition (preposition or postposition) can develop from the category of verb by a process of grammaticalization (the English preposition *regarding* is an example of this). It is natural, therefore, that the order of verb and object noun should coincide with the order of adposition and noun. (Payne 1994: 4848)

Derivation from psychosocial principles is not the only way to explain linguistic universals.

The hypothesis that common implicature conventions were inherited from a common ancestor would seem testable in the hands of a good linguist. Analogies aside, it is speculation on my part. The explanation has to be more plausible than the Gricean explanation, if only because the view that implicatures are derivable from general psychosocial principles is completely untenable. Grice thought the determinacy of implicatures obviated the need for historical research:

It might be objected that whether one sense of a word is to be regarded as derivative from another sense of that word should be treated as a question about the history of the language to which the word belongs. This may be so in general (though in many cases it is obvious, without historical research, that one sense must be secondary to another), but if I am right in thinking that conversational principles would not allow the word *or* to be used in normal circumstances without at least an implicature of the existence of nontruth-functional grounds, then it is difficult to see that research could contribute any information about temporal priority in this case. (Grice 1978: 47)

Grice is assuming the strongest form of determinacy and calculability here, which, as we have seen, is falsified by the arbitrariness of implicature conventions. The Gricean explanation of common implicatures is also undermined by the existence of nonuniversal implicature conventions.

6.7 CONCLUSION

Grice's Cooperative Principle, the associated maxims, and other conversational rules concerning politeness, style, and efficiency have an important reciprocal influence on the communicative intentions of speakers and on semantic conventions. As normative rules they identify goals that all people try to achieve in their speech, and to some extent they are rules people explicitly try to follow. Both forms of motivation lead to speech that contributes to the truth of the principles as descriptive generalizations.

The other principles of Grice's theory are all false. These include the theoretical definition of implicature in terms of the Cooperative Principle, which introduces the cooperative presumption, determinacy, and mutual knowledge conditions; the Calculability Assumption, stating that conversational implicatures can be worked out or inferred from the conversational principles; the Generative Assumption, stating that conversational implicatures are generated by and predictable from the satisfaction of those conditions; and Grice's Razor, according to which it is more economical to postulate conversational implicatures rather than conventional implicatures, senses, or semantic presuppositions because conversational implicatures can be derived from and explained by conversational rules. These principles seriously underestimate both the intentionality of speaker implicature and the conventionality of sentence implicature.

To understand speaker implicature, we must view it as a species of speaker meaning or implication. We should focus on broadly Gricean definitions of speaker meaning in terms of speaker intention rather than on Gricean definitions of speaker implicature in terms of the Cooperative Principle. To comprehend sentence implicature, we have to study and carefully describe the actual linguistic conventions of language communities. Rather than trying to deduce arbitrary practices from some general psychosocial principles, we must look at the social functions that particular conventions serve. And we should look to historical linguistics for their origins.

In sum, Gricean theory fails because speaker implicature is a matter of intention, sentence implicature is a matter of convention, and neither is calculable from or generated by psychosocial principles. Conversational rules instead codify social goals motivating intentions and sustaining conventions.

References

Adler, J. (1987). Comparisons with Grice. *Behavioral and Brain Sciences,* **10,** 710–711.

Alston, W. P. (1964a). *Philosophy of Language.* Englewood Cliffs, N.J.: Prentice-Hall.

Alston, W. P. (1964b). Linguistic Acts. *American Philosophical Quarterly,* **1,** 138–146.

Anttila, R. (1989). *Historical and Comparative Linguistics.* Philadelphia: John Benjamins.

Atlas, J. D. (1979). How Linguistics Matters to Philosophy: Presupposition, Truth, and Meaning. In *Syntax and Semantics, 11: Presupposition,* ed. C. Oh and D. A. Dinneen, pp. 265–281. New York: Academic Press.

Atlas, J. D. (1989). *Philosophy Without Ambiguity.* Oxford: Oxford University Press.

Atlas, J. D., and Levinson, S. C. (1981). It-Clefts, Informativeness, and Logical Form: Radical Pragmatics (Revised Standard Version). In *Radical Pragmatics,* ed. P. Cole, pp. 1–61. New York: Academic Press.

Avramides, A. (1989). *Meaning and Mind: An Examination of a Gricean Account of Language.* Cambridge, Mass.: MIT Press.

Bach, K. (1987). *Thought and Reference.* Oxford: Oxford University Press.

Bach, K. (1994a). Conversational Impliciture. *Mind and Language,* **9,** 124–162.

Bach, K. (1994b). Meaning, Speech Acts, and Communication. In *Basic Topics in the Philosophy of Language,* ed. R. M. Harnish, pp. 3–21. Englewood Cliffs, N.J.: Prentice-Hall.

Bach, K., and Harnish, R. (1979). *Linguistic Communication and Speech Acts.* Cambridge, Mass.: MIT Press.

Ball, C. (1986). Metalinguistic Disjunction. *Penn Review of Linguistics,* **10,** 1–15.

Bar-Lev, Z., and Palacas, A. (1980). Semantic Command over Pragmatic Priority. *Lingua,* **51,** 137–146.

Bennett, J. (1976). *Linguistic Behavior.* Cambridge: Cambridge University Press.

Berg, J. (1991). The Relevant Relevance. *Journal of Pragmatics,* **16,** 411–425.

Bertolet, R. (1983). Where Do Implicatures Come From? *Canadian Journal of Philosophy,* **13,** 181–192.

Bickerton, D. (1979). Where Presuppositions Come From. In *Syntax and Semantics, 11: Presupposition,* ed. C. Oh and D. A. Dinneen, pp. 235–248. New York: Academic Press.

Bird, G. (1979). Speech Acts and Conversation, Part II. *Philosophical Quarterly,* **29,** 142–152.

Blackburn, S. (1984). *Spreading the Word.* Oxford: Clarendon Press.

Blakemore, D. (1987a). *Semantic Constraints on Relevance.* Oxford: Blackwell.

Blakemore, D. (1987b). Linguistic Constraints on Pragmatic Interpretation: A Reassessment of Linguistic Semantics. *Behavioral and Brain Sciences,* **4,** 712–713.

Blakemore, D. (1992). *Understanding Utterances.* Oxford: Blackwell.

Boër, S., and Lycan, W. (1973). Invited Inferences and Other Unwelcome Guests. *Papers in Linguistics,* **6,** 483–506.

Brown, P., and Levinson, S. C. (1978). Universals in Language Use: Politeness Phenomena. In *Questions and Politeness,* ed. E. Goody, pp. 56–311. Cambridge: Cambridge University Press.

Brown, P., and Levinson, S. C. (1987). *Politeness: Some Universals in Language Use.* Cambridge: Cambridge University Press.

Burge, T. (1975). On Knowledge and Convention. *Philosophical Review,* **84,** 249–255.

Burton-Roberts, N. (1984). Modality and Implicature. *Linguistics and Philosophy,* **7,** 181–206.

Carston, R. (1987). Being Explicit. *Behavioral and Brain Sciences,* **10,** 713–714.

Carston, R. (1988). Implicature, Explicature, and Truth-Theoretic Semantics. In *Mental Representations: The Interface Between Language and Reality,* ed. M. Kempson, pp. 155–181. Cambridge: Cambridge University Press.

Cherry, E. C. (1953). Some Experiments on the Recognition of Speech, with One and with Two Ears. *Journal of the Acoustic Society of America,* **25,** 975–979.

Chierchia, G., and McConnell-Ginet, S. (1990). *An Introduction to Semantics.* Cambridge, Mass.: MIT Press.

Clark, H. (1987). Relevant to What? *Behavioral and Brain Sciences,* **10,** 714–715.

Cohen, L. J. (1971). The Logical Particles of Natural Language. In *Pragmatics of Natural Language,* ed. J. Bar-Hillel, pp. 50–68. Dordrecht: Reidel.

Cole, P. (1975). The Synchronic and Diachronic Status of Conversational Implicature. In *Syntax and Semantics, 3: Speech Acts,* ed. P. Cole and J. L. Morgan, pp. 257–288. New York: Academic Press.

Cole, P., ed. (1981). *Radical Pragmatics.* New York: Academic Press.

Cowie, A. P. (1994). Phraseology. In *The Encyclopedia of Language and Linguistics,* ed. R. Asher, pp. 3168–3171. Oxford: Oxford University Press.

Cowie, A. P., Mackin, R., and McCaig, I. (1983). *Oxford Dictionary of Current Idiomatic English.* Oxford: Oxford University Press.

Crimmins, M. (1992). *Talking About Belief.* Cambridge, Mass.: MIT Press.

Croft, W. (1994). Universals, Linguistic. In *The Encyclopedia of Language and Linguistics,* ed. R. Asher, pp. 4850–4852. Oxford: Oxford University Press.

Cruse, D. A. (1986). *Lexical Semantics.* Cambridge: Cambridge University Press.

Cutler, A. (1987). The Task of the Speaker and the Task of the Hearer. *Behavioral and Brain Sciences,* **10,** 715–716.

Davis, W. A. (1992a). Speaker Meaning. *Linguistics and Philosophy,* **15,** 223–253.

Davis, W. A. (1992b). Cogitative and Cognitive Speaker Meaning. *Philosophical Studies,* **67,** 71–88.

Davis, W. A. (Forthcoming). *Meaning, Expression, and Thought.* New York: Cambridge University Press.

Davison, A. (1975). Indirect Speech Acts and What to Do with Them. In *Syntax and Semantics, 3: Speech Acts,* ed. P. Cole and J. L. Morgan, pp. 143–184. New York: Academic Press.

Fasold, R. (1990). *The Sociolinguistics of Language.* Oxford: Blackwell.

Fodor, J. (1975). *The Language of Thought.* New York: Thomas Y. Crowell.

Fraser, B. (1988). Motor Oil Is Motor Oil: An Account of English Nominal Tautologies. *Journal of Pragmatics,* **12,** 215–220.

Gazdar, G. (1979). *Pragmatics: Implicature, Presupposition, and Logical Form.* New York: Academic Press.

Geis, M., and Zwicky, M. (1971). On Invited Inferences. *Linguistic Inquiry,* **2,** 561–566.

Goldman, A. (1970). *A Theory of Human Action.* Englewood Cliffs, N.J.: Prentice-Hall.

Gordon, D., and Lakoff, G. (1975). Conversational Postulates. In *Syntax and Semantics, 3: Speech Acts,* ed. P. Cole and J. L. Morgan, pp. 83–106. New York: Academic Press.

Grandy, R. (1977). Review of *Convention* by David Lewis. *Journal of Philosophy*, **74**, 129–139.

Green, G. M. (1975). How to Get People to Do Things with Words. In *Syntax and Semantics, 3: Speech Acts,* ed. P. Cole and J. L. Morgan, pp. 107–141. New York: Academic Press.

Green, G. M. (1989). *Pragmatics and Natural Language Understanding.* Hillsdale, N. J.: Erlbaum.

Green, M. (1995). Quality, Volubility, and Some Varieties of Discourse. *Linguistics and Philosophy*, **18**, 83–112.

Grice, H. P. (1957). Meaning. *Philosophical Review*, **66**, 377–388.

Grice, H. P. (1968). Utterer's Meaning, Sentence Meaning, and Word Meaning. *Foundations of Language*, **4**, 225–242.

Grice, H. P. (1969). Utterer's Meaning and Intentions. *Philosophical Review*, **78**, 147–177. Reprinted in H. P. Grice, ed., *Studies in the Way of Words* (Cambridge, Mass.: Harvard University Press, 1989), 86–116.

Grice, H. P. (1975). Logic and Conversation. In *Syntax and Semantics, 3: Speech Acts,* ed. P. Cole and J. Morgan. New York: Academic Press. Reprinted in H. P. Grice, ed., *Studies in the Way of Words* (Cambridge, Mass.: Harvard University Press, 1989), 22–40.

Grice, H. P. (1978). Further Notes on Logic and Conversation. In *Syntax and Semantics, 9: Pragmatics,* ed. P. Cole, pp. 113–128. New York: Academic Press. Reprinted in H. P. Grice, ed., *Studies in the Ways of Words* (Cambridge, Mass.: Harvard University Press, 1989), 41–57.

Grice, H. P. (1981). Presupposition and Conversational Implicature. In *Radical Pragmatics,* ed. P. Cole, pp. 183–198. New York: Academic Press. Reprinted in H. P. Grice, ed., *Studies in the Way of Words* (Cambridge, Mass.: Harvard University Press, 1989), 269–282.

Grice, H. P. (1982). Meaning Revisited. In *Mutual Knowledge,* ed. N. Smith, pp. 223–243. New York: Academic Press.

Grice, H. P. (1989). *Studies in the Way of Words.* Cambridge, Mass.: Harvard University Press.

Harnish, R. M. (1976). Logical Form and Implicature. In *An Integrated Theory of Linguistic Ability,* ed. T. G. Bever, J. J. Katz, and T. Langedoen, pp. 313–392. New York: Thomas Y. Crowell.

Heim, I. (1988). On the Projection Problem for Presuppositions. In *Proceedings of the Second West Coast Conference on Formal Linguistics,* ed. D. Flickinger, pp. 114–115. Palo Alto: Stanford University Press. Reprinted in S. Davis, ed., *Pragmatics: A Reader* (Oxford: Oxford University Press, 1991), 397–405.

Hewitt, B. G. (1994). Greenberg Universals. In *The Encyclopedia of Language and Linguistics,* ed. R. Asher, pp. 1500–1504. Oxford: Oxford University Press.

Hinkelman, E. (1987). Relevance: Computation and Coherence. *Behavioral and Brain Sciences,* **10,** 720–721.

Hirschberg, J. (1991). *A Theory of Scalar Implicature.* New York: Garland.

Holdcroft, D. (1979). Speech Acts and Conversation, Part I. *Philosophical Quarterly,* **29,** 125–141.

Horn, L. R. (1972). *On the Semantic Properties of Logical Operators in English.* Ph. D. Thesis, UCLA.

Horn, L. R. (1984). Towards a New Taxonomy for Pragmatic Inference: Q-based and R-Based Implicature. In *Georgetown University Round Table on Languages and Linguistics,* ed. D. Schiffrin, pp. 11–42. Washington, D.C.: Georgetown University Press.

Horn, L. R. (1989). *A Natural History of Negation.* Chicago: University of Chicago Press.

Horn, L. R. (1992). Pragmatics, Implicature, and Presupposition. In *International Encyclopedia of Linguistics,* ed. W. Bright, pp. 260–266. New York: Oxford University Press.

Hugly, P., and Sayward, C. (1979). A Problem about Conversational Implicature. *Linguistics and Philosophy,* **3,** 19–25.

Hungerland, I. C. (1960). Contextual Implication. *Inquiry,* **3,** 211–258.

Hungerland, I. C., and Vick, G. R. (1981). Hobbes's Theory of Language, Speech, and Reasoning. In *Thomas Hobbes: Part I of De Corpore,* pp. 1–70. New York: Abaris.

Karttunen, L., and Peters, S. (1979). Conversational Implicature. In *Syntax and Semantics, 11: Presupposition,* ed. C. Oh and D. A. Dinneen, pp. 1–56. New York: Academic Press.

Kasher, A. (1982). Gricean Inference Revisited. *Philosophica,* **29,** 25–44.

Kates, C. (1980). *Pragmatics and Semantics.* Ithaca, N.Y.: Cornell University Press.

Keenan, E. O. (1975). The Universality of Conversational Implicature. In *Studies in Language Variation,* ed. R. Fasold and R. Shuy, pp. 255–268. Washington, D.C.: Georgetown University Press.

Kempson, R. (1975). *Presupposition and the Delimitation of Semantics.* Cambridge: Cambridge University Press.

Kempson, R. (1979). Presupposition, Opacity, and Ambiguity. In *Syntax and Semantics, 11: Presupposition,* ed. C. Oh and D. Dinneen, pp. 283–297. New York: Academic Press.

Kempson, R. (1986). Ambiguity and the Semantics-Pragmatics Distinction. In *Meaning and Interpretation,* ed. C. Travis, pp. 77–103. Oxford: Blackwell.

Kripke, S. (1982). *Wittgenstein on Rules and Private Languages.* Cambridge, Mass.: Harvard University Press.

Kroch, A. (1972). Lexical and Inferred Meanings for Some Time Adverbs. *Quarterly Progress Report of the Research Lab of Electronics, MIT.*

Lakoff, R. (1975). *Language and Women's Place.* New York: Harper & Row.

Lakoff, R. (1977). What You Can Do with Words: Politeness, Pragmatics and Performatives. In *Proceedings of the Texas Conference on Performatives, Presuppositions and Implicatures,* ed. R. Rogers, R. Wall, and J. Murphy, pp. 79–106. Arlington, Va.: Center for Applied Linguistics.

Leech, G. (1983). *Principles of Pragmatics.* London: Longmans.

Lehrer, A. (1974). *Semantic Fields and Lexical Structure.* Amsterdam: North Holland.

Lehrer, A. (1992a). Principles and Problems in Translating Proper Names. In *Translation and Meaning, II,* ed. B. Lewandowska-Tomazczyk and M. Thelen, pp. 395–402. Rijkschogeschool Maastricht.

Lehrer, A. (1992b). Names and Naming: Why We Need Fields and Frames. In *Frames, Fields, and Contrasts,* ed. A. Lehrer and E. F. Kittay, pp. 123–142. Hillsdale, N.J.: Erlbaum.

Lehrer, A., and Kittay, E. F., eds. (1992). *Frames, Fields, and Contrasts: New Essays in Semantic and Lexical Organization.* Hillsdale, N.J.: Erlbaum.

Levinson, S. C. (1983). *Pragmatics.* Cambridge: Cambridge University Press.

Levinson, S. C. (1987a). Implicature Explicated? *Behavioral and Brain Sciences,* **10,** 722–723.

Levinson, S. C. (1987b). Minimization and Conversational Inference. In *The Pragmatic Perspective,* ed. J. Verschueren and M. Bertuccelli-Papi, pp. 61–129. Amsterdam: Benjamins.

Levinson, S. C. (1989). Review of Relevance. *Journal of Linguistics,* **25,** 455–472.

Lewis, D. (1969). *Convention.* Cambridge, Mass.: Harvard University Press.

Lewis, D. (1975). Languages and Language. In *Minnesota Studies in the Philosophy of Language,* ed. K. Gunderson, vol. 7, pp. 3–35. Minneapolis: University of Minnesota Press.

Lewis, D. (1979). Scorekeeping in a Language Game. In *Semantics from Different Points of View,* ed. R. Bäuerle et al., pp. 172–187. Berlin: Springer.

Loar, B. (1976). The Semantics of Singular Terms. *Philosophical Studies,* **30,** 353–577.

Loar, B. (1981). *Mind and Meaning.* Cambridge: Cambridge University Press.

Lycan, W. (1984). *Logical Form in Natural Language.* Cambridge, Mass.: MIT Press.

Lyons, J. (1971). *Introduction to Theoretical Linguistics.* Cambridge: Cambridge University Press.

Martinich, A. (1984). A Theory of Metaphor. *Journal of Literary Semantics,* **13,** 35–56.

Matsumoto, Y. (1995). The Conversational Condition on Horn Scales. *Linguistics and Philosophy,* **18,** 21–60.

McCawley, J. D. (1978). Conversational Implicature and the Lexicon. In *Syntax and Semantics, 9: Pragmatics,* ed. P. Cole, pp. 245–258. New York: Academic Press.

McCawley, J. D. (1987). The Multidimensionality of Pragmatics. *Behavioral and Brain Sciences,* **20,** 723–724.

Mey, J. (1993). *Pragmatics: An Introduction.* Cambridge, Mass.: Blackwell.

Miller, G., and Johnson-Laird, P. (1976). *Language and Perception.* Cambridge, Mass.: Harvard University Press.

Millikan, R. (1987). What Peter Thinks When He Hears Mary Speak. *Behavioral and Brain Sciences,* **10,** 725–726.

Morgan, J. L. (1978). Two Types of Convention in Indirect Speech Acts. In *Syntax and Semantics, 9: Pragmatics,* ed. P. Cole, pp. 261–280. New York: Academic Press. Reprinted in S. Davis, ed., *Pragmatics: A Reader* (Oxford: Oxford University Press, 1991), 242–253.

Morgan, J. L., and Green, G. M. (1987). On the Search for Relevance. *Behavioral and Brain Sciences,* **10,** 725–726.

Nunberg, G. (1981). Validating Pragmatic Explanations. In *Radical Pragmatics,* ed. P. Cole, pp. 199–222. New York: Academic Press.

O'Grady, W., Dobrovolsky, M., and Aronoff, M. (1993). *Contemporary Linguistics: An Introduction,* 2nd ed. New York: St. Martin's Press.

Oh, C., and Dinneen, D. A., eds. (1979). *Syntax and Semantics, 11: Presupposition.* New York: Academic Press.

Pawley, A. (1985). Lexicalization. In *Language and Linguistics: The Interdependence of Theory, Data, and Application,* ed. D. Tannen and J. E. Alatis, pp. 98–120. Washington, D.C.: Georgetown University Press.

Payne, J. R. (1994). Universals of Language. In *The Encyclopedia of Language and Linguistics,* ed. R. Asher, pp. 4847–4850. Oxford: Oxford University Press.

Pierce, C. S. (1931–1935). *Collected Papers.* Cambridge, Mass.: Harvard University Press.

Posner, R. (1980). Semantics and Pragmatics of Sentence Connectives in

Natural Languages. In *Speech-Act Theory and Pragmatics,* ed. J. Searle, F. Kiefer, and M. Bierwisch, pp. 169–203. Amsterdam: Reidel.

Quine, W. V. O. (1936). Truth by Convention. In *Essays for A. N. White-head,* ed. O. H. Lee. New York: Longmans. Reprinted in *Ways of Paradox* (New York: Random House, 1966), 70–79.

Reboul, A. (1987). The Relevance of *Relevance* for Fiction. *Behavioral and Brain Sciences,* **10,** 729.

Recanati, F. (1986). On Defining Communicative Intentions. *Mind and Language,* **1,** 213–242.

Recanati, F. (1987). Literalness and Other Pragmatic Principles. *Behavioral and Brain Sciences,* **10,** 729–730.

Rooth, M. (1992). A Theory of Focus Interpretation. *Natural Language Semantics,* **1,** 75–116.

Rosenberg, J. (1974). *Linguistic Representation.* Dordrecht: D. Reidel.

Russell, B. (1921). *The Analysis of Mind.* London: Allen and Unwin.

Russell, S. J. (1987). Rationality as an Explanation of Language. *Behavioral and Brain Sciences,* **10,** 730–731.

Sadock, J. M. (1972). Speech Act Idioms. In *Papers from the Eighth Regional Meeting of the Chicago Linguistic Society,* ed. J. Peranteau, J. Levi, and G. Phares, pp. 329–339. Chicago: Chicago Linguistic Society.

Sadock, J. M. (1974). *Toward a Linguistic Theory of Speech Acts.* New York: Academic Press.

Sadock, J. M. (1978). On Testing for Conversational Implicature. In *Syntax and Semantics, 9: Pragmatics,* ed. P. Cole, pp. 281–297. New York: Academic Press.

Sadock, J. M. (1981). Almost. In *Radical Pragmatics,* ed. P. Cole, pp. 257–272.

Sag, I. A. (1981). Formal Semantics and Extralinguistic Context. In *Radical Pragmatics,* ed. P. Cole, pp. 273–293.

Sainsbury, M. (1984). Saying and Conveying. *Linguistics and Philosophy,* **7,** 415–432.

Schiffer, S. (1972). *Meaning.* Oxford: Clarendon Press.

Schiffer, S. (1987a). *Remnants of Meaning.* Cambridge, Mass.: MIT Press.

Schiffer, S. (1987b). The 'Fido'-Fido Theory of Belief. In *Philosophical Perspectives, 1, Metaphysics,* ed. J. Tomerlin, pp. 455–480. Atascadero, Calif.: Ridgeview.

Schiffrin, D. (1994). *Approaches to Discourse.* Oxford: Blackwell.

Schmerling, S. F. (1975). Asymmetric Conjunction and Rules of Conversation. In *Syntax and Semantics, 3: Speech Acts,* ed. P. Cole and J. L. Morgan, pp. 211–232. New York: Academic Press.

Searle, J. (1965). What Is a Speech Act? In *Philosophy in America,* ed. M. Black, pp. 221–239. London: Allen and Unwin.

Searle, J. (1969). *Speech Acts.* Cambridge: Cambridge University Press.

Searle, J. (1975). Indirect Speech Acts. In *Syntax and Semantics, 3: Speech Acts,* ed. P. Cole and J. L. Morgan, pp. 59–82. New York: Academic Press. Reprinted in S. Davis, ed., *Pragmatics: A Reader* (Oxford: Oxford University Press, 1991), 265–277.

Searle, J. R. (1982). Metaphor. In *Metaphor and Thought,* ed. A. Ortnony. Cambridge: Cambridge University Press.

Seuren, P. A. M. (1987). How Relevant? *Behavioral and Brain Sciences,* **10,** 731–732.

Smith, N., and Wilson, D. (1979). *Modern Linguistics: The Results of Chomsky's Revolution.* Harmondsworth: Penguin.

Sperber, D., and Wilson, D. (1981). Irony and the Use-Mention Distinction. In *Radical Pragmatics,* ed. P. Cole, pp. 295–318. New York: Academic Press.

Sperber, D., and Wilson, D. (1986a). *Relevance: Communication and Cognition.* Cambridge, Mass.: Harvard University Press.

Sperber, D., and Wilson, D. (1986b). Loose Talk. *Proceedings of the Aristotelian Society,* **86,** 153–171. Reprinted in S. Davis, ed., *Pragmatics: A Reader* (Oxford: Oxford University Press, 1991), 540–549.

Sperber, D., and Wilson, D. (1987). Précis of *Relevance: Communication and Cognition. Behavioral and Brain Sciences,* **10,** 679–754.

Stalnaker, R. (1974). Pragmatic Presuppositions. In *Semantics and Philosophy,* ed. M. K. Munitz and P. K. Unger, pp. 471–481. New York: New York University Press.

Sterelny, K. (1982). Against Conversational Implicature. *Journal of Semantics,* **1,** 187–194.

Strawson, P. (1964). Intention and Convention in Speech Acts. *Philosophical Review,* **73,** 439–460. Reprinted in S. Davis, ed., *Pragmatics: A Reader* (Oxford: Oxford University Press, 1991), pp. 293–302.

Suppes, P. (1986). The Primacy of Utterer's Meaning. In *Philosophical Grounds of Rationality: Intentions, Categories, Ends,* ed. R. Grandy and R. Warner, pp. 109–129. Oxford: Clarendon Press.

Thomason, R. (1990). Accommodation, Meaning, and Implicature: Interdisciplinary Foundations for Pragmatics. In *Intentions in Communication,* ed. P. R. Cohen, J. L. Morgan, and M. Pollack, pp. 325–63. Cambridge, Mass.: MIT Press.

Van Kuppevelt, J. (1996). Inferring from Topics: Scalar Implicatures as

Topic Dependent Inferences. *Linguistics and Philosophy*, **19,** 393–443.

Walker, R. (1975). Conversational Implicatures. In *Meaning, Reference, and Necessity: New Studies in Semantics,* ed. S. Blackburn, pp. 133–181. Cambridge: Cambridge University Press.

Ward, G., and Hirschberg, J. (1991). A Pragmatic Analysis of Tautological Utterances. *Journal of Pragmatics,* **15,** 507–520.

Wierzbicka, A. (1985). Different Cultures, Different Languages, Different Speech Acts. *Journal of Pragmatics,* **9,** 145–178.

Wierzbicka, A. (1987). Boys Will Be Boys: "Radical Semantics" vs. "Radical Pragmatics." *Language, 63,* 95–114.

Wierzbicka, A. (1991). *Cross-Cultural Pragmatics: The Semantics of Human Interaction.* New York: Mouton de Gruyter.

Wierzbicka, A. (1994). "Cultural Scripts": A Semantic Approach to Cultural Analysis and Cross-Cultural Communication. *Pragmatics and Language Learning,* **5,** 1–24.

Wierzbicka, A. (1995). In Defence of Australian Culture. *Quadrant Magazine,* **39**(11), 17–22.

Wilks, Y. (1987). Relevance Must Be to Someone. *Behavioral and Brain Sciences,* **10,** 735–736.

Wilson, D., and Sperber, D. (1979). Ordered Entailments: An Alternative to Presuppositional Theories. In *Syntax and Semantics, 11: Presupposition,* ed. C. Oh and D. A. Dinneen, pp. 299–323. New York: Academic Press.

Wilson, D., and Sperber, D. (1981). On Grice's Theory of Conversation. In *Conversation and Discourse,* ed. P. Werth, pp. 155–178. New York: St. Martin's Press.

Wilson, D., and Sperber, D. (1986). Inference and Implicature. In *Meaning and Interpretation,* ed. C. Travis, pp. 377–393. Oxford: Blackwell.

Wright, R. A. (1975). Meaning$_{nn}$ and Conversational Implicature. In *Syntax and Semantics, 3: Speech Acts,* ed. P. Cole and J. L. Morgan, pp. 363–382. New York: Academic Press.

Yu, P. (1979). On the Gricean Program About Meaning. *Linguistics and Philosophy, 3,* 273–388.

Ziff, P. (1960). *Semantic Analysis.* Ithaca, N.Y.: Cornell University Press.

Index

metaphor, 12, 59, 61, 65, 71, 73, 125, 184, 187; *see also* idioms

.